JOSHUA JARVIS

KINGDOM DRIVEN LEADER

**FROM SUCCESSFUL ENDEAVORS
TO A SIGNIFICANT MISSION**

Kingdom Driven Leader™
Copyright 2018 © by Joshua Jarvis

All rights reserved. This book or any portion thereof may not be reproduced or used in any manner whatsoever without the express written permission of the publisher and author except for the use of brief quotations in a book review.

Printed in the United States of America

First Printing, 2021

Website: https://jrjarvis.com

ISBN: 978-1-7372428-0-2 (International Trade Paper Edition)
ISBN: 978-1-7372428-1-9 (Hardback)
ISBN: 978-1-7372428-4-0 (ebook)

TABLE OF CONTENTS

Introduction 05
Chapter 1: What It Means to Be A Kingdom Driven Leader 11

SECTION 1: PREPARATION 37
Chapter 2: Prepare to Rule 39
Chapter 3: 100% Submitted to Christ 63
Chapter 4: Receiving the King's Mandates 77
Chapter 5: Speak to The King of Kings 89
Chapter 6: Has Integrity 97
Chapter 7: Servant to The People 103
Chapter 8: Holy Discontent 109
Chapter 9: Be Humble 121
Chapter 10: Tithe 131
Chapter 11: Gain Wisdom 139
Chapter 12: Finding Prophets (Wise Counsel) 155
Chapter 13: Excellence in Everything 169

SECTION II: LEADING — 179

Chapter 14: Begin to Reign — 181

Chapter 15: Tear Down Strongholds — 197

Chapter 16: Build A Network — 223

Chapter 17: Grow Your Giving — 245

SECTION III: REIGNING WITH CHRIST — 251

Chapter 18: Reigning with Christ — 253

Chapter 19: Launch Offensives — 263

Chapter 20: Claim Territory — 277

SECTION IV: ENEMIES OF A KING — 289

Chapter 21: Enemies of A King — 291

Chapter 22: Traps of The Enemy — 307

Chapter 23: Leading A Dynasty — 317

Conclusion — 325

ACKNOWLEDGEMENTS — 329

Notes — 331

INTRODUCTION

For most of my life, I've wanted to find my purpose. Wanting to find the answer to why I was put here on earth, I've read numerous books and attended seminars, webinars, and conferences. In every avenue in which I've looked, whether it be spiritual or secular, I've come away with only more questions.

When I launch a new business, the same feeling of hope and excitement accompanies each one. Each time, I think, "Maybe this time I'd find my purpose!" I thought success, specifically, financial success equated purpose. I also equated success with value. I believed a lie that my life wasn't valuable to God or anyone if I wasn't a success.

Moderate success or relative success wouldn't do either. If my life wasn't a success in the world's eyes, then I was a failure. A psychologist would tell you that I had father issues. I worked hard to strive for success to capture his attention and approval. The reality was that I didn't just have father issues in the earthly sense; I had Father issues in the spiritual sense.

With so much weight placed on business success, I was susceptible to huge letdowns when I failed. And I failed often. I only received financial gains from running businesses because God blessed me despite my failed business plans. He always provided.

Religion compounded this problem. When I fully committed my life to Jesus, I had new problems. I no longer measured success in financial metrics, but now I measured success in religious ones like reading the Bible more, praying more, and doing more. If I wasn't a pastor or missionary, how could I possibly be valuable to God? After all, pastors and missionaries are leading people to Christ and spending all their time working for Him. How could I compete when all I did was sell real estate?

At a church event that I attended for business leaders, I discovered, to my astonishment, there were others like me! There were others seeking purpose, fulfillment, and a sense of value. CFOs of large corporations, small business owners, and tech gurus attended the same church I attended. All of us were struggling in quiet desperation, waiting for the moment we would get "called" to something greater. The wonderful reality is that we *are* called to something greater. However, it would take me a while before I realized it.

My problem was that I believed success would fulfill my purpose.

ANSWERING THE WRONG CALL

I thought the game of life was about financial success and business growth. I was wrong. Not only could I not win the supposed game of life, but I was playing the wrong game. God cares very little about my financial possessions but a great deal about how humble and loving my heart is. The game isn't about how much I can gather but how much I'm using what I have to serve others.

There was a time when I was utterly consumed with trying to find my special calling. During that time, I asked a friend and mentor to lunch to discuss how I might discover this calling. My mentor, George, is an old-school, "man's man" complete with the oversized belt buckle. He told me, "I don't think God gives a rip about what you do." I have to admit, for a few years, this statement stung. However, over time I've learned that George might not have had the best words, but he was right. To put it another way, God is less concerned about what you do and more concerned about who you are.

INTRODUCTION

Whether I work in a field that some might consider as lowly work or work in a high profile job, it makes very little difference in this game. As a Father, God certainly wants me to be happy. He cares about where I work and what I do. However, He cares much more for my soul than my vocation.

If you're like me and always wondered what you are called to or if you've ever been envious of pastors and missionaries, this is the book for you. For you to discover your true purpose, you'll need first to accept who you are. You'll then have to start living like what your calling is. Finally, as you understand the full weight of the responsibility, you'll begin conquering for the kingdom.

The foundation of your life is built on knowing who you are. If you've accepted Jesus as your Lord, then you're a child of God. It says in the first chapter of Ephesians that God decided in advance to adopt us (verse 5). If we are adopted as sons and daughters, then we have the same rights that children naturally do. This includes delegated authority and an inheritance, among other things.

However, like children, we aren't given these tools without training. In order to be the leader that God's called all of us to, we have to prepare. We will need to grow ourselves spiritually to accomplish the mission He's laid out for us.

Once that preparation is ongoing, we can then progress through maturity to do great things for the Kingdom. Preparation is similar to physical training, which consists of two major phases. The first phase is general acclimation. If you're training as a bodybuilder, you don't just lift weights. You learn the proper form first. Once you've learned that, your real training begins with increasing difficulty.

Our growth as leaders is very much like bodybuilding. For example, we must first learn how to humble ourselves before we can begin the process of growing in humility.

This journey will uncover your purpose, but this process to discover your purpose is not for the faint of heart. Let me warn you. It will require everything. This process is very much like what God asked of Abraham in Genesis 22 - to sacrifice his son. Isaac was the son that God had promised Abraham, the son for whom Abraham waited patiently.

Like Abraham, you'll have to take every dream and place it on the altar. Only when you're willing to sacrifice your Isaac, will you receive the blessing that Abraham received. And just like Abraham, you'll need to trust God to provide.

WHY READ THIS BOOK

This book has several purposes but has only one major goal: For you to live out your mission to impact the world. You're going to discover principles of business found in the Bible and learn about the tools to apply these immediately.

It's time to shed the self-image the world has given you. This is an incorrect self-image that measures your value by what social media says you are, by what your dad called you, or by what your friends said you are. This isn't how God sees you. It's time to see what the truth is and step into what it means to be a kingdom driven leader. Even if you don't agree completely with everything you read, understand that, as a follower of Christ, you are a kingdom driven leader regardless of whether you feel you are or not.

If you've accepted the adoption into God's family, God has called you His sons and daughters, brothers and sisters to Jesus the King. Just based on family ties alone, we are royalty.

In my church, we have a group of marketplace leaders who come together to do life and discuss business. The men's group is called "Kings." Every year when new men are invited to the Kings group, they always

INTRODUCTION

question their qualifications. Most try to disqualify themselves. "I'm not a leader, I just work at IBM," or "I'm a professor at the local college, I'm not a kingdom driven leader."

Being a kingdom driven leader isn't about your title, but it is about your position, your position in the kingdom. It's as easy as answering this question. Are you a child of God ready to conquer the mission He made you for? If you answered yes, you are positioned as a kingdom driven leader. As a child of God, you have all the support and tools to become a great leader. Your vocation doesn't matter because God can use you wherever you are.

If you want to learn the Biblical principles of what it takes to lead and grow as a kingdom driven leader, as God calls you to be, then read on. This is for those who wish to go from successful endeavors to a significant mission and see their influence grow.

1

What It Means to Be A Kingdom Driven Leader

When you think of the word "king," do you think of good kings, warrior kings, or evil kings? Do you imagine royalty, family dynasties, or dictatorship? The Bible has quite a lot to say about kings – so much so that more than six books of the Old Testament are specifically dedicated to the subject. One thing is certain; kings shaped our world since the term was created. Before the word "king" was ever used, there were many different names that could all be summed up in one word, "leader."

What if I told you that God considers you to be a king? Because Jesus is King of Kings, you may have wondered, "what kings are Jesus king of?" Scripture tells us we are joint-heirs with Christ (Romans 8:17). This means we are essentially the "of kings" part of that. A king has a kingdom to rule and reign over, resources to steward, and a mission to execute. This is about the opportunity you and I have been given to steward the kingdom entrusted to us.

Genesis 3:1 … "Did God really say?"

The original sin of mankind was introduced in the Garden of Eden when Satan asked Adam and Eve, "Did God really say…? (Genesis 3:1)" The enemy of our souls and our kingdom asks this most deadly question over and over again in our lives. There are many sins that tempt and trap us but doubting God's word is chief among them. I argue that this little bit of doubt is stopping people from going from survival to success and from success to significance.

This doubt comes in when businessmen and women believe that their vocation and their calling are separate. When we leave Jesus at home and go to work, we miss the opportunity to be used for significance in the workplace.

> "As He was setting out on a journey, a *businessman* ran up to Him and knelt before Him, and asked Him, "Good Teacher, what shall I do to inherit eternal life?"
>
> And Jesus said to him, "Why do you call Me good? No one is good except God alone.
>
> You know the commandments, 'Do not murder, Do not commit adultery, Do not steal, Do not bear false witness, Do not defraud, Honor your father and mother.'"
>
> And he said to Him, "Teacher, I have kept all these things from my youth up."
>
> Looking at him, Jesus felt a love for him and said to him, "One thing you lack: go and sell all you possess and give to the poor, and you will have treasure in heaven; and come, follow Me."
>
> But at these words he was saddened, and he went away grieving, for he was one who owned much property.
> **— Mark 10:17-22 NIV**

WHAT IT MEANS TO BE A KINGDOM DRIVEN LEADER

The enemy's lie tells us that we can do this life without giving 100% of our lives away. Notice Jesus didn't mention the first commandment (You shall have no other gods before me. Exodus 20:3) in His listing. Yet, that was the very thing missing from this young businessman. It's also what's typically missing from our lives. God has asked us for 100% of our lives.

Sometimes we can give up to 99% of our lives to Him. However, when it comes down to that last 1%, we ask, did God really say to that part too?

The Bible has given us enough information on how to not only live in victory but how to rule the kingdom. I hope to challenge you to go deeper to learn the principles of what being a great kingdom driven leader truly is so you can live like one and have victory in your life.

I want to be clear. This is not about God's acceptance or another way to earn His love. He loves you. He is calling you to rule with Him. There is nothing you can do to cause God to love you less or more. **This journey is about being the best you can possibly be infused with God's power while following His principles.** This also isn't about living a life of luxury. There may not be any material rewards from your arduous effort, but you will reap eternal rewards.

OF KINGS AND PRIESTS

> "To Him who loved us and washed us from our sins in His own blood, and has made us kings and priests to His God and Father, to Him be glory and dominion forever and ever."
> **— Revelation 1:5-6 NKJV**

The typical Sunday message about kings and priests goes something like this. God calls some to be kings and others to be priests. Priests are the ones that do the serving, teaching, and general caring part of the ministry. Kings go out and work and bring money into the storehouse.

I'm here to tell you that these are not mutually exclusive. There is often a clear distinction between those called to full-time ministry and those called to full-time missions. (See what I did there? If you didn't catch it, we are *all* called to the mission field).

For me, when I heard this message, it caused confusion. A message on kings and priests that was surely meant to unite the Church, left me feeling like an outsider. It was as if there were only two groups, and I didn't see myself as either. Priests were people who work for the church and kings were everyone else. I certainly didn't see myself as a priest. However, as delighted as I was to hear about this kingly classification, I didn't know what that meant or whom I could look to as an example of someone living out their kingly calling well. There were also a number of underlying questions that tugged at my mind. Does my work matter? Is there any true-life giving work in business? Am I essentially only working to bring money into the church? Are the only people making a difference doing so in the nonprofit sector? Are only successful companies able to give?

I wrote this book to answer these questions. True life-giving vocational work is "found" when you're found on mission... being a king.

MODERN-DAY KING

It was Sunday at Victory World Church. Pastor Dennis Rouse, the author of "10 Qualities of a Disciple," was preaching a year-end message, where he typically covers the finances of the church, our giving, and Victory's vision.

About mid-way through his message, Pastor Rouse began to reveal how he personally feels about giving. He also shared how close he felt we were to be able to give at a level that made a real difference. He began to outline the cost of the world's problems relative to our giving. Essentially, he was saying that it's possible that this church in Norcross, GA, could have the potential to eliminate thirst and provide clean water to an entire nation or any other "world problem."

To illustrate his point, he began talking about a man who had a vision of something eternal, Jace Rabe. He was an average man with a deep passion for business. Later, when I heard Jace speak, he said that in his younger years, his hero was Gordon Gekko, the Michael Douglas character from Wall Street. A villainous businessman.

Jace was a commodity broker, specifically with ties to dried fruits and nuts. What made him special was not that he uprooted his family from Atlanta, GA, to move to Benin, Africa. It wasn't that he saw the opportunity of cost-effective labor in a cashew-rich country that could benefit from modernized processes and systems.

What made him special was *why* he did it. His purpose was not just to make a huge profit. He wanted to make a huge profit to give back to that community.

Jace's business, Tolaro Global (www.tolaroglobal.com), fuels hospital construction, water well digging, and schools being built. His labor force is the highest-paid cashew processors in the entire country.

Jace is a born-again Christian, and yet most of his workforce are Muslim. His company is one of the most respected companies in Benin with ties to European investors. One of the many initiatives that his company has employed is training farmers on how to grow cashews better, as well as how to evaluate them when it comes time to sell. Benin now has some of the most knowledgeable farmers, thanks to education received from Jace's company. A move that might seem counterproductive has garnered loyalty from the farmers.

It's easy to see why I might have been enamored with this story of this man, whom I'm lucky enough to call a friend now. It wasn't about how great Jace is but rather that I finally had heard of a model of a business that was doing what I thought every business was designed to do.

Jace's company influences not only his employees and customers but also the community. Through his non-profit (www.projectsforprogress.com), Jace has funded new schools, water wells, and other necessities right inside that community. He is impacting an entire nation. I'm sure you can agree that businesses have the potential to change the world. Jace's impact on every facet of his business and community, all for God's glory, is the picture of a modern-day kingdom driven leader.

BIBLICAL BUSINESS

I often find frustrating when I meet great godly business people who are brilliant, yet they do not see what type of impact, influence, and power they have to shape the community they serve. They are ignorant about their potential and unintentional in their mission. Most well-meaning businesses help their community by default or proximity.

The Bible didn't leave us hanging. It's just that the pattern of how to live like a kingdom driven leader is often skipped over because the reader finds the information rather boring and perhaps difficult to read. These life-changing lessons are found in the books of Kings, Chronicles, and throughout the Bible. Every Old Testament passage, even in Kings, like most of the Bible, highlights the very nature of the one True King, Jesus.

Most of this book focuses on leadership and the kings of Israel. When I started this book, it was as if God was showing me something special. Locked away in what I thought were the most boring sections of the Bible were patterns of kingly identity and behavior. If it's in the Bible, it has a purpose. I sought out that purpose. I asked, why did He include this story and that story?

Stories that we often hear from the perspective of a Sunday School lesson now came alive in a business context. Take Esther, for example.

In modern-day terms, we find her in a position of influence within an evil, powerful conglomerate. She could have complained or quit, but she instead chose to influence from within. In fact, she was able to influence the CEO despite her position. You could look at Moses to see how to delegate, to Joshua for how to trust God for victory, to Caleb for the way to finish, to even to the shrewdness of Jacob to teach us lessons. These lessons are great, but in and of themselves, most fail to give us a complete blueprint to live like a kingdom driven leader.

As I researched, I found principles that characterized good kings, and I started recording many patterns and characteristics. Most of these characteristics, like humility or wisdom, are easy to identify. Not truly satisfied with this list, however, I realized something was missing. I then examined the life of Jesus, looking for any similarities between stories of good kings and His life.

That was my light bulb moment. I saw the patterns, and they matched up with what Jesus did. Jesus not only had the heart characteristics of good Old Testament kings, but He did many of the same actions, such as tearing down strongholds and taking captives. The last step for me was translating all these actions and characteristics into our daily lives and doing so from the perspective of a business leader.

If you don't see yourself as a kingdom driven leader yet, hang in there. Everyone has the ability to be a leader. Every leader starts leading the same way. They must learn to lead themselves. My hope is that by reading this book, you will come to realize your royal heritage as well.

King David didn't start as a king. Before he was king, he was a shepherd. In today's religiousfied world, a shepherd has a nice sounding connotation because of the parallels to Jesus. However, during that time, David would have been featured on an episode of "Dirty Jobs." He was essentially a janitor to the janitorial staff. Not only that, but as the youngest in the family, he was about as non-essential of an employee as you could get. Yet, God called him to be Israel's greatest king.

Before I ever had a relationship with Jesus, I always thought that businesses could change the world. Not just in shaping economies per se, but rather in the impact that a business can have on the lives of the employees, the lives of the customer, and the lives of the community that it's in.

Maybe it's a generational thing that social entrepreneurism is on the rise. However, I like to think it is part of God's calling for all of us to see ourselves as the kings we are.

Before we get too far ahead, let's get into the scripture here and discuss what foundation there is to be calling ourselves kings and our area of influence - our kingdom. After all, any business endeavor that lacks clarity is destined to fail.

WHAT THE BIBLE SAYS ABOUT KINGS

Calling yourself a kingdom driven leader comes from an attitude that is different from what the world promotes an understanding of who you are in Christ. In addition, some have abused the word "kings" to mean something other than how we are using it in our context. Let's journey through the Bible to ensure a good theological foundation.

Kings have been around as far back as 2,500 BC. Small tribal groups might have had a leader, such as Abraham, or a spiritual Judge (See Judges) but rarely an official king unless there was a city or some sort of fortification. That's where the word "kingdom" comes from - the domain or dominion of the king.

You might remember that Israel didn't have an official king until they defiantly rejected God's way and wanted to follow the world's way. Let's look at this story.

> "Then all the elders of Israel gathered together and came to Samuel at Ramah, and said to him, 'Look, you are old, and your sons do not walk in your ways. Now make us a king to judge us like all the nations.'
>
> But the thing displeased Samuel when they said, 'Give us a king to judge us.'
>
> So, Samuel prayed to the Lord.
>
> And the Lord said to Samuel, 'Heed the voice of the people in all that they say to you; for they have not rejected you, **but they have rejected Me**, that I should not reign over them.'"
> **— 1 Samuel 8 5:7 NIV**

Up until this point, Israel was a tribe of people that relied on God and the prophets who had a close relationship with God to direct them. The history of that time suggests that having a king would be a natural progression. I wonder what would have happened had Israel not asked for an earthly king. God warns them of this decision:

> "This will be the behavior of the king who will reign over you:
>
> He will take your sons and appoint them for his own chariots and to be his horsemen, and some will run before his chariots.
>
> He will appoint captains over his thousands and captains over his fifties, will set some to plow his ground and reap his harvest, and some to make his weapons of war and equipment for his chariots.
>
> He will take your daughters to be perfumers, cooks, and bakers.

> And he will take the best of your fields, your vineyards, and your olive groves, and give them to his servants.
>
> He will take a tenth of your grain and your vintage and give it to his officers and servants.
>
> And he will take your male servants, your female servants, your finest young men, and your donkeys, and put them to his work.
>
> He will take a tenth of your sheep. *And you will be his servants.*
>
> And you will cry out in that day because of your king whom you have chosen for yourselves, and the Lord will not hear you in that day."
> **— 1 Samuel 8:10-18 NIV** (italics mine)

Essentially, God warned them that a king would make them servants. It sounds like a bad deal to me. The people wanted to go from trusting God's direction to having a man rule them while hoping he was humble enough to submit to God. Essentially, they wanted to replace God with a man.

When Jesus came to break the chains of the curse of sin, I believe this was one of the links that were broken. Instead of restoring the old order of priests, we can hear directly from God. Instead of the idea of a king turning his subjects into servants, the king is now the greatest servant.

> "In the past God spoke to our ancestors through the prophets at many times and in various ways, but in these last days he has spoken to us by his Son, whom he appointed heir of all things, and through whom also he made the universe."
> **— Hebrews 1:1-2 NIV**

We know from this passage that a king leads his people, manages resources, stakes a claim in the lives of his subjects for better or worse, and manages the military campaigns. Notice the implication here is that if a kingdom driven leader does not heed the voice of the Lord, those they influence will be crying.

Before we go too much further, let's not miss this important point — **If we don't heed the voice of God, we could cause the ones we lead to cry out**. This is what happened to the Israelites. Hosea recorded God as saying, "In My anger I gave you kings and, in My anger, I removed them" (Hosea 13:11).

Israel, God's chosen people, had their first king in Saul, and so goes the history of kings, which we will cover in more detail later. After King David, Israel's kings either were born into the office of the king or fought for it. This is an important distinction because Jesus qualifies by doing both. The fact that Jesus, having been born through the line of David, as the son of God and came here to fight to get the authority back, more than qualifies Him to be king by any possible standard.

Fast forward to the New Testament, where we find Israel under Roman occupation, and there's a rumor of a new king that will free everyone. In fact, the ruling governor at this time was so scared of this "messiah" that he killed all the newborn babies in Bethlehem to try to stop this prophecy from coming true.

You likely know the Christmas story. What you might miss is that Jesus is the King. He was the King in the Old Testament, and He put on a human body to free us. He did that to offer us the opportunity to be adopted into the family. When we accept Jesus, we become part of the royal bloodline.

CO-REGENCY

> "God sent His Son, born of a woman, born under the law, to redeem those under the law, that we might receive adoption to sonship.
>
> Because you are His sons, God sent the Spirit of His Son into our hearts, the Spirit who calls out, "Abba, Father."
>
> So, you are no longer a slave, but God's child; and since you are His child, God **has made you also an heir**."
> — **Galatians 4:4-7 NIV**

Once the king selected the heir to the throne, their son was involved in every aspect of ruling until he was made co-king, crown prince, or as a historian would say, "co-regent." He got the opportunity to practice being king while his father had all the final authority. In this way, you'd have a smoother transition of succession and dynasty of rulers from the same family with a stable kingdom.

Co-regents weren't simply "assistant to the assistant vice president" or a title with no power. They carried the weight of kingly responsibilities of kings. In some cases, co-regents were co-kings and ruled one district. In other instances, such as the case with Uzziah's rule, who as a co-regent had to rule because his father had leprosy. As co-heir with Christ then, we are co-regents in this world.

> "Now if we are children, then we are heirs--heirs of God and coheirs with Christ, if indeed we share in his sufferings in order that we may also share in his glory."
> — **Romans 8:17 NIV**

There are two ways to walk in this "Kingship." One is understanding that you are part of the royal family and, therefore, a rightful heir to the kingdom. As heir, you have a provision of authority that has been given to you through the ultimate King, Jesus. You see yourself as a co-regent.

The other understanding is what Jesus said about the kingdom of Heaven. He'd often say, "the Kingdom of Heaven is here" or "the Kingdom of God is near." When I first read that, I often misunderstood it, as if He meant, "you better repent because this world is ending soon, and heaven or hell are close at hand."

In some ways, I guess that's true too, but I think what He was saying was that Jesus, the King, has freed us from the sin of this world, and thus His domain and dominion can now reign wherever He was exercising that authority. In fact, in the Gospels, we see Jesus giving His authority to His disciples.

Lucky for us, this kingdom of Heaven didn't end with Jesus' death, resurrection, and ascension. He gave the authority to us. You can read Acts and the rest of the New Testament to see how, even long after Jesus' ascension, normal people like us were operating under the authority and with the authority of Jesus.

I admit this is a bit of a rabbit trail, but I think it's important for us to understand that we have authority given to us. The degree to which we operate in it is up to us.

For example, let's say a King said to you that you could have all the land in a particular valley. It's a vast 1,000-acre valley with rich fertile land. It has some breathtaking waterfalls, beautiful fruit trees, and amazing fauna. He's given this land to you to manage and steward. Because of the land's fruit trees, he's counting on your tract of land to produce fruit for the kingdom. At the end of your reign, you'll have to give an account of how you managed it and receive your reward.

This valley, although rich and fertile, also has a few problems. The waterfall pours into a river, and although it's beautiful, it's overgrown with thorns and wild vines. As a result, the fruit trees are overrun with disease and insects. In addition, the land is full of vicious wild animals. Knowing this, the king has given you full authority to command his army and recruit other leaders to take back any occupied land.

After receiving this land, you roll up the deed and begin packing. You march outside the city gates. You then march along the wall of the kingdom. Not too far from the gate, you notice that there is a plot of land for rent that was already cleared during the construction of the wall. You start building a home there, complete with a 2-car garage. You think to yourself, why bother ever venturing out to the valley when you have everything you need here? Every day you do some good things, pay the tribute of a tenth of your income to the King, and then go home and shut your garage doors.

That may sound farfetched, but that's what many Christians have done today with what God has given them. Some Christians in this scenario do not even do this much. Instead, they spend all their time trying to spy on other prince's domains and petitioning the King to swap out the land. This isn't just about marketplace leadership; this is about leading yourself.

I know I'm personally guilty of all the above, and I've been in enough small groups and meetings to know the problem is a common one among believers. Understand this, though; you are part of the royal family and have been given authority from the King of the universe. In ancient times, those two factors alone would have made you the ultimate type of King, one of blood and authority.

The Bible does a great job illustrating delegated authority through the story of the Centurion.

> "When Jesus had entered Capernaum, a centurion came to Him, asking for help.
>
> "Lord," he said, "my servant lies at home paralyzed, suffering terribly."

Jesus said to him, "Shall I come and heal him?"

The centurion replied, "Lord, I do not deserve to have You come under my roof. But just say the word, and my servant will be healed.

For I myself am a man under authority, with soldiers under me. I tell this one, 'Go,' and he goes; and that one, 'Come,' and he comes. I say to my servant, 'Do this,' and he does it."

When Jesus heard this, He was amazed and said to those following Him, "Truly I tell you, I have not found anyone in Israel with such great faith.

I say to you that many will come from the east and the west and will take their places at the feast with Abraham, Isaac and Jacob in the kingdom of heaven. But the subjects of the kingdom will be thrown outside, into the darkness, where there will be weeping and gnashing of teeth."

Then Jesus said to the centurion, "Go! Let it be done just as you believed it would." And his servant was healed at that moment.
— Matthew 8:5-13 NIV

The centurion clearly understood delegated authority because, during the era of the Roman Empire, Caesar did not make every decision. No leader can do this. This is why you see many companies fail. They don't empower their employees. Caesar delegated his authority, and those leader's authority was delegated down to the lowest level. It's this authority that allowed the Roman empire to grow. It's this kind of leadership that will cause your endeavors to grow as well.

God is infinitely more capable than any human. He gives us commands and directives and then empowers us with the most powerful authority there is in the universe.

> Then Jesus came to them and said, "All authority in heaven and on earth has been given to Me.
>
> Therefore, go and make disciples of all nations, baptizing them in the name of the Father and of the Son and of the Holy Spirit, and teaching them to obey everything I have commanded you.
>
> And surely, I am with you always, to the very end of the age."
> **— Matthew 28:18-20 NIV**

> "Very truly I tell you, whoever believes in Me will do the works I have been doing, and they will do even greater things than these, because I am going to the Father.
>
> And I will do whatever you ask in My name, so that the Father may be glorified in the Son.
>
> You may ask Me for anything in My name, and I will do it."
> **— John 14:12-14 NIV**

To step into your kingly calling, you must understand *whose* you are. You are God's, and He is yours. To truly live, you must submit everything to Him. Only then will you be able to carry out His will for your life.

Before we move on, it's worth recapping your first criteria to understand your kingship. The reason I want to invest so much time in this piece is that it's the foundation of everything. Until you understand whose you are and how valuable you are to the King, you'll never fully grasp the value of the mission He has for you.

1. You're adopted by the King of the universe - you're essentially a crown prince - a co-regent or co-king. (Galatians 4:4-7, Romans 8:17)

2. Your King has delegated authority and power to you. (John 14:12, Acts 1:8)

KINGLY DEFINITION

For the context of this book, here's your kingly definition:

> A kingdom driven leader is someone who, understanding the power and responsibility given to them, gathers and stewards resources for the kingdom. A kingdom driven leader intentionally expands the kingdom of their influence and willingly takes ownership of supporting the greater kingdom, often through partnership with a Priest.

CHARACTERISTICS OF A KING

When I examined the kings of Israel from Saul to Zedekiah and compared them to Christ, I was lit on fire. Finally, Chronicles had a purpose in the Bible! Like Leviticus, Chronicles was a book I skipped when reading through previously. I never truly understood the connection until this examination.

What matched up is inside the chapters of this book. I purposefully restrained myself from only focusing on Saul, David, and Solomon. Those kings are likely the ones you are most familiar with. David is the closest perhaps to living like Christ, but each king's reign has a story to tell and a lesson. My hope is that you'll see these characteristics and actions as helpful.

That's an important point that might be missed in the text of this introduction. It's not just characteristics; it's also actions. Integrity is where actions meet words. You can't have humility without action, wisdom is useless without action, and you'll devalue the advice you receive if you don't act on it. Living like a kingdom driven leader is about understanding your authority and about taking action.

PREPARE TO REIGN

As you go on this journey with me, here's a preview of what you'll find. At the beginning of the journey, you'll want to understand the foundations of a dynasty. We are not endeavoring to simply learn about godly principles but rather to put them into action. We aim to build a life that impacts generations. This first section of the book is all about preparing your heart. Every good king had some measure of these characteristics. Though, a great kingdom driven leader is also never satisfied with the quality of these characteristics.

The greatest kings to appear in the Word were characterized by humility and wisdom. This is especially true with how they stewarded resources. They listened to the wise counsel of their inner circle, and they pursued excellence in all things.

What I love about this study of kings is that it translates very easily to modern-day leadership principles and values.

BEGIN TO REIGN

While "heart work" is never done, a kingdom driven leader truly becomes a kingdom driven leader when they decide to take action. It's the intentionality behind the decision and the willingness to take that first step toward becoming a better leader that makes the difference. When a kingdom driven leader takes full responsibility for their decisions as it relates to the kingdom, only then can they call themselves a leader worth following.

Every good king in the Bible knew the "why" of their mission. They attacked spiritual strongholds and tore them down. The best of the best were intentional networkers, and they always had generous hearts.

REIGNING WITH CHRIST

In order to build a dynasty, kings had to be intentional about reigning. They needed to continue to grow themselves and intentionally grow what they were reigning over. Much like the parables of the talents, we, too, are called to multiply our influence.

Great kings and Christ did this with intentionality. They grew in influence by valuing people while at the same time being laser-focused on the mission. This focus produced growth in influence and responsibility.

ENEMIES OF THE KING

Almost every Old Testament king had a downfall of some kind. Unfortunately, most of them failed to finish well. It is said that failure is the best teacher. We cannot just learn from their mistakes, but we also see what Jesus did to defeat these temptations. Temptations like pride, lust, and envy aren't unique in and of themselves, but they do present themselves in unique ways to leaders.

THE RHYTHM OF A DYNASTY

One of my passions is businesses that have a kingdom mission. Businesses that are designed to generate enormous profit and create an enormous impact are kingdom driven. As I have looked at businesses making an impact, I noticed they have characteristics that you and I can follow.

As I started to write this book, I began to solicit opinions from friends and business people alike about what makes a great leader that is driven to impact the kingdom. What I found was that their responses to my questions were uncannily like what I had discovered through research. Questions as to what makes a godly leader different from a non-godly one were surprisingly similar. Furthermore, what was also interesting is how surprised they were when their story matched that of a king in the Bible.

One of those friends is Jace Rabe, the cashew processing businessman from earlier. Jace most closely represents a "kingdom driven leader," in my mind. You'd be hard-pressed to find a man that loves the Lord more than Jace and has impacted an entire nation. When I asked him how he'd define a kingdom driven leader, I started to see how universal his ideas were. Unprompted and unaware that I was currently writing this book, he said,

» A kingdom driven leader is someone who recognizes the supreme authority of Christ and is submitted to that authority.

» A kingdom driven leader takes discerned risks by sowing in new directions and in unplanted fields with the goal of bringing in an increase for the kingdom.

» A kingdom driven leader is explicit and intentional in expanding the kingdom by focusing on the areas that maximize his returns that grow the kingdom in terms of resources, land, influence, and power.

» A kingdom driven leader recognizes his human limits and develops his people by entrusting them and empowering them to take responsibility and ownership in the kingdom they are growing together.

» A true kingdom driven leader has advisors everywhere but understands that God has placed him in this position of authority; thus, he makes all decisions at the throne of God.

OF KINGDOMS

There are two types of kingdoms that we will refer to in this book, God's kingdom and the one He's entrusted to us to steward. God's kingdom is everything, it's all His, and there is no disputing that. You have been given gifts to help grow His kingdom in different ways. I often see this play out in the business world with how people invest their money. Essentially, God's kingdom is the one we want to grow intentionally.

The second kingdom mentioned in this book is our kingdom. This is the area that God has given us to rule, steward, and reign. A stay-at-home mom has one of the most impactful and deep kingdoms there is. This mom (through Christ) influences her husband and assists in raising a new generation of world changers. She controls the atmosphere in the home and can set the tone for everyone else. She is truly the queen of the home.

A CEO might have a broad influence over hundreds of employees and thousands of customers, but many of those customers will fall outside the gates of his immediate kingdom. The more a leader is responsible for, the more he needs to set his priorities.

The purpose of this book is really to take you a few steps further in your discipleship journey beyond just being a good tither or offering a few hours each week in service. The purpose is to help you create a bigger impact by leveraging the kingdom resources you have been given. In other words, I hope this book helps grow your influence and leverage your systems in new ways to reach people for Christ.

A problem arises when we look out over our balcony from our kingdom and envy other people's kingdoms. We were never meant to compare ourselves to others. We were only meant to compare ourselves to Jesus. When you read this, try to hold the "yeah buts" until the end. I hope to show you that God has given you a kingdom, whether you are a CEO, an entrepreneur, or a stay-at-home mom. He has a specific mission just for you.

Unfortunately, some will never fully see their kingdom's legacy. You, however, must have faith that God is using you for a mighty work no matter what you can see with your eyes. Our entire life is a love affair with a God that created us to be in relationship with Him first and for us to help Him heal and love others that He created for that same purpose.

In "The Purpose Driven Life," Rick Warren says that we're ultimately created to worship God. That's absolutely correct, but I think we get the word 'worship' twisted. We often imagine bowing down or some boring chanting with some deity keeping us at arms' length. Our God thought about us before the world was formed (Ephesians 1:4), knows everything we will do and think (Psalm 139), and still wants to have a relationship with us. This relationship is one of a loving Father who wants to have fun with us, wants us to conquer a mission, and look up and say, "Wow, Dad, look what you did through me!"

Many of us have a wrong perspective of God's love and His design. We must set the foundation correctly. We need to get where we can see everyone as God sees them. The only way we can do that is if we spend enough time with Him to learn how He sees us.

There's a saying that you should trust a tour guide more than a travel agent. The reason is that the tour guide is there, knows the area, and is an expert, while the travel agent has only read the brochure. It's hard to share your experience with God with others if you have not had your own personal experience. When it comes to helping people, you need to be a tour guide and not a travel agent. You must have God as your number one priority.

BELIEF

This book is about you. I mentioned before that I believe businesses have the biggest opportunity to change the world. Chances are high that you work as a leader in the marketplace or in your sphere of influence. Like your kingship, you might not have accepted the authority, but you are a leader. Leadership is not the same thing as a positional title. I'm talking specifically about the level on which you use your influence intentionally.

What does *"living like a Kingdom Driven Leader"* mean?

> **Kings are intentional in wielding their influence to grow and steward God's kingdom.**

Throughout the rest of this book, we'll be covering the Biblical principles of how to grow your God-given kingdom. We'll compare what the Bible tells us about successful kings in the Old Testament, match that to Jesus' life and what He did, and compare that to what we can do in the marketplace. We'll cover how to steward the kingdom and ultimately how to diagnose problems within your kingdom so that you can rule effectively.

If you don't connect directly with the business leanings of this book, don't be discouraged. Revert to that first part in understanding that even a position considered "lowly" by some in our western society has the influence to wield. You don't need a massive business or an important position to make an impact. Your workplace and sphere of influence are your mission field.

Consider the generation we live in now. Even if you have "employee" status and benefits, you essentially are a long-term contractor for the company. I believe my parents' generation might be the last to work at a company for 30 plus years at the same company and retire. To some extent, this is a great thing. You are the company of you. You must take responsibility for growing yourself and look for opportunities. This mindset is useful in understanding your role as a leader.

If you go back to my allegory of being given a tract of land, realize that not everyone is given a 1,000-acre valley. Some may be given a quarter acre of thorns. Regardless of what you've been given, it's yours to steward. God sometimes allows instances in our life to create the kind of character He's looking for. In order to be used by God, you must be usable. It's often how we steward the situations we find ourselves in that reveal whether we're ready for the mission or not. I think the Bible says it best.

> "But blessed are those who trust in the Lord and have made the Lord their hope and confidence. They are like trees planted along a riverbank, with roots that reach deep into the water. Such trees are not bothered by the heat or worried by long months of drought. Their leaves stay green, and they never stop producing fruit."
> **— Jeremiah 17:7-8 NLT**

As a kingdom driven leader, it's your job to shine a light even in the midst of a vocational season that you'd describe as a drought. However, this isn't just about being salt and light. That's a prerequisite. If you call yourself a Christian, this is your responsibility. However, as a kingdom driven leader, you're called to so much more. You are called to make an eternal impact.

You don't have to be an entrepreneur or high-level manager to get this concept. It's all how you perceive yourself. When I decided to write this out, I wanted you to see yourself as God sees you, as a son and daughter first, and also as a kingdom driven leader who is a warrior, adventurer, and one under the authority of God.

Please re-read that. You cannot live like a king if you don't accept your adoption first. This is where the authority comes from. It's from the Father through you. This is how you can rule because it's your right as an heir. This is why it's repeated over and over again throughout Scripture.

> "But when the right time came, God sent His Son, born of a woman, subject to the law. God sent Him to buy freedom for us who were slaves to the law, so that He could adopt us as His very own children."
> **— Galatians 4:4-5 NLT**

Successful kings lived through four main stages: Preparation, Reigning, Ruling, and Dynasty. These stages are not necessarily sequential, with the exception of starting with preparation, but like life, there is a natural progression between them. There are always times when you may be preparing to move into new territory and rule in a new area of life. In addition, I've met great leaders that are building a dynasty of leadership in one area of their life while continuing to mature in other areas of life. The great news is that while God may have completely wiped the slate clean to start fresh with your heart, He's able to use so much of your life experiences for the Kingdom that nothing is wasted.

Like any king, you must start with preparation. Even Jesus had thirty-three years to prepare for His mission. Once you start operating with this authority, you need to establish your kingdom. The act of reigning lays the foundation for your expansion. Never stagnant, once a king's domain is stable, they plan offensives to expand the Kingdom. Ruling from an understanding of who you are ruling for allows you to create a dynasty. All of these thoughts are huge shifts in paradigms from what I experienced as a young Christian entrepreneur. Each one is worth spending time understanding what the Bible says about becoming a kingdom driven leader.

SECTION I
PREPARATION

2

Prepare to Rule

Before there were kings in the Bible, there were leaders. Every story points to leadership. Noah, Abraham, and Joseph were all steadfast in their love of God and were blessed because of it. However, there is one leader that could be called the greatest Old Testament leader, Moses.

Moses' highlight reel includes the plagues of Egypt, freeing the Israelite nation, the splitting of the Red Sea, and delivering the ten commandments. What is usually missed in this notable list of things remembered about Moses is the interesting way in which God prepared him to lead.

During Moses' birth, the Israelites were slaves in Egypt, but God continued to bless them, and their population grew. The Pharaoh, or king, of that time, decided to kill the male babies of the Israelites to control the population.

As the story goes in Exodus 2, Moses' mother placed him in a basket in the river. Moses' basket miraculously floats to where the princess of the pharaoh is bathing. In God's divine plan, Moses ends up being one of the only Jewish baby boys that get spared after being adopted by the princess.

In the king's household Moses was groomed to assist in ruling the nation. In other words, he was being prepared to lead. However, when he reached adulthood, he was still not ready. After seeing the plight of his people, Moses tried to take matters into his own hands and killed a man.

Forced to flee, Moses spent the next 40 years as a shepherd before God called him via a burning bush.

For brevity's sake, I'll skip ahead to the time after the Israelites were freed and they were in the wilderness. Moses wasn't done growing in leadership. As he listened to the Israelites problems, he took the advice of some wise counsel to delegate some authority and manage the people.

All throughout Moses' story, we read about him in a state of constant growth and preparation.

While you can never grow enough, preparing to be a kingdom driven leader is a process that can't be overlooked or underemphasized. You can never grow enough. Preparations build a foundation for you to reign with Christ. These lessons in the first part of this book are the ones I can point to almost every time I have experienced a breakthrough.

There is a saying that says your life's past events are preparation for your current circumstances. I know God works together for our good (Romans 8:28). If we can't see it now, He has great plans for us, and the opportunities come so fast that we may feel unprepared. In fact, Israel's first king was anointed in this very manner. But as history goes, Saul is not remembered as a great king.

AN UNPREPARED KING

When we see Israel's first official king arrive on the scene in the book of 1 Samuel, Saul was looking for his father's donkeys. He searched high and low, and then he decided to give up on his mission and go back home. It was his servant that urged him to visit the "man of God," who just happened to be in the city at the time. Saul didn't immediately think this was a good idea.

Let's pause here for a second and read I Samuel 9.

You may have noticed in your reading that Saul not only wanted to give up on the mission, but he only acquiesced when it didn't cost him anything to continue. **How often have we missed God by not finishing the assignment we start or stopping it when it costs too much?** If Saul's servant didn't persist or have the money to give as an offering, then Saul may have never been made king.

To an average person, Saul looked like a king should look. He was tall and handsome, came from a wealthy family, and appeared to be humble. His heart was humble enough to receive the anointing and allowed his heart to be changed.

Clearly, Saul was flawed. Yet, God chose someone that was a representation of what the people wanted. In other words, their perception of what a great king would be was wrong.

There are two clear thoughts here. The first is that what we want is often not exactly what God wants. We need to seek His answers to our problems versus what we think the answers are because what He wants is what's best for us.

The second, and possibly just as important thought, is that often we don't see ourselves as God sees us. Going around calling yourself a king may feel weird. God sees us as His children, so elevating our self-view is hard, especially if we've been brought up in church culture that identifies pride as the ultimate sin.

Remember, you were handcrafted in your mother's womb (Psalm 139:13) for this mission, so you have everything you need with God's help to accomplish it. We have the Father's words, a relationship with Jesus, and the guidance of the Holy Spirit to accomplish our mission. The challenging part of this is that we often envision the calling through our own worldly lens. We measure the success or failure of the mission based on what we know here on Earth. Our perceptions and expectations of what God wants are often wrong. He wants you to be an eternal success, not just a temporal one. Thank God His ways are better! We should be thankful that He's written so much down for us.

WHY PREPARE?

1 Samuel 10:9 says, "God changed Saul's heart." So, you might think to yourself that Jesus changed your heart, so you must be ready. Unfortunately, if Saul is any indication, just receiving the power of the Holy Spirit and having a changed heart is not enough. In fact, at the very moment that Saul is being announced as king, he is found running and hiding from his responsibility in the baggage.

> "So, Samuel brought all the tribes of Israel before the Lord, ... And finally, Saul son of Kish was chosen from among them. But when they looked for him, he had disappeared! So, they asked the Lord, 'Where is he?' And the Lord replied, 'He is hiding among the baggage.
> **— 1 Samuel 10:20-22 NLT (edited)**

Saul's life is an example of what happens when we pursue things outside of God's timing. Often, we want something to change in our life and become frustrated with God for not changing it. In these instances, two things tend to happen, we grow further away from God and become more frustrated. What we don't fully appreciate is that God is using our current circumstances to prepare us for what's ahead.

God knows what you need when you need it. He's timeless. He knows the past and the future and sees it all at the same time. What He is doing now may very well be preparing you for the future.

For those unfamiliar with the story, Saul became prideful. How quickly he went from God's anointed, to hiding in the baggage to thinking he was the one in control.

Saul chose not to wait on God and did things for himself, and it immediately caused his downfall. As we'll see later in this book, choosing not to wait on God was the turning point. A new king was anointed, and

Saul began to lose his mind.

That new king was David. Contrast David with Saul. Here was a young man that had been walking with God and trusting Him for all his victories. When I read the two books of Samuel, I find myself convicted with how much David relied on communication with God. David was intentional with his relationship with God and was prepared when the call came.

Prepared Old Testament kings were relatively good kings. You know the name Solomon, but what about Josiah? Like Solomon, one of Josiah's first recorded actions as king was to seek wisdom.

If you're concerned that time has passed you by or that you're not in the right position, don't be. Consider Jeroboam. He worked with such excellence as superintendent of his tribesman in building parts of Jerusalem that he was noticed by King Solomon and by God. He was prepared. Jeroboam was in leadership but had no hopes of being king. He didn't know what God knew about the future division of Israel. It's a great reminder to be faithful where you are because even if you're in the middle of the journey, you can still prepare to rule.

> **We must prepare if we are truly to live like kingdom driven leaders.**

The journey is long and full of challenges, and you might wish to quit. Preparing is not the process of doing things under your own power but rather studying God's Word and what He wants from us and for us. You can't only prepare yourself in a traditional physical sense. You must also prepare your heart. Be intentional about ordering your footsteps to steward the kingdom God's given you and the future opportunities to expand His kingdom that He wants to give you.

Paul said it best.

> "But He said to me, 'My grace is sufficient for you, for My power is made perfect in weakness.' Therefore, I will boast all the more gladly about my weaknesses, so that Christ's power may rest on me. That is why, for Christ's sake, I delight in weaknesses, in insults, in hardships, in persecutions, in difficulties. For when I am weak, then I am strong."
> **— 2 Corinthians 12:9-10 NIV**

Preparing yourself is not about your strength. The only strength that is required from you is to receive what God has for you.

Imagine for a second you are a child. Today is "Take Your Child to Work Day" at your dad's office, so you go with him, and everything about the day feels larger than life. From the moment you wake up, you're excited with anticipation. Your best clothes are laid out for you. Your hair is perfect. Even the drive to the office is filled with excitement.

As you arrive, that feeling is still there. The building feels gigantic. The security desk gives you the sense that you're on a mission. The elevator swallows you up as you ride to the workspace. Ding! The doors open, and the cubicle walls tower over you like the walls of Jericho!

Throughout the day, you have a sense of awe. When you discover that the chairs spin around, you think to yourself that this is the coolest job in the world. Throughout the day, your dad introduces you to all his co-workers. Your dad must be the boss because they all treat him with respect and honor and greet you like royalty.

Occasionally during this day, your dad gives you special assignments. He asks you to take extremely important papers across the office. He has you push the enter key on an urgent e-mail.

After work, he takes you for ice cream and asks what you thought of the day. You recount how much work you put in and how exciting it was.

Your dad then tells you that he is proud of you. He says he is particularly proud of your maturity in the office and how attentive you were.

Just as earthly fathers want us to experience the privileges and blessings of sharing in his work, our Heavenly Father wants to take us to work with Him too.

EXAMPLE OF PREPARATION

Truly our only real example of a great King is Jesus. We'll continue to review Israel's flawed kings for instructions, but Jesus is the prototype. Often, we think we can never achieve what Jesus did, and yet He's the one that says we'll do greater things through Him!

> "I tell you the truth, anyone who believes in Me will do the same works I have done, and *even greater works*, because I am going to be with the Father."
> **— John 14:12 NLT (emphasis mine)**

Jesus had a life of preparation. From an early age, He was found at the synagogue learning God's Word. Then we saw Him being baptized and immediately tested in the desert before launching His ministry.

I know it's an odd thing. How and why did Christ, fully God, fully man, perfect in every way, need to learn anything? Hebrews 5:8 in the Amplified version tells us clearly, what happened. "Although He was a Son [who had never been disobedient to the Father], He learned [active, special] obedience through what He suffered..." Verse 9 tells the reason for the necessity of His preparation.

> "And having been made perfect [uniquely equipped and prepared as Savior and retaining His integrity amid opposition], He became the source of eternal salvation [an eternal inheritance] to all those who obey Him"
> **— Hebrews 5:8-9 AMP**

> Jesus chose to fully experience what it means to be human so that He could become relatable to us, to be our source. Hebrews again gives us insight into this, "For we do not have a High Priest who is unable to empathize with our weaknesses, but we have one who has been tempted in every way, just as we are—yet He did not sin"
> **— Hebrews 4:15 NIV**

Remember when I referenced the tour guide versus the travel agent? In the context of our life and our walk with Jesus, this little analogy is profound. We can truly trust Jesus because He's been through anything and everything we've had to or will face.

If you are to step into ruling the kingdom God has given you, you need to prepare your heart. You need to be humble, willing to follow God, and constantly seeking His wisdom. You will also need to understand the very practical and biblical law of reaping and sowing to steward God's resources. To put it plainly, you need to learn how to manage yourself, your influence, and your finances.

ALL THINGS ANALOGOUS

Most salespeople that achieve success rarely do so without training and preparation. An inexperienced salesperson will often say something like, "I don't need a script. It won't sound authentic." However, any skilled salesperson will tell you that the script is everything. Internalizing it gives you control in a conversation. This control is not meant to be abused or used to manipulate your audience, but rather it should help remove objections so that the client can decide.

Sales training is valuable preparation, and I don't believe in coincidence. If you went through years of such training (or any other training), God had a purpose for it. It could be to be His salesperson of the Gospel, but more than likely, it will be used as part of several key missions.

As you prepare yourself to be a kingdom driven leader and as you look at the tools and training you have already been given, don't make assumptions. Don't make the mistake of measuring your mission by the world's standard. The size of your mission does not correlate to the impact that it will have. Sometimes God has us on a training regimen that might seem like a waste of time, but in reality, it's preparing us for a future mission. Take sales, for example.

I struggled greatly with my calling while I was in sales. Before my sales role, I didn't know how to talk with people or understand other people's decision-making processes. Learning about sales, however, gave me confidence in a job interview and confidence to speak with strangers. Sales also gave me skills to generate income. Being in a sales role allowed me to value relationships as a long-term resource.

I see sales as part of God's training regimen for me. Now when I'm with an unbeliever, I'm able to understand, at least partly, their decision process and see the objections they have to following Christ. Because I value relationships in the long term, I've had the opportunity to connect with individuals that have blessed me and others in very special ways.

Other training, such as computer programming, may not be as obvious. Be very aware that this is a war to win souls and resources. Whether your training allows you to be a big earner or perhaps be an infiltration unit with the ability to influence from within, all things work together for our good and His mission. The point is that the training you've had up until this point is for a purpose.

REMEMBER THE ONE

> What do you think? If a man owns a hundred sheep, and one of them wanders away, will he not leave the ninety-nine on the hills and go to look for the one that wandered off? And if he finds it, truly I tell you, he is happier about that one sheep than about the ninety-nine that did not wander off."
> — **Matthew 18: 12-13 NIV**

Before we jump into how you can prepare yourself, let me offer you what may be an eye-opener to you. God is all about the one. I know some churches talk about this in an effort to get you excited about inviting people to join you in church. That's good. However, what I'm talking about is a mission to get to one person. Like the movie "Saving Private Ryan," don't be surprised if God has you on this long, arduous journey to reach one person.

In the movie "Saving Private Ryan," a band of soldiers are tasked with going behind enemy lines to rescue Private Ryan during World War II. In the process of doing so, six out of the eight men on this mission died. All of this effort was to save one soldier. When people watch this movie, they are moved by the mission meant to save one person. Yet our God sent His only Son behind enemy lines for you! (John 3:16). To me, it only makes sense then that our mission is often for the one.

I can remember very clearly when this realization hit me. In my prayer time, I felt like God was asking me to create an event. I liked Catalyst at the time and felt like there needed to be a "business" version of that event. The idea was to get business owners to think like kings, taking them from a sense of success to significance.

The event was a non-profit event with the proceeds going to a local charity as well as a foreign one. The name "Heroic" became the theme for the event, and Heroic Event was born. Paperwork was filled out and a non-profit officially started. Everything I did felt so God-inspired. I knew this was going to be a huge success.

However, I'm not an event planner. There are times in our life when we face certain tasks or obstacles, and we just know, "that's not me." Event planning is not me.

I did what I honestly should do with everything. I just relied on God to make it happen. That does not mean that I simply sat on my hands.

I started soliciting help from friends and contacting various speakers whom I thought would be good. I started with the best of the best and quickly realized that with no budget and no experience, I was completely out of my depth. I had no idea what those highly sought-after speakers would cost. In at least one instance, I would have had to mortgage my home to get that caliber of speaker there.

However, the price didn't stop me. It compelled me to be more creative and prayerful. By doing so, I was able to line up Jim Reese, former CEO of Randstad and head of Atlanta Mission, Jace Rabe, the CEO of Tolaro Global, and Marci Fair, a co-owner of a large real estate franchise. We even had Aurea McGarry, Emmy Award-winning MC and author.

I just kept calling and talking about the event, and God helped me take baby steps. During this process, one area I was confident in was selling tickets. I gave very little thought or time to it because I knew that was a strength. Unfortunately, I was surprised to realize that everything I did was failing in this area. Friends were too busy to listen or attend. Colleagues and even vendors who rely on my business to succeed couldn't make it either.

Lucky for me, I did tell enough friends who helped bring their own people to attend. One special friend assembled a small team and began to sell tickets. I was told that most of the ticket sales wouldn't happen until the day before. So even though we only had about 40 tickets sold, I was confident that more would be sold the day of the event.

That confidence was misplaced. When only 45 or so people showed up, including my mom, in a room designed to hold 300, I was a bit dumbfounded. The lineup was great, the price was less than $50, and it was a full day of awesome content. Not to mention the funds all went to advertised charities.

The show must go on, as they say, and the event started, and every one of the speakers was professionals. They spoke as if the room was standing room only, and it was a great event. There was even one woman in the audience who was moved to tears.

As I was packing up, this woman came and told me, "*This* is what I needed to hear." After thanking her, I packed up and headed back to the office to drop off a few items before heading home.

On my way, I was praying. "Lord, I asked You to use me, and You told me I must become usable. I did everything You asked. I uncharacteristically waited on You to tell me the next steps. I did things that were going to be huge embarrassments if You didn't come through. Why then, did You not come through for me when it mattered at the end?"

I felt like God then said to me, "If you want to be used, you don't get to choose how you're used." I don't know if that's theologically correct, but that's the message I got. He followed up with, "What if I loved that woman so much, I caused you to act." Then He reminded me of the scripture mentioned at the beginning of this section. He came for the one.

What if, after 33 years of life, all that agony and suffering, and the death and resurrection Jesus endured, only one person got saved. God would still say it was worth it. It suddenly struck me that, I too, must be ok with impacting only one; whether it was a lesson in humility or a lesson in the importance of the mission, I'll never really know. However, I've learned a few things I want to pass on to you as you prepare for your mission.

» God's view of success is very different from the world. My event was a miserable worldly failure but very well could have been a godly success.

» God uses those that are usable. I've heard pastors put it this way, "It's hard to steer a parked car."

A KING'S MISSION

The mission of a king is rarely a simple and quick task. It's a growing process. During your life, if you place your value in the size or growth of your kingdom, your own estimate of your value may waiver. You may be doubting your power. You might be wrestling with your heart. The Bible is clear that we can be free from these things, but I cannot write this and not be honest that there are times in my own life where this is a struggle. Whether it was sales, the seemingly failed event, or even the process of writing this book, I have asked God, "Why?" I assumed that if God's called me to do something, it should be grandiose and excellent for all to see. My false assumption is that it should be attractive to the world.

Your mission will differ not only from everyone else's mission, but you most likely will have multiple missions throughout your life. The previous premise still applies in each instance. Through God's delegated authority, you have the power to complete it, and your mission will require you not just to serve people but take responsibility for them.

A business is a tool to generate profit. I believe God put businesses in our hearts. Our civilization cannot survive without businesses. Business, at its core, is simply people solving each other's problems and creating monetizable value from that solution. However you describe businesses, it always sounds similar to me at the end. It sounds a lot like serving to me.

The challenge that most businesses have is that they stop with profit. That's their main focus. God's purpose for businesses was never a place to hoard resources or to extract as much profit from its customers without providing value. No, God's purpose for the profit was progress in growing the Kingdom.

At a base level, a business can give some of its profits to the church or an organization and accomplish this. This is good, but it is not necessarily missional. Missional efforts take you from good to great and from success to significance.

THREE STAGES OF A KINGDOM DRIVEN LEADER'S REIGN

Churches and businesses are very similar. Obviously, there *are* differences, but there are enough similarities that it's worth looking at it from the perspective that they are similar. God calls the church the Body, and each member is valuable. A business then is an organism, and its people make up its body. It needs constant growth to survive long term, and its health can be measured. In this light, it's easy to see why when you evaluate businesses, it can be uncanny how much they mirror personal life.

One of the most impactful sermons I can remember from my pastor, Dennis Rouse, is one in which he explained the stages of most people's walk. They go from survival to success, then to significance. I'd argue that most businesses find themselves in similar stages. However, for a business with a kingdom mindset, I'd reword the stages as Gather, Give, Go

GATHER

A business purpose, as defined by the world, is simply to derive profit. It makes sense then that all businesses start with the initial purpose of gathering income. Accordingly, the first stage every business starts with is the "Gather" stage.

Most businesses, entrepreneurs, and new marketplace leaders are in this stage. There's nothing inherently wrong with gathering. Most businesses are "bootstrapped," that is, they have to start and launch with little or no funding. Gathering resources is a perfectly acceptable and financially sound stage. There's no shame in being in a gathering stage, just as there is no shame in being in a survival state. Statistically, over 80% of small businesses fail in the first 2 years, and even fewer make it to year 5. [iii]

The challenge is moving forward out of the gathering state. Many businesses intentionally or unintentionally stay in this state. Many of the world's non-Christian business owners stay here because there is no need to push beyond it. It keeps them financially sound and usually makes a few people wealthy.

While this may be a seemingly safe and comfortable place to remain, God has called us to do more. In Luke, Jesus tells the parable about the rich fool who decides to increase his storage for wealth.

> "Then he said, 'This is what I'll do. I will tear down my barns and build bigger ones, and there I will store my surplus grain. And I'll say to myself, 'You have plenty of grain laid up for many years. Take life easy; eat, drink and be merry.' But God said to him, 'You fool! This very night your life will be demanded from you. Then who will get what you have prepared for yourself?' This is how it will be with whoever stores up things for themselves but is not rich toward God."
> **— Luke 12:18-21 NIV**

We can read that parable and easily see this as folly. However, we need to re-examine our financial budgets to make sure we aren't guilty of the same thing. When you realize that you are simply a steward for God's resources and that you are supposed to be a river and not a reservoir of resources, you move to the second stage. Give.

GIVE

Most organizations I've had the pleasure to know that make it out of that dreadful first 2 or 3 years are in this category. They have a surplus, so they are actively giving to their community or to a charity. What's exciting is that many members of the millennial generation often go into business with this goal in mind.

In and of itself, a business is just a system built to solve a problem. This problem solving produces a value that is exchanged into profit. However, the power of the business profit is that it can do so many things to impact the lives of the employees, the customers, and the community. No law says a business or a business leader must give. I personally feel that it's every leader's responsibility to search for those opportunities where their business can make a positive impact. Most great businesses create excess. In addition, as Christians, we are called to stand out.

> "But you are a chosen people, a royal priesthood, a holy nation, God's special possession, that you may declare the praises of Him who called you out of darkness into His wonderful light."
> **— 1 Peter 2:9 NIV**

Sadly, it is often the non-Christian business owners that outgive the Christian business leaders! Look at a business like Toms Shoes that gives a pair of shoes to those in need whenever they sell a pair of full-priced shoes. In researching Toms Shoes, I found nothing Christian about the company. You could say that Toms Shoes is only giving because it's good press. Where Toms Shoes is different than say Goodwill is that Toms is giving the shoes away. Whether it's 5% or 10%, it's still an amount that's been set aside to give.

That's a key takeaway. You must be proactive and take a step. To be an effective giver, you must set aside the resources to give. You must look at your budget and earmark the amount to give. I use percentages, but you could have a giving goal that isn't percentage-based.

You'll never accomplish great things if you don't take the first step. Giving, even something small is often the first step to bigger things for the kingdom. There is something that happens when you essentially "give back" what you were given. It reveals that you trust God as your provider enough to give.

An entrepreneur or marketplace leader is in this stage when they are giving over and above their tithe. If you aren't at the "give" stage yet, then aspire to be. Giving is not a someday destination. It's a decision that you can make that God will bless. Often giving can open doors to new opportunities, whether it be good press or new relationships. It's a Biblical principle, give, and you will be given to. Another way the Bible says, you're blessed to be a blessing. Read Jesus's words in Luke 6:38 NLT.

> "Give, and you will receive. Your gift will return to you in full--pressed down, shaken together to make room for more, running over, and poured into your lap. The amount you give will determine the amount you get back."

Need more examples from Scripture? Read Deuteronomy 15:10, Proverbs 11:24, 22:9, 2 Corinthian 9:6-7.

Many businesses give to the Red Cross or give to special projects at the church and call it a day. This is a great place to be, and there are many great examples of givers, both Christian and non-Christian. However, for businesses and leaders to be driven by eternity, there's another stage that I'd like for you to strive for.

GO

> "Therefore, go and make disciples of all nations, baptizing them in the name of the Father and of the Son and of the Holy Spirit."
> **— Matthew 28:19 NIV**

> ".... and you will be My witnesses in Jerusalem, and in all Judea and Samaria, and to the ends of the earth."
> **— Acts 1:8 NIV**

Few Christian leaders ever reach this stage. It's the mixing and melding of a business and a mission. Very, very few non-Christian companies get here either. It'd be easy to herald businesses that do well that are openly Christian, but international businesses rarely allow this sort of freedom. For a leader engaged in this stage, you need to be engrossed in Kingdom work.

This doesn't mean you have to build churches or orphanages. And it doesn't mean you have to pay to help Bible smugglers. You could be building hospitals or providing clothing and food to the needy. It's a subtle difference that makes a similar impact.

"Going" looks different than Giving. It's taking a specific action or physically going somewhere. The key factor in "going" is responsibility. It's taking it upon yourself to not just give to a charity but be committed to the work. The difference between the Give and the Go stages is that in the Go stage, you are using your time and talent, not just your treasure, to impact God's kingdom.

My hope is that as you grow from gathering to giving, that you'd create enough momentum to begin "Going." This is where your business can leave a legacy because of the impact that was left.

SUCCESS VS. SIGNIFICANCE

I'm from Atlanta, and I'm what they call a "homer." For those unfamiliar, a "homer" is basically someone who loves all things from their hometown. Usually, this term is meant to describe someone who discards the reality of the losing sports team in their city and still believes their team will win the big game. I love my city and pretty much anything it produces. I love the fact that in every town I've visited, none of them come close to the diversity of Atlanta. While New York has its burrows and "blocks," Atlanta is just one big sprawling city of diversity.

Just like the sports teams, the companies founded in Atlanta are the best. You've got Chick-fil-A, Home Depot, Delta, and Coca-Cola, just to name a few. Each is incredibly successful in its own right, so what I'm about to do is admittedly unfair. I'm going to measure a company against a standard that they do not strive to achieve. I'm going to look at one of my favorite companies that is, in many ways, excellent. I'm going to examine this company from a "kingdom perspective," though they do not intentionally operate from this perspective. The fact that I'm using this company is a testament to how great it is, not an indictment.

The Coca-Cola Company is, by all accounts, a successful company. They sit atop of the world of beverage companies with width and depth that only allows one real competitor. They have multiple brand lines within the company and many other successful endeavors.

The Coca-Cola company even has a great mission statement:

"Refresh the world. Make a difference." [3]

That sounds amazing, and it matches their brand. If you're like me, then this is the very first time you've ever read this or heard about it. You're starting to see the drift from good to great and from success to significance before I even make the case, aren't you?

The Coca-Cola company does many good things for charities, and they spend a great deal of effort making their company more sustainable. If you read all their marketing, you'll find that they often "give" through sponsorships or donating to education. It's easy to miss the brand because it's ever-present in our lives. Much to the dismay of every northern traveler that asks for a "pop" and gets a look that can only suggest that the traveler was indeed from outer space, there are no pops or sodas in the South. The only carbonated beverage is a "coke" in the South.

The list of accomplishments by any other standard is great. Who's to say that the CEO or the Board aren't all born-again Christians? What I am pointing out is glaringly obvious.

If their mission was to refresh the world, why not end world thirst? I'm in no way calling out Coca-Cola. I'm a huge fan of the Atlanta-based company, and they do a ton of great charitable giving. It's not their responsibility to fix the world. It's *ours*, as Christians. With that out of the way, let's go a bit deeper into the numbers.

It's estimated that Coca-Cola Enterprises globally brings in $41 Billion[4]. According to the UN, it's going to cost $30 Billion to fix not just the world's food problems but also the world's water problem. However important, it's not about the money. I can't stress this point enough.

Business is a tool. In a sense, a successful business is made up of humans integrated into systems to help it perform. Coca-Cola is a great example of this. It has hard assets like patents and real estate, but more importantly, it has the logistical supply chain and workforce.

I found this Huffington Post article by Auren Kaplan[5] that points out that it's going to take some money (relatively speaking) and a Coca-Cola-like supply chain to fix this problem. She sees the potential in a company like Coca-Cola that I did.

Imagine if Coca-Cola said they would earmark $500 million a year to end world hunger and thirst. Keep in mind that depending on the financial report, Coca-Cola reportedly spends over $5 Billion a year in marketing globally. Taking the lead in ending world thirst would be far better for their brand than any reformulation of "the original coke" or buying the next Vitamin Water. Their profits would soar, and at the same time, they'd make a very tangible impact on the world. The magnitude of potential impact gives me chills just typing this out. This is business as a mission, and it's that kind of business that kingdom driven leaders are called to run.

It's not fair to critique a great company like Coca-Cola against a standard they never chose. Instead of picking on a great company, let's look at one that measures itself against our kingly standards.

MY PLEASURE

It's easy to pull a mission out of Chick-fil-A. You only have to order one sandwich to realize they are doing something missional with their employees. When you drive up for the first time, Chick-fil-A just seems like a slightly cleaner fast-food place. However, there is something magical about a teenager delivering your food with a smile that just makes you want to say thank you. You will then hear those magical words, "My pleasure," in response.

Chick-fil-A doesn't have a mission statement. They have a purpose. Read it and see if it doesn't remind you of something right away.

> "To glorify God by being a faithful steward of all that is entrusted to us. To have a positive influence on all who come in contact with Chick-fil-A." [6]

To me, Chick-fil-A's statement sounds almost like a Bible verse. It reminds me of one of my life verses, Colossians 3:23, which says, "Work willingly at whatever you do, as though you were working for the Lord rather than for people (NLT)." Chick-fil-A is still a privately-owned family business. When you read through the pages on their website for "about us" and dive into what they are doing, there is an air of humility.

I may not agree with every decision they make, but I think much of what Chick-fil-A has prioritized is right. I appreciate that they choose to influence their family first. You can see this visibly by them being closed on Sunday to honor God and the families that work there. If you read the history of the company, you'll see that family values are at the core of what they do.

After family, Chick-fil-A prioritizes the people that serve at the restaurant. Notice they didn't say "work"; they said, "serve." It's an attitude shift that is reflective of Chick-fil-A's values.

From there, they serve the customers that come to the restaurants. When all of that is working, the local Chick-fil-A operators can invest in the community.

Chick-fil-A, like Coca-Cola, is at the very top of its field. This business is the most profitable fast-food restaurant in the US, period, and it does it six days a week. It's not just the $19 Million in scholarships through the Peach Bowl[7], the $92 Million in scholarships from the company's scholarship program[8], or the other millions spent on community efforts. It's because Chick-fil-A follows kingdom principles of priority.

The point of the comparison is not to glorify Chick-fil-A and potentially demonize Coca-Cola. The point is to show how much potential a kingdom driven business has to impact the world. Chick-fil-A is arguably doing this, so much so that many people use their business as a reference when talking about a good company. When someone says, "they are the Chick-fil-A of" that business niche, they are usually suggesting that the company possesses Christian values.

The key part missing from these comparisons is all the people and leaders that make these businesses run. When you look at a business's impact as a whole, you rarely look at the most valuable asset, the people.

Usually, it's the leader in charge that gets the credit. However, neither one of these companies become worth writing about without strong leadership at every level.

As a kingdom driven leader, your mission might be to lead a team of one, it might be to influence a department from within, or it could be to lead an entire organization. None of us know God's plan, but we do know that His plan is better than ours (Isaiah 55:8-9). This is why we need to prepare because whether we realize it or not, our mission matters. However, it's easy to lose sight of this in our busy lives. This is why as leaders, we need to be 100 percent submitted to Christ.

3

100% Submitted to Christ

"Therefore, I urge you, brothers and sisters, in view of God's mercy, to offer your bodies as a living sacrifice, holy and pleasing to God—this is your true and proper worship."
— **Romans 12:1 NIV**

Unlike some historical kings who were simply born into royalty, we get to choose whether we want to follow Christ. However, similarly to historical kings, He demands our 100% devotion. Like a Father that has a zero-tolerance policy for drugs or alcohol in the house, Christ wants 100% of your heart.

This shouldn't be any surprise to any of us. What is surprising is how often we stray from keeping our Father first. The militaristic side of kings offers great metaphors of the spiritual battles we are facing. Our King doesn't demand our submission because he needs a loyal subject. He wants our submission so that when He calls us to action, we move.

This section is short because it's the simplest. Personally, in my life, I know that when I think I've given Him 100%, He asks for another part of my life, or He opens up a new level of understanding.

As business owners and leaders, it's easy to compartmentalize our life into our business life and our church life. God never meant for us to separate those two. This isn't about your vocation just being a mission field. It's about growing His kingdom by making intentional choices to grow as a disciple. The most important of those choices are the ones that impact your relationship with Him.

> "But seek first His kingdom and His righteousness, and all these things will be given to you as well."
> **— Matthew 6:33 NIV**

One of the biggest mistakes that I've ever made was getting my priorities out of order. I often would pay lip service to God first, and then I was off to my work. I believed the lie that I was the provider. I would make choices that didn't line up with the Bible, such as not taking a sabbath. Then I saw the patterns I mentioned earlier in the Bible. These patterns were not just for behaviors or values but also priorities.

Even the arrangement of kingdoms spoke to me in terms of priorities. When you look at most kingdoms and cities of the Old Testament, there were often the king's quarters. The king's home, if you will, usually had its own wall and gates, but it was also set in a larger area with some other important buildings. The concentric shape reminded me of how our soul, spirit, and body are often depicted.

From the king's quarters and area, there was a wall around much of the city itself. Often the king would spend time at the gates of the city judging the citizens and hearing their complaints. However, the city itself didn't end at the gates as there was usually farmland and other residents outside the city gates.

As a young entrepreneurial believer, I got my calling confused with my priorities. I would pray fervently for God to reveal more of my calling while neglecting my wife and children. I'd invest in other relationships, not realizing that God had called me to be a husband and father first.

The Bible is clear about priorities. Your first relationship is with God. This would be the bullseye and the most important circle. If you're still tracking with the kingdom analogy, this would be like the king's residence. This relationship supersedes everything else and directs everything.

The second circle would be your spouse.

> "That is why a man leaves his father and mother and is united to his wife, and they become one flesh."
> **— Genesis 2:24 NIV**

When you get married, you should no longer decide big things without being in unison. From a biblical perspective, you become "one" as if one organism. The priority that must be given to a spouse is one of the major reasons I believe Paul recommended that some stay single if at all possible. There are fewer "cares" of this world to attract your attention than when you are married.

Outside that circle would be your family. You could go much deeper here and try to figure out the priorities, but for the sake of brevity, I won't do that here. Outside your spouse and children, the circumstances can dictate different arrangements.

When you have a new lens, it changes the answers to questions. In many cases, it might cause you to ask new ones.

» Does this opportunity take you away from your family or your church?
» Does this new opportunity take anything away from the work you're currently doing for the Lord, such as ministry?
» Will it enhance what you're already doing in ministry?

Not every opportunity is a good one. The question should be, "Is this good or God?" Some things that are masquerading as "ministry" are going to drain you as well.

As business people, we're used to saying "yes" to tasks and projects and love to get things done. When you say yes to something, you're saying no to something else. I heard a good question posed about this: "For every one new thing you start, what two things will you stop doing?" That's a great way to look at our most precious commodity, time.

God will never truly be "first" in your life until you can evaluate the time you spend with Him. I must check myself constantly on this. Am I simply settling for a "drive-thru" experience? I read His word, pray, and sometimes even worship in the morning, but if I'm honest, sometimes it's just a box to check and not a real, intimate experience.

For you to reach the pinnacle of God's calling, you're going to have to settle the priorities in your life. Is God really your provider, or are you? If He is God, then let's treat Him like He's really God. Let's work and make decisions unto and for Him.

> "And whatever you do, whether in word or deed, do it all in the name of the Lord Jesus, giving thanks to God the Father through Him." — **Colossians 3:17 NIV**

CALLING VS PRIORITIES

There are people in life who never do what God's called them to do and use family as an excuse. They will say things like, "Little Timmy is too young to go to a third-world country. God couldn't so possibly ask me to uproot my young family to be missionaries right now." Or "What about Esther and her music studies at the high school? Surely God wouldn't take her out of that situation at such a critical time in preparation for her college career." These are common excuses to avoid heavenly callings.

Let's say God's clearly called you to serve in Zimbabwe. If He's truly called you to serve that country, I believe He'll help you be in agreement with your spouse. If you have children, they don't get a say at this point, but you must be confident that God will protect their best interest as well.

However, I've also seen the other side when someone feels led by God to do something, and they take off on their own to accomplish it. If God calls you to the mission field, He's called your family, your kingdom to go, not just you. Rarely have I ever seen it work where one person in the family is called to do something, and that calling doesn't include plans for the spouse and children.

The Apostle Peter is a good example of this. Jesus came to him and called him, and by all accounts of the Bible, it looks like he left his job, his wife, and his kids to follow Jesus.

> "Jesus was walking by the Sea of Galilee. He saw two brothers. They were Simon (his other name was Peter) and Andrew, his brother. They were putting a net into the sea for they were fishermen. Jesus said to them, 'Follow Me. I will make you fish for men!' At once they left their nets and followed Him."
> **— Matthew 4:18 NIV**

This scripture and the disciples' actions are often the basis of this argument. However, the Bible doesn't leave us hanging. I think there isn't much in the Bible regarding this because the unity of a couple would seem so obvious to readers at that time. Paul gives a brief look.

> "Don't we have the right to take a believing wife along with us, as do the other apostles and the Lord's brothers and Cephas?"
> **— 1 Corinthians 9:5 NIV**

Are there instances where one spouse is called to preach, teach, or run a company, and the other is called to something seemingly altogether different? Sure, I believe this can be true without being contradictory. The key is the unity between the husband and wife. They have to have agreement.

I believe God has a big plan for my wife, Sythan. I don't know if she'll be speaking, traveling, writing, or simply continuing to impact her small group. What I do know is that we are both submitted to Christ and to each other. I don't like the idea of being without her, but I know God will give me peace if He should call her for an extended period of time away from our family. I also know that if we have arguments and strife over it, it's time to pause and check if I'm 100 percent submitted in every area of my life to Christ. God is not the author of confusion and chaos (1 Corinthians 14:33). It's only through this total submission that I'll be able to differentiate between an attack from the enemy that is designed to delay or stop a decision and an attack designed to distract.

This is the testing question: Do you feel peace or strife with what you believe God has called you to?

Do not mistake strife for fear of failure. Strife could be fear, but its source is likely fear of losing comfort or fear God won't do what He said. However, regular fear of failure is a bit different. Most of the Biblical leaders were fearful at first. Joshua was told three times to be "strong and courageous." Moses, Gideon, Jonah, and Jeremiah all openly told God they were fearful or that He was mistaken. If you don't have peace, it's a great moment to self-analyze and get with God on why.

I know too many people that have left churches, started ministries, launched businesses, and even become missionaries because "God told them to" and had their endeavor fail. When you unpack their stories, there is one thing in common. The initial idea caused strife, and instead of getting unity and patience around the idea, they forged ahead. If you have peace, and you're in unity, then you are most likely in the best position to go for it!

Much like Abraham, who took matters into his own hands and created

Ishmael, I think kingdom driven leaders tend to be prewired for action. I think God gives us a dream so that we're willing to endure the trials to be molded into the kind of person that He can use for this dream. When we act before we're ready, it not only often crushes the dream, but it can often destroy us as well.

Many business owners are task-oriented. I know I am very guilty of having this predisposition. I'll have anxiety about not finishing some menial tasks while I should be enjoying dinner with my family. In this orientation, it's easy for leaders to lose sight of their most precious kingdom real estate (their relationship with God, themselves, and then their family). This is one of the biggest challenges of a king. Therefore, preparation is so important. Getting the priorities down is, the most important task a king can undertake because it's what can guide his whole reign.

Later we'll see that often a good king would start to rule Israel, and he would uncover the law, and immediately repent and call a nationwide church service to get right with God. They would then start removing the idols and worship centers. The reign of Asa, a king that the Bible calls good, started off this way. As his priorities shifted toward God, his kingdom flourished. When his priorities started to shift again, he became more concerned with man's opinions, and he lost his reign.

In the Old Testament, we see Israel turn down a relationship with God for a relationship with a man who has a relationship with God.

> When the people saw the thunder and lightning and heard the trumpet and saw the mountain in smoke, they trembled with fear. They stayed at a distance and said to Moses, "Speak to us yourself and we will listen. **But do not have God speak to us or we will die.**" — **Exodus 20:18 NIV**

Now not only did they want to be removed from a direct relationship with God, but now they wanted a man that was influenced by another man who had a relationship with God. They keep adding people in between them and God, feeling satisfied with a second – and even third – hand-word from God.

If we look around at the West, we can see this is not too far from how many people live today. How many of us choose to let the sermon prepared for by our pastors and delivered in a concise pocket of time on Sunday be the only time we hear from God?

Lucky for us, Jesus came and re-established the ability we have for a one-on-one relationship with God. We no longer have to go to the Priest or wait for a Prophet; we can go directly to God and get the Word from Him (Ephesians 3:12, Hebrews 4:16).

JESUS IS THE MODEL

If you want to live like a king, then you need to live like *the* King. If you want to lead like the King, then you must learn how to serve like the King. We can see this submission from Jesus at several crucial parts of His ministry. This is good news because we have an example, and we'll likely be facing this "trial" ourselves throughout our entire "campaign."

AT THE BEGINNING OF HIS MINISTRY

The act of coming to Earth was one of obedience in and of itself. Everything that Jesus did was preordained in Scripture and direct revelation from the Father. You could sum up His mission in John 14:31 NIV, "but he comes so that the world may learn that **I love the Father** and **do exactly what my Father has commanded me.**"

As I'm writing this, it is dawning on me how profound that one little sentence is. When I first "accepted" Jesus, I wasn't aware of the relationship I could have, but after I finally decided to give it all to Him and attempt to grow an actual relationship with Him, my love for Him and the Word grew. It's only out of this love that I can even attempt to do what I was commanded to do.

This explains why Jesus was baptized. Jesus didn't need to be baptized. Jewish tradition at that time dictated that being baptized was a ritual that one performed to be pure before coming to worship. Jesus was already pure. However, He was on a mission. He had to become like us and join us in fallen humanity. He had to show us the way. He did that by being submitted to the Father's mission. We see that again right after the baptism in His temptation.

DURING HIS MINISTRY

Every word that Jesus spoke and every action taken was all the will of the Father. John 12:49 says, "For I did not speak on my own, but the Father who sent me commanded me to say all that I have spoken" (NIV). He executed His mission so carefully to be an example to His brothers and sisters. The Bible calls Jesus the firstborn, and we are all His siblings. His ministry was an example of the obedience and submission that we need to have. Matthew 12:50 lays it out for us. "For whoever does the will of my Father in heaven is my brother and sister and mother" (NIV).

EVEN TO THE CROSS AND BEYOND

Every Christian knows the story of the cross, but I think we miss the turmoil right before what took place there. Christ went through tremendous anguish of suffering before Judas ever laid a kiss on His cheek. It was agony and anxiety at such a level that it caused His blood vessels to rupture!

As I write this, childhood memories of awaiting punishment from a parent are replaying in my mind. The punishment itself wasn't what broke me. It was waiting for it to occur. We often think of scenarios before they ever play out. This helps anticipate challenges and avoiding situations. However, in a situation like this, it can break a person down.

I don't think we realize the level of obedience that was required of Christ in this moment. We dismiss the story because Jesus is God. I'll let you use your imagination, but I'd venture to say any thought you've had, Jesus had. Certainly, He defeated these thoughts, quite possibly easier or quicker than you or I. He's not just God; He's our Brother, our King. He led the charge, and we get to charge behind Him!

Let's look a little closer. Luke 22:44 states it like this: "And being in agony [deeply distressed and anguished; almost to the point of death], He prayed more intently; and His [a]*sweat became like drops of blood*, falling down on the ground" (AMP, emphasis mine).

According to Wikipedia, "Hemosiderosis is a condition in which capillary blood vessels that feed the sweat glands rupture, causing them to exude blood, occurring under conditions of *extreme physical or emotional stress. Severe mental anxiety* activates the sympathetic nervous system to invoke the stress-fight or flight reaction to such a degree as to cause hemorrhage of the vessels supplying the sweat glands into the ducts of the sweat glands."[9]

This condition is very rare, but every account of it is related to the most severe of mental anguish possible. Jesus didn't just beam here, heal people, and then march off to die. He wrestled with obedience in the very same way we do. I'd wager that nothing in your life has caused you so much mental anguish that you sweated blood over it. Yet our Brother and Savior went through that.

In a later chapter, we'll talk about forming a band of brothers, but at this moment, it's worth pointing out that Jesus, forever the leader, gives us the example to follow. He used scripture, prayer, and the support of His disciples to get through this moment. Matthew 26:38 says, "Then He said to them, 'My soul is deeply grieved, so that I am almost dying of sorrow. Stay here and stay awake and keep watch with Me'" (AMP).

I write all of this to remind us who gave us the authority to rule on His behalf. This is a lesson in submission - total submission. We can often get frustrated when we don't feel like we are in control. Maybe you volunteer at your church and have a "leader" over you that isn't doing what you think is best. Perhaps this causes you spiritual grief.

Ok, I'll come clean. That was me. I can remember serving at our church and starting in the parking lot. It was such a joy just to be able to serve, and I took this attitude with me. Within just a few months, the church expanded and put me as a leader on the parking lot team. I still maintained an attitude of joy and was happy to serve, but I also started to develop a little pride. After all, I'm the leader of a new church parking team. I had "minions" now.

In my mind, I was leading as a businessperson would, but something sinister was growing in my heart. Through the grace of God, the parking team grew large enough that I was able to ask for more opportunities. I started to see the church like the marketplace and looked for advancement opportunities. I wanted more power and control.

It was during this next assignment, one I thought might be a new area to rule, that I learned of being humbly submitted to authority.

It wasn't that the leader of this ministry was incompetent or particularly bad, but I did not like the way he did things. I had taken this new role based on my perceptions of new power and control and had elevated my opinion over pretty much everyone else.

It's true that oftentimes church people do things differently than businesspeople, and it can cause frustration. I do think it is worth reviewing because I know there are churches where mismanagement happens. However, even that needs to be handled humbly. We all answer to the same God for our actions, and that frees you up to be able to serve faithfully.

At my church, the only mismanagement that was going on was my mismanagement of my heart—everything this leader did just rubbed me the wrong way. I knew I could do a better job than he was doing. This led to passive-aggressive behavior with the leader and much cynicism on my part. It became so bad that it was driving a wedge in between God and myself. I couldn't figure it out.

After a lot of prayer, I realized that the problem wasn't the leader. It was actually me. God worked it out so that I could learn how to serve His leaders and humble myself. There's a certain freedom in just doing the very best you can, whether that's in business or at the church. I had to learn that it's up to me to fulfill my responsibility and serve the best I can, let go of control, and let God do the rest.

Letting go of control, however, isn't sitting on your hands. It's like the serenity prayer,

> God grant me the serenity
> to accept the things I cannot change;
> courage to change the things I can;
> and wisdom to know the difference. [10]

It's taking ownership of your day, every day, and doing the absolute best you can by relying on God and being submitted to Him first. If He has placed a bad boss or perhaps even a gifted leader that you don't agree with, it does not matter. Your first act as King is to submit to the ultimate authority and serve.

WHAT SUBMITTING TO AUTHORITY TEACHES YOU

In a very practical way, I think God wants us to learn to serve and be submitted to others, particularly in the church environment, to show us what obedience truly is. In our submission, we often learn what to look for in others to help us lead more effectively. This is a truly difficult lesson for those used to leading or those with "high drive" personalities.

It's often tough to learn how to take your leadership to the next level without first learning how to be submitted to authority. Luckily, I believe leadership is a skill and can be taught and learned.[11]

My friend, Aaron, says it this way: "In the Marines, whether you are a leader or not, every Marine learns to fight the same way, to stand guard duty in the cold and rain while sleepy, and to endure forced marches under a heavy load with blistered feet. This way, the leader will remember what his men are experiencing when he is placing demands on them or giving orders."

In my case, I know this was true. I finally had to repent to someone who was my leader, and once I did, there was a weight off my shoulders. I could serve him as unto the Lord, and it changed everything. It changed the questions I asked him about his decisions. It changed the speed at which I acted on the needs he had. It changed how I approached him with suggestions for improvements that I saw we could make as a team. After all, if we're to use the sports metaphor, the game is on, and we are here to win souls. We must act as a team.

Again, being submitted and humble doesn't mean being subservient. It means understanding your responsibility in the role God has you in the moment and being the very best you can be. It means being respectful of the authority in place and having a servant's heart when it comes to being submitted.

Recognizing that God comes first and that it is He who should create the lens through which we view life is a great challenge. However, it's in this act of submission that creates humility. We can choose to do things from our own free will, or we can submit to His will. The Bible says that God resists the proud but favors the humble (James 4:6). As we're preparing, we begin to turn our hearts toward God. As a result, this act of submission prepares our hearts to receive what God has to say to us.

4

Receiving the King's Mandates

"My sheep listen to My voice; I know them, and they follow Me. I give them eternal life, and they shall never perish; no one will snatch them out of My hand."
— **John 10:27-28 NIV**

Recently I was driving to the gym. I always pray on my way, not because I'm a good Christian, but because it's become a habit. This morning my head was very busy. Still half asleep, my mind went to conversations around a TV show, to what I was going to do that day, and the progress of my side projects. I tried to shake off the thoughts and focus on my prayer.

I asked the Lord why was it so difficult to pray and hear from Him? If I'm honest, it wasn't a prayer but a complaint; I was already near the gym and was just kind of fed up and a bit frustrated. Frustrated that I couldn't think coherently and frustrated with how God speaks to us. I was reminded of this scripture:

> "Go out and stand before Me on the mountain,' the Lord told him. And as Elijah stood there, the Lord passed by, and a mighty windstorm hit the mountain. It was such a terrible blast that the rocks were torn loose, but the Lord was not in the wind. After

the wind, there was an earthquake, but the Lord was not in the earthquake. And after the earthquake, there was a fire, but the Lord was not in the fire. And after the fire, there was the sound of a gentle whisper."
— 1 Kings 19:11 NLT

Then He told me, "I'll never raise My voice at you. You're struggling to hear Me because of what you've filled your mind with." It's not that He's not talking, and it's not that I am not listening. It's that I can't hear Him over the noise. Then I was reminded of a particular verse in Mark 4.

"And the cares of this world, and the deceitfulness of riches, and the lusts of other things entering in choke the word, and it becometh unfruitful."
— Mark 4:19 NKJV

CARES OF THIS WORLD

Depending on the version of this verse you examine, it's easy to gloss over it. We consider deceitfulness and lust as the context. Look at the first part, "cares of this world." Cares is translated as worry or anxiety here[12]. While that is certainly something that can take you away from God and hinder you from hearing from God, I think it can include some of the senseless cares that we add to our lives unintentionally.

This world or this life means the current world. In other words, the worries of our current life. In this technology-infused information age, meditate on what that might look like?

If I were to list out all my cares of the current world, it might look like this. Will I ever see another Iron Man movie? How many subscribers, followers, or fans do I have on social media? Will Star Wars ever be good again? Will my sports team ever draft the right player?

At an initial glance, some of these cares seem innocuous. You might think I've gone too far here, and if you think that, then you went too far. I'm not suggesting that entertainment is bad. Rather, what I am suggesting is that if you fill yourself with entertainment and neglect God's word, you're not likely going to hear from Him. In the same way, I was guilty of letting my dreams and goals cloud my mind versus what was most important.

WE NEED FOCUS TO HEAR GOD SPEAK

In ancient battlefields, there were no sat phones or drones overhead. Military commanders had to use runners, flags, and their voices to help direct the troops. During a battle, a soldier had to keep their ears and eyes tuned to the fight while looking for the signals from their commander. They didn't have time or need to worry about anything other than the mission at hand.

Unlike our brothers and sisters in the east, we, as Christians in the west, generally don't have the intense focus of a soldier when it comes to practicing our faith. We can do so without persecution. Of course, social media and mainstream media aren't always kind to Christians overall, but that's another topic for another day. Regardless, make no mistake. We are in a spiritual battle with the enemy of our souls. To be victorious, we must be submitted and tuned into His voice to execute the plans He has for us.

With the understanding that it will require a clear focus, let's look at some practical ways we can hear from God.

HOW DOES GOD SPEAK TO US?

God talks to us in a few different ways. If you are someone who says, "I've never heard from God," then I challenge you right now to say a prayer. Here's a sample:

> "Heavenly Father, I have heard You speak to others, I believe You have something to say to me. Please open my mind, eyes, and ears to hear You today."

You must first believe that He wants to talk to you and that He does actually speak to you. If you are a believer, then you've already experienced Him speaking to you first hand.

> "My sheep listen to my voice; I know them, and they follow me."
> **— John 10:27 NIV**

I know God talks to me, but I've never heard His voice with my ears. It's always a voice in my mind that sounds a little like my voice but with some distinct differences. What's spoken is immensely wise, much wiser than I ever could be. It's always loving. What's said, even in correction, is always edifying. It always matches His word in specificity or in character. Sometimes it's future-oriented, and sometimes it's a revelation of something in the past.

God doesn't just "speak to your mind." There are three main ways He speaks to us. The first and most obvious one is His word. The second way is often through other people. The final way is through our worship, specifically through prayer, fasting, and actual worship.

GOD SPEAKS TO US THROUGH HIS WORD

"Thy word is a lamp unto my feet, and a light unto my path." — **Psalm 119:105 KJV**

If you haven't heard from God in a while, what He might be saying is, "I already wrote down what you need in this season." In my life, I'll often read a scripture that I've read many times before and skimmed over only to realize that it had something very applicable to my current situation.

Recently I read James 1:6. "But when you ask, you must believe and not doubt *(waver)*, because the one who doubts is like a wave of the sea, blown and tossed by the wind" (NIV, emphasis mine). I have read this verse over 100 times. I love the book of James. I've always read over this one because I thought I really believed God and didn't waver in my faith. I thought that verse addressed salvation. However, when I began to understand it more, the Holy Spirit caused me to understand what the word "waver" really means.

I had a few setbacks over the last few years, and I began not to believe that God was going to move these mountains, not because He couldn't but because I thought He didn't want to. I stopped praying about them. In other words, I wavered. God showed me this scripture with fresh eyes and then reminded me that prayer is a long-term endeavor. Like the parable of the woman and the judge, she kept coming to the judge until he gave in (Luke 18:1-8). This expanded my understanding and renewed my faith.

Many believers haven't had a real experience with God because they haven't expected one, and they haven't been reading and studying the Word to receive one.

GOD SPEAKS TO US THROUGH OTHERS

Many times, you'll hear a message from a pastor and feel like that message was crafted just for you, or perhaps you'll talk to a friend, and they'll say something that opens your eyes. Internally you'll say, "that's so good." This can be evidence of God speaking to you.

The danger of hearing God through others is we'll often make this the only way we hear from Him. Our walk is a process, and there are seasons. In some seasons, we'll need to hear from others to take another step. However, we cannot become reliant on others because they are human and can, at times, speak from places of bias instead of truth. And at the same time, we need to remain humble enough to listen when someone speaks and take it to God for confirmation.

The key to hearing God through others is asking, "Does what he just said line up with the Word?" If you are going through a tough time in your marriage and everything seems chaotic, and a friend automatically suggests a divorce, then you know that's not from God. However, if that same friend, who understands the covenant relationship, suggests counseling or getting help or forgiveness, then you have something to work on within this difficult time.

There have been many times where I've felt like I was going through a "wilderness" season. It was a time when God fell silent, and I struggled to find purpose in my circumstances. I'd read the Bible and pray, but if I'm honest, I was going through the motions in those areas. God would send a friend or acquaintance to renew my strength in this area. They would be dealing with something and share a revelation they had. That revelation would then spark something in me.

One test is that spark. There is something about hearing from God via His word, worship, or through others that causes a spark on the inside. That spark can be the catalyst to get us moving again.

GOD SPEAKS TO US THROUGH WORSHIP

Probably one of the best ways to hear from God is through worship. It's great because it forces you to get rid of anything in your mind that has nothing to do with Him. It's a simple concept, but it's not easy to do. I struggle in this area. I love to worship in a song, but my mind is often thinking about tasks to accomplish or plans I need to make. It takes a significant amount of energy to get focused completely on Him.

Worship can come in many forms. Biblically, this could be through songs and hymns. It could simply be through prayer with an expectancy of receiving a response. Another way to worship is through fasting. Fasting often helps you unclog your ears, eyes, and heart. I've seen people receive breakthroughs because they fasted. The lack of food is simply one way to deny your fleshly desires to build stamina in your faith, but that alone isn't what brings the life change. It's the focus. Often in a fast, you choose to remove distractions like social media and other forms of entertainment. This declutters your mind.

If we're honest, we give worship to so many other things that it's no wonder many people struggle with hearing from God. I'm guilty of this.

There are books that explain at a much deeper level how to hear from God if you still have questions (see recommended reading at the end of the book). I can tell you that for me, no book has changed my life more so than the Bible. The turning point for me was when I expected an answer back to the questions I posed while reading and praying over what I read.

While there are many methods to try to hear from God, it's likely He's been speaking to you this whole time. The key is to tune your ear to Him. Sometimes He speaks, and it's easy to identify His voice, and other times, He comes in a whisper which requires us to focus on Him.

There are seasons where He seems quiet, and other times He seems to be speaking in every key moment. One thing that is clear is He never gives us the full plan. It can be quite frustrating to hear in part, but He wants us to stay close as He reveals as we go. One of the things I like to say is that God has us on Street View.

GOD HAS US ON STREET VIEW

We're all familiar with the map apps. While there are other apps out there, such as Waze or MapQuest, the go-to app for me is Google Maps. Ultimately, they all work similarly, though. They use your location and the place you want to go to give you a bird's eye view before zooming into the street view. The biggest problem with this is that the street view is only useful if you aren't moving. If you've ever gone to a new place and were rushed and just entered the address and left, it's a bit maddening. You go into an unknown area and have to completely trust your map app not to drive you into a lake. I like to see the entire map with the anticipated turns and all the streets ahead of time so that I'm not in the wrong lane when it's time to turn or I don't take a route I know will have construction or perhaps include small, unfamiliar roads. Unfortunately, for me and anyone else wired this way, God has us on street view.

I used to cry out to God for more direction, for more purpose, and to see the plan to no avail. Why? Why would my loving Father not reveal the entire plan for my life so that I could execute on it? It seems to me that would be a good idea. However, I now understand that if He did give us all the steps, we'd run off without Him.

I don't want to get into a free-will discussion here, but I believe God wants us to make a choice to follow Him and be dependent upon Him for our turn-by-turn directions in life. It's not just a choice to follow because many of us will say we're Christians, but do we trust God to be our provider? Do we so completely trust Him with a "reckless faith" that we move away from things that give us pleasure in the short term for things that will bring eternal rewards?

When I began to seek out answers here, I was brought to this scripture:

> "The steps of a [good and righteous] man are directed and established by the Lord, And He delights in his way [and blesses his path]."
> **— Psalms 37:23 AMP**

Notice it says "steps," and in one translation, it says footsteps. I can already hear some of you whisper to yourself, "baby steps." You're absolutely right. If you read the Bible, you start to see the theme that God wants us to rely on Him daily.

In the Old Testament, the Israelites had just left Egypt, crossed through the parted Red Sea to get to the desert. Their 40-year wandering in the wilderness was marked with the idea of daily provision.

In Exodus 16, God gave them manna, a type of bread that miraculously appeared like dew on the ground. Manna would fall from heaven every day to prove His provision to His people and, in turn, test that they are faithful. When a few people failed to trust God and collected more manna than a day's worth, their manna rotted with worms. He told them upfront that He was only going to provide one day's worth of bread. They had to trust Him for their future.

Then, in the New Testament, the Lord's Prayer famously teaches us to pray, "Give us this day our *Daily* Bread" (Matthew 6:9-13, emphasis mine). And there are more than 50 references to footsteps in the Bible, indicating God's desire and intent to guide His children. There's a biblical pattern of trusting God "daily" for direction, purpose, and fulfillment.

Researchers on leadership have also found that small victories lead to momentum for most successful leaders. In fact, it's the ultimate way to accomplish a huge goal; break it down into small chunks that you can accomplish[13].

There's still a part of me that wonders why we can't at least get a glimpse of what's ahead. How do we ever get off street view? Are we stuck there?

What about Abraham, Joseph with his dreams, David, the Prophets, John, Jonah, and others? Why did they all get divine revelations from God? It goes back to the beginning. From the beginning, God wanted a relationship with us. From the beginning, He's wanted to be our Father. Are we intentionally choosing to trust Him daily? How are we stewarding our daily opportunities? These are all questions I ask myself, and I challenge you to consider asking them each day yourself.

Our Old Testament heroes of the faith trusted God daily for years, decades, or their entire lives before they ever received a divine vision. Here's the thing about trusting God daily that I've found. I must be happy with the journey day-to-day when I trust He knows better than I know.

> "'For My thoughts are not your thoughts, Nor are your ways My ways,' declares the Lord. 'For as the heavens are higher than the earth, So are My ways higher than your ways And My thoughts higher than your thoughts.'"
> **— Isaiah 55:8-9 NKJV**

Ultimately, if you want to get off street view, you must go deeper with God. We have something our Old Testament heroes did not have. We have the privilege to build a personal relationship with the Creator of the universe. We don't need a burning bush or a dream and an interpretation. We can have a conversation... daily.

> "But first and most importantly seek (aim at, strive after) His kingdom and His righteousness [His way of doing and being right—the attitude and character of God], and all these things will be given to you also."
> **— Matthew 6:33 AMP**

If you want to walk with God daily, you must make time for it. Follow Jesus' example and get up early when no one is awake and read His Word. I challenge you to do this for one week, with one simple prayer, "Father, I want to hear your voice." If you do this, I have no doubt that He will meet you where you are, one step at a time.

John Eldredge, author of *Wild at Heart*, said in a video series that God doesn't give us a master plan. Instead, he gives us a loving Father to hold our hand on the adventure with Him. What a wonderful picture.[14]

As a kingdom driven leader, you are continuing a pursuit to grow as a disciple through preparation. You've completely submitted your will to Christ's. This submission allows you to hear from God in a deeper way. This relationship is a great reminder that you aren't leading alone. You are allowing yourself to be led so that you can be a better leader in every area of your life.

This has profound implications in the marketplace. When you start to get new ideas, a sense of what to do, or new opportunities, you now have a deeper understanding of how to evaluate these. However, more importantly, you will start developing a recognition that these "gut feelings" and "coincidences" are actually promptings from the Holy Spirit.

It's one thing to study His word and listen patiently for His voice, but it's a completely different thing to have an ongoing conversation. As a kingdom driven leader, you are leading in your home, your community, and the marketplace. These burdens aren't there for you to carry alone. Counseling and friends are amazing, but nothing takes the place of a loving Father, and you can speak to Him directly.

5

Speak to The King of Kings

In the last chapter, we talked about hearing from God. In this one, we'll dive into speaking to the King of kings. I don't think you achieve anything great without prayer. Nowhere is this tougher in my mind than in business. Most business leaders I know are driven and decision-oriented. When a new opportunity pops up, it's easy for most of us to charge forward or dismiss it quickly without asking what God thinks about that opportunity.

In the Old Testament, it was common for kings to speak with one another. However, even more interesting is that kings often wanted to hear from God. Even the evil kings, such as Ahab, wanted to hear from God. In addition, our perfect example, Jesus, prayed or taught about prayer quite frequently.

> "Then Jesus told His disciples a parable to show them that they should always pray and not give up."
> **— Luke 18:1 NIV**

Prayer is so important that there are over 100 verses from the Old and New Testaments about prayer. Prayer is a conversation you have with God. He's your loving Father, and although He knows all, He genuinely wants to listen and speak to you where you are.

Many of us have not had this modeled by our earthly fathers, but our Heavenly Father is the perfect picture of a father – one who takes time to listen and nurture our hearts and provide direction and wisdom.

In the Old Testament, there wasn't any story quite so moving to me as to see how God responded to ungodly men. King Manasseh, son of one of Judah's greatest kings, Hezekiah, was one of those men. He seemed to be on a mission to undo all the good his father did. He not only rebuilt the places of worship for idols but even forced his son to "go through the fire." This wasn't just idol worship or child sacrifice. This was a practice of sacrificing children by burning them alive in a furnace that was carved into the statue of the idol. Some accounts suggest that they would remove babies after a period, and the ones that lived were revered as great warriors.

Both books of Kings and Chronicles tell us that Manasseh was one of the most despicable Kings Judah ever had.

> "But Manasseh led Judah and the people of Jerusalem astray, so that they did more evil than the nations the Lord had destroyed before the Israelites."
> **— 2 Chronicles 33:9 NIV**

After sending prophets, God finally lifted His hand of protection, and Judah was taken. Manasseh had his nose forcibly pierced to be dragged around like a piece of cattle and was taken into captivity with bronze fetters. I'm sure most of us, and the Israelites, for that matter, would say, "serves him right."

Then something unexpected in the story happened. Manasseh's heart changed. Like the prodigal son, he was humbled and at his lowest with no hope.

> "In his distress he sought the favor of the Lord his God and humbled himself greatly before the God of his ancestors. And *when he prayed to Him, the Lord was moved by his entreaty and listened to his plea*; so, He brought him back to Jerusalem and to his kingdom. Then Manasseh knew that the Lord is God."
> **— 2 Chronicles 33:12-13 NIV (emphasis mine)**

Manasseh went on to rebuild Jerusalem and tear down the idols and high places that he helped build. This is a great example of the promise that God hears every prayer, knows our heart and our thoughts. He wants us to rely on Him.

My opinion is that God wants us to make decisions on our own but also wants us to consult with Him. In cultivating a relationship with Him, He's constantly in our thoughts. We don't have to run to a closet or get on our knees to ask Him about every little thing. Often, simply praying or talking about what's going on in our lives with our Father can help us release the burden.

As you grow in your relationship, you will notice different seasons of the relationship. Like earthly relationships, things need to be freshened up every now and then. Don't misunderstand me, though; your relationship adjustments with God are not riddles to solve because God's not gimmicky. I would more so liken it to working out because you will need to make it a habit that appears consistently on your calendar, and you will need to be open to changing up your routines when needed.

Some time ago, I started jogging, and to be honest, I hated it at first. However, over time, I developed a habit of it. I still don't like it, but now I automatically drive myself to the park to jog. Creating a daily prayer habit is a lot like that. At first, it might be tough, but eventually, you'll find yourself waking up to spend time with God, which yields way more rewards than jogging!

There is a bit of a dark side to habits, though. Have you ever driven somewhere and not remembered how you got there? This was a habit at work, allowing you to think about other things while your body drove you to your destination dangerously. While habits allow us to do more, sometimes, that same wiring makes it difficult to keep the relationship fresh. By turning the familiar into a habit, your brain is free to do other things. However, it is your mind that you want to engage when you're spending time with God.

Bodybuilders experience this as well and must change up their routine to keep their muscles and their minds engaged. Their calendar stays the same, but what they do during that time changes.

Some ideas to keep your relationship fresh are praying scripture, changing up your schedule, or reading through a book about prayer such as Mark Batterson's "Prayer Circles" or Philip Hunter's "Promise Principle." One tactic that's helped me tremendously is praying scripture.

PRAYING SCRIPTURE

What I do is write down the scripture on an index card but insert my name so that I'm praying His blessings over myself. You could almost do this with the entire book of Psalms! Here's an easy example from Psalm 90.

> "Father, May [Your favor] rest on me; establish the work of my hands for [my family, my workplace, etc.] yes, establish the work of [my] hands"
> **— Psalm 90:17 NIV [personalization in brackets]**

PAUL'S PRAYERS

There are four prayers that the Apostle Paul prayed that have gotten me on fire for praying scripture. I've taken the liberty of changing them so that they are personalized for you.

> "[Father, I ask that You] may give me the Spirit of wisdom and revelation, so that [I may know You] better. I pray that the eyes of [my] heart may be enlightened in order that [I] may know the hope to which [You have] called me, the riches of [Your] glorious inheritance in [Your] holy people, and [Your] incomparably great power for [me, the one that believes]."
> — **Ephesians 1:17-19 NIV [personalization in brackets]**

> "I pray that out of [Your] glorious riches [You] may strengthen [me] with power through [Your] Spirit in [my] inner being, so that [You/Christ] may dwell in [my heart] through faith. And I pray that [I], being rooted and established in love, may have power, together with all the Lord's holy people, to grasp how wide and long and high and deep is [Your love], and to know this love that surpasses knowledge—that [I] may be filled to the measure of all the fullness of [You/God]."
> — **Ephesians 3:16-19 NIV[personalization in brackets]**

> "And this is my prayer: that [my] love may abound more and more in knowledge and depth of insight, so that [I] may be able to discern what is best and may be pure and blameless for the day of Christ, filled with the fruit of righteousness that comes through Jesus Christ—to the glory and praise of God."
> — **Philippians 1:9-11 NIV [personalization in brackets]**

> "[I will continually ask] [You] to fill [me] with the knowledge of [Your] will through all the wisdom and understanding that the Spirit gives, so that [I] may live a life worthy of the [You] Lord and please [You] in every way: bearing fruit in every good work, growing in the knowledge of [You] God, being strengthened with all power according to [Your] glorious might so that [I] may have great endurance and patience, and giving joyful thanks to [You, the Father], who has qualified [me] to share in the inheritance of [Your] holy people in the kingdom of light."
> **— Colossians 1:9-12 [personalization's in brackets]**

PRAYER OF JABEZ

There was a small book that popularized a verse in Chronicles highlighting a businessman. Amidst the historical genealogies is a man named Jabez that is found to be honorable. In Chapter 4, verse 9 tells us this. We can only tell he is a businessperson from looking at his request. It's a simple yet powerful reminder about prayer.

> "Jabez cried out to the God of Israel, 'Oh, that you would bless me and enlarge my territory! Let Your hand be with me and keep me from harm so that I will be free from pain.' And God granted his request."
> **— 1 Chronicles 4:10 NIV**

One word of caution is to be careful when praying for the enlargement of your "territory," as it often comes with increased responsibility. It's not a prayer for the faint of heart.

LORD'S PRAYER

This one needs little introduction. However, I didn't have a full understanding of this prayer until I heard a Pastor go over it as a template for prayer and not just reading it like a chant as I had previously experienced each time it was recited in church.

> "This, then, is how you should pray: 'Our Father in heaven, hallowed be Your name, Your kingdom come, Your will be done, on earth as it is in heaven. Give us today our daily bread. And forgive us our debts, as we also have forgiven our debtors. And lead us not into temptation but deliver us from the evil one.'"
> **— Matthew 6:9-13 NIV**

The oversimplification of this is that every prayer should contain:

» Acknowledgment of God's Lordship
» Thankfulness for What You've Received
» Praying for the Will of God
» Prayer/Request for Provision
» Repentance/Forgiveness
» Prayer for protection and against even the temptation of evil.

You can do the same thing with many scriptures in the Bible. Every time someone prays, you can personalize it to help you. A great reference is the "Power of a Praying..." series of books from Stormie Omartian.

WHO'S LEADING YOU?

Ever since the beginning of Genesis, God has wanted us to express our free will. When you study His word, listen for His voice, and talk with Him through prayer, you're showing humility and submission. You're allowing God to lead you. This leadership in your life is critical for everyday life, not just marketplace leadership.

Once you understand that you are a leader and that God loves you and has a special assignment for you, then you can begin preparing. Your growth as a kingdom driven leader and a disciple will come directly through how much communication you have with your leader. It's this communication that prepares your heart. It's this realization - that the relationship is real - that will give you the strength to have the integrity you need to lead.

6

Has Integrity

"As for you, if you walk before Me *faithfully with integrity of heart* and uprightness, as David your father did, and do all I command and observe My decrees and law. I will establish your royal throne over Israel forever."
— 1 Kings 9:4 NIV (emphasis mine)

At first, integrity almost feels like a cliché leadership characteristic. Almost every Christian book will reference it. It's the foundation of many marriage books. We see it over and over again. However, unfortunately when it comes to leaders in power, many lack integrity. Whether it's a scandal involving CEOs or one involving Presidents, we've heard our share of stories that reveal a deficit in this area.

When God met with Solomon, He gave him guidelines so that his reign could be part of a great legacy. One key ingredient to his success was integrity. I'd even argue that integrity was more important to Solomon's wealth than his wisdom. It's that important, but it's pretty simple in theory. It's doing what you say you are going to do.

Further, if you look up integrity in any dictionary, you'll find that integrity is simply being steadfast against a moral or ethical framework. It means that if you have integrity, you live by a code or standard and that the more integrity you have, the more likely you are to adhere to this code. Integrity asks the question, "How flexible are you on your morals and ethics?"

Integrity is also often tied to honesty and faithfulness. It is so closely related to honesty that governments use tests to see how honest someone is. One German study suggests that people with low integrity are more likely to abuse drugs, commit crimes.[15]

"Do not lie" (Leviticus 19:11) is more than just a commandment. Rather, it's a code on how to operate your life. If integrity is a code to follow and our first commandment is to follow God, then the true measure of integrity for a believer isn't just doing what we say we will do but doing what He said we should do. Doing what He says is the reason God tells Solomon to have integrity first.

God knew that the more integrity a man has, the more likely he is to follow God's commands. Therefore, if Solomon chose to follow God with integrity, everything would go well for him. And you can read in Kings how well it did go for Solomon. He was one of the richest and wisest kings ever in the world by any standard.

However, in 1 Kings 11:9, it says God was angry with Solomon. Solomon had achieved everything there is to achieve in this life and still found it to be lacking. I don't think God was primarily angry with Solomon for overindulging in sensuality (1 Kings 11:1), forming questionable partnerships (1 Kings 10:11), or even for enslaving a nation (1 King 5:13). I think what angered God the most was that Solomon forgot his first love, God. Instead of living for the Creator, he chose to live for himself.

The more worldly success he experienced, the more lacking he was in integrity. This resulted in him worshipping idols. As 1 Kings 11 opens, it reveals that Solomon was doing exactly what God told him not to. He lacked integrity in this one area, and it cost him the kingdom.

THE INTEGRITY CHALLENGE

The challenge with integrity is that you cannot claim to have it. You must be judged to have it. I cannot look at a person and decide if they have integrity or not. They must show me through their actions that they have it. For a person to declare another person as integrous, they must see that their actions are congruent with who they are.

Before you go around judging people or anointing them as someone of integrity, God is the only person that can see our hearts, our intentions, and our actions. He's the ultimate authority on integrity.

One of my favorite books in the Bible is James. He's so direct, and almost the entire book is a lesson on integrity. He puts "faith" together with "actions" or deeds in chapter 2. Deeds won't get you into heaven, but your actions do show that you have faith. This is why baptism is a crucial part of the walk. It's not just some religious activity, but rather a step of action that says to everyone, "I believe."

It'd be easy to skip this chapter; I know I wanted to skip writing it. After all, most of us think we have a good "degree" of integrity. If you say something, then do it. It's pretty simple. Except it's never that simple.

How are we doing on the small things? That's where I see a lot of people miss it. When we see big integrity failures, it's never the result of a one-time lapse in judgment. When we examine the situation closely, we can see a lot of little failures that happened and accumulated over time. This is like when a dam breaks; it never happens instantaneously. Instead, small cracks form, which lead to bigger cracks that eventually lead to collapse.

It would be easy to pull a headline out of the news and discuss integrity but let's look at one example that is a bit closer to home for me especially. As I mentioned, I live in Atlanta. It's probably one of the toughest cities in the world to get anywhere on time. However, I've learned that the little thing of not showing up on time can often cost you your integrity with others waiting on you. I'm not saying if you're late that you are evil or are going to fall into sin. However, if you told someone you'd be in a place at a certain time, and you didn't show up at that time by your miscalculation or negligence, how can you say you have integrity? You didn't do what you said you would do.

That might sound harsh, but in a very real sense, you've devalued the other person's or other people's time by doing something that is frankly very selfish. It sometimes happens in situations in which we can't control the outcome, and we tend to brush off tardiness because it's so common today. However, the devaluing - the lack of integrity - is still there to deal with.

Having integrity is a simple thing, and sometimes in certain contexts, this would be a very silly discussion. Atlanta traffic isn't anything new. You were late, and it couldn't be helped even though you planned ahead and left early. Hopefully, if this was you, you at least called ahead.

You might dismiss this example; however, I can tell you that I have seen firsthand where tardiness has cost many opportunities. I've even seen where it cost a CEO the opportunity to hire talent because the tardiness of the CEO left a bad impression on the new hire. Being on time is one simple way to show you have integrity.

Like respect, the title of integrity is earned over time, and showing up on time is a way to build that integrity account up.

INTEGRITY IS KEY FOR KINGDOM DRIVEN LEADERS

As a leader, you lead your team. Although some leaders lead a team in an official name or title, all of us lead others in some compacity. Those people that we influence can be considered "our team."

In Patrick Lencioni's excellent book *The Five Dysfunctions Of A Team*, he says, "Trust is the foundation of real teamwork."[16] I would take that even a step further and suggest that trust is the foundation of *any* relationship.

To have trust, there has to be honesty and consistency. In any relationship, not just in the marketplace, people need to know what you say is true, and they need to be able to predict how you will behave in any given situation.

Successful entrepreneurs are often celebrated for being creative and unpredictable. However, when it comes to leading people or even growing relationships, predictability can be a good thing. I'm not talking about being boring. What I am suggesting is that people want to know if they can count on you when the time comes. That's trust. Having integrity, meaning you adhere to a set of standards, means you'll predictably respond in certain situations. Integrity then brings peace, security, and trust into a relationship.

For a kingdom driven leader, you can build trust by consistently holding to biblical values and being 100 percent submitted to Christ. Doing this puts you in a position to receive the blessings that God has promised (like Solomon).

Remember, God is a good Father and wants to bless us (Luke 11:13). Just like our earthly relationships, this integrity influences our Heavenly relationship, and better helps us to hear from God and influences our prayer life.

Integrity is the word for the boundaries that you are willing to embrace around your life. These boundaries not only breed peace, but you gain a sense of confidence. If you know what you will and won't do ahead of time, then decision-making is much easier. This practice will help you become a better leader. Then, from this position of confidence, you can grow in serving your people. As a servant leader, you have confidence in who you are as a leader, and your team will have a leader they can trust.

7

Servant to the People

> "I have set you an example that you should do as I have done for you. Very truly I tell you, no servant is greater than his master, nor is a messenger greater than the one who sent him. Now that you know these things, you will be blessed if you do them."
> **— John 13:15-17 NIV**

When the kings of Israel truly followed God's commands and served Him, life was good for the people. They flourished. In fact, as painful as it is read, the Old Testament is much like our lives. When we are passionate about God, life is good. When we start to create idols and move away from our relationship with God, life isn't so good. Our loving Father and King calls us back to Him, often only to have the cycle repeated.

Thankfully, unlike the experience of the Israelites plight to follow the law without success, we have the gift of the Messiah whose sacrifice on the cross atoned for our sins, once and for all. His grace covers our sin, and the Holy Spirit helps us overcome so we don't have to repeat the negative part of this cycle. It doesn't mean we need Him any less or that there is permission to willfully walk in disobedience (Romans 6). It just means we have the assurance that our sin is covered.

However, although we live in victory, it doesn't always mean that we will be in a period of "worldly success." As we'll see throughout this book, there are parallels to both Jesus' life as well as the kings of Israel.

Jesus came to serve people. It's one thing even non-believers can agree on. As the perfect combination of King and Priest, it's often hard to see the King in Jesus. In the church world, I think it's even harder. Most images I've seen of Jesus while in a church setting are of a loving, gentle nomadic man with flowing hair holding lambs. I've rarely seen the kingly Jesus that intentionally led His disciples. And I've rarely seen the version of Jesus with fire in His eyes, tattooed, and dripping in blood as depicted in Revelation 19:11-16. However, Hollywood gets it. The most creative minds in the world have taken His story and tried to make stories of what happened, albeit poor counterfeit ones.

The most powerful being that ever was or will be, came to planet Earth, which He created. Jesus, the King, took responsibility for His people's eternal destiny. It was His mission to sacrifice Himself to save us. He got His hands dirty for us.

Likewise, a kingdom driven leader's job isn't behind a desk, although that might be where they do most of their duties. A kingdom driven leader's job is to take responsibility for those in their care. Usually, that's family first and emanates out from that, as we discussed earlier.

It's not the job or the role that matters. It is the heart a leader has for the people he or she serves. You don't have to be a priest or a prophet, but you do need to have a heart for the people, *your* people.

Earlier I wrote about your value as a person and as a son of the King. It's important for you to see others how you now see yourself. It's the key to understanding the heart that you need to perform your mission.

Like humility and submission, the word servant gives the same weak word image. The word slave often comes to mind. Now Paul, the writer of almost a third of the New Testament, might tell you that you are a slave to Christ. As someone who sees himself as a leader, I have a tough time imagining myself as a slave or servant. This is not because I think I'm better than they are but because I've rarely served at that level.

SERVANT KINGS

When you examine the Bible, you'll notice that Saul lost his kingdom to David when he stopped listening to God. David and Solomon's kingdom's suffered similar fates. However, what you might miss is who steps in as the next leader was often the greatest servant.

The easiest of these to point out is David. He was a man after God's own heart (1 Samuel 13:14, Acts 13:22) because he understood what it meant to serve others. The youngest son in a large family and the one to tend to the sheep, he often had to serve his older brothers, his father, and the king. Later as king, we see him leading into battle and leading in worship, so it's no wonder he's the prototypical kingdom driven leader.

Kings in the Old Testament didn't just sit on a throne and eat grapes. Often kings would sit near the entrance to the city and listen to people's problems, acting as a judge. The Bible says that people would come from all around the world to hear the wisdom of Solomon through one of these sessions.

Kings that failed to judge properly often had unrest in their kingdom. After David's famous sin with Bathsheba, he lost his kingdom to his third son Absalom. We'll discuss this more in detail later in this book, but what's important to note is how Absalom rises to power. It all started when he stepped up to serve the people. He went where kings were supposed to go - to listen to the people's problems.

With a king's son to listen to them, the people's hearts began to turn toward Absalom instead of David. Accordingly, the people felt like they would be served better by Absalom than David in this case.

A kingdom driven leader isn't a title; it's an opportunity. It's an opportunity to serve God by serving His people.

In my mind, the best way to describe this servant's heart is to look to the business world. The best presenters, salespeople, and frankly, businesses are great because they focus on one thing, the customer. The very best focus so fully on the customer that it consumes them. They don't just solve a problem; they attempt to anticipate the needs of the customer before the customer even knows it's coming up.

No one thinks less of these companies. The last time I checked, everyone would love to stay at the Ritz Carlton. Even NorthPoint Church, a church out of Atlanta, spent time with leaders in the Ritz Carlton organization to learn how they created a culture of service.

I'll never forget my 10th anniversary with my wife. We went on a Royal Caribbean cruise on their largest ship in the ocean at that time, the Oasis of the Seas. What struck me about the trip wasn't that the ship was magnificent, though it truly was. It was a floating paradise, complete with a mall, restaurants, a zip line, a surfing wave, and exquisite cuisine. While all of that was impressive, what impressed me most was the service we received.

We talked to attendant after attendant and were just blown away. Here are people living at the bottom of the ship in close quarters, working long hours, taking long "contracts" away from home, and still serving us with a smile.

However, when we engaged the people in conversations that dug a little deeper, we often discovered they didn't love their job. When I heard this, I was dumbfounded. How could someone serve me so well, seem to genuinely care about me, ask insightful questions, and do it with a smile, all the while hating their job? It touched a nerve for me personally because, as I've alluded to a few times in this book, I've often questioned my purpose and it seemed to me like what they were doing was meaningful service.

I know what some of you are thinking. Yes, they were trained extremely well, or perhaps some of you explain it away by thinking most cruise lines are simply made up of cultures that serve well. I know you are thinking about these things because I did too.

Cultures that serve well are vital to an organization's success. I realize that, but I also had to internalize this as a problem for which I needed to learn to stop making excuses. What your team does for a huge profit will be your profit too. Don't just volunteer at your church but serve with anticipation. If you get this one thing alone, it can be life-changing. This is how we should serve unto the Lord. It's how we should serve our spouses. If we have this attitude of anticipatory service, it can allow us to gain influence.

One of the biggest mistakes I see people make is a lack of focused intentionality. They don't realize that the position that they are in now is often meant to groom them for something much larger later. Your boss might not see you, but God sees you. You might miss the opportunities that are there, but God doesn't miss them. God loves you passionately.

Of course, this does not mean that once you grasp this that you'll cruise through life. If you were a billionaire, you might be inclined to give your children everything, but that rarely works out in the best interest of the child. Life is a training ground, and this is one of the lessons you have to learn. Just remember that even if you struggle being submitted to your earthly authority, that ultimately your true "boss" is your Heavenly Father.

> "When pride comes, then comes disgrace, *but with humility comes wisdom*"
> **— Proverbs 11:2 NIV (emphasis mine)**

A kingdom driven leader has a mission and a calling. However, Jesus always turned people's perceptions inside out. Our calling as leaders can be reminiscent of Jesus summing up the commandments. First, we're to love Him with all our heart (Matthew 22:37). That's why we study the word, listen for His voice, and speak with Him.

Next, we're to love our neighbor as we love ourselves (Matthew 22:39). There is no greater calling than to love our neighbor.

And finally, as no leadership book is complete without mentioning the importance of humility, there is no calling from God that does not include serving others (1 John 3:10). Love can look different when expressed by different people, so different in fact that you might not call it love.

Often when I think about conversations I've had around calling and mission, I think about the "what." What country will I go to? What business will I be involved in? How many systems will I create that are conversation points? The "what" is just part of the journey, but the "who" are the people God has called us to serve. Every mission is about the who.

When you serve others, you create an opening for trust to build. True kingdom driven leadership is servant leadership. When you serve your team, you are adding value to them. What's great about serving is that it's very actionable. You can do it even if you don't feel like it, and as you do it, you will often find that you will want to serve even more.

Continuing to challenge yourself to serve others keeps you as a leader in a position to continually receive God's new assignments. From the beginning of this book, I've been encouraging you to prepare. You need to have a close relationship with God and be a person of integrity to have the resolve to keep your heart pure enough to serve others willingly.

As you practice this, you'll often find a special group of people that causes a holy discontentment in your heart. It's not that serving one group is better than serving another group; it's that God may have a special group that is open to receive what you have to give. As you begin serving in the season of life and place that you are, you may find a special assignment waiting for you to take it on.

8

Holy Discontent

"What is the one aspect of this broken world that, when you see it, touch it, get near it, you just can't stand? Very likely, that firestorm of frustration reflects your holy discontent, a reality so troubling that you are thrust off the couch and into the game. It's during these defining times when your eyes open to the needs surrounding you and your heart hungers to respond that you hear God say, "I feel the same way about this problem. Now, let's go solve it together!"
— **Bill Hibels, Holy Discontent** [17]

As you begin to serve people, inevitably, there will come a time when you feel drawn to a specific cause or group. There are a lot of causes that will break your heart. As believers, we're called to care for orphans, widows, and disenfranchised. We should care deeply for those that have been marginalized by society. There is likely one group, cause, or location that pulls your heart, a mission that stands out.

There are two keys to finding your special cause: a feeling and a desire for action. The best way for me to describe holy discontentment is a feeling. It's that same feeling you get when you witness an injustice knowing that it's not right. For example, perhaps you find your heart breaking and your mind fixed on children without fathers. You know it's unjust that they don't have strong male figures in their lives providing guidance, support, and an example of how a man cares for and provides for his family. This feeling then compels you to the second key, a desire for action. Seeing how fatherlessness affects young children and teens may move you to want to become a mentor or a Sunday School teacher so you can have an eternal impact on those kids who may not otherwise have godly men in their lives. When you combine your life experiences with these feelings and a willingness to get involved, I think you'll find which cause is right for you.

I share all of this because many times, people will ask me, "How do I find my mission?" I reply by asking what breaks their heart and God's. Often, they have experienced life experiences that draw these out. For some of you, it will be human trafficking or the plight of the farmer in South America or inner-city youth.

I'm personally passionate about what a business can do to change a person's life. I'm extremely passionate about getting those that are successful and connecting them to their causes. I also have a very special place in my heart for the country of Cambodia. Do I want to help those in Africa, South America, or Europe? Absolutely! However, when I dream, the people I dream of helping are Khmers.

I'm married to a Khmer woman who introduced me to the plight of the people of Cambodia. When I learned how family members were suffering and how it wasn't just a few people but almost an entire country, it caused something in me to want to do something. When I took action to do something about it, it was based on the idea of a business impacting the community.

Once you have some semblance of your mission, you can endeavor to integrate that into what you're doing. If you own your own company, you can begin thinking not just in terms of money but also in logistics.

While I believe there are causes that are specifically for you, I also believe that you can't pick wrong here. When you take action toward growing the kingdom, I believe God will guide you to the right path. I'd encourage you to read this book and take action. In business, when you take a risk, you could lose finances and valuable time. However, taking a risk here only offers eternal rewards.

A lot of times, we hear the word "calling" or even the word "mission" and think of something grandiose. We might think there needs to be a moment like when God spoke to Moses through a burning bush to tell him that he was going to be used to free the Israelites. However, your particular mission may not look anything like that. Let's look at a real-life example.

BOBBY MALONE

We've likely heard the stories about a person's own burning bush moment and wondered when it would happen for us. We wonder when God will come and speak to us in an audible voice about our purpose. The reality is that the burning bush is the exception, not the rule. A friend of mine has an incredible story that almost sounds like a business version of Forrest Gump. From his perspective, it's just one event that led to another, but as you read it, you'll see the grander picture of a life well-lived.

Bobby was a UPS driver and a church drummer when he visited a prison with his church group. This prison made all the men keep close shaved beards or none at all, and everyone needed to be well-groomed. This attention to grooming caused a shift in how the prisoners carried themselves and how those outside the prison saw the young men. Bobby noticed this shift in his view, and he saw the men as men and not as criminals. "I had this thought, 'I wish I could help them.' Then, 'How can I help them?' Then, 'They will need jobs.'"

From then on, Bobby had in the back of his mind that given the opportunity to hire, he would consider qualified, talented men no matter their background. Often men getting out of prison have a difficult time finding jobs. They are often stuck working at places that offer lower wages even if they have the skills and talents to do more. Bobby's compassion for them in this area sparked a desire to do something that would allow for their advancement.

At the time with his UPS job, Bobby had a thought that he says God gave him to launch a private valet business. At the time, this idea was revolutionary because taxi apps didn't exist. The only private valet services were limo drivers and drivers for people with enough income to pay a driver a salary. "What made the idea even more profound was that pretty much all I knew was lower-middle-class America, definitely not the target market for a private driver." Instead of just launching and floundering as many would-be entrepreneurs do, Bobby went to work at a restaurant to understand the valet business and to get acquainted with the clientele.

It's worth noting how slowly all this was progressing and how faithful Bobby was. At the time, Bobby will tell you that life wasn't perfect, but it was progressing. The income and the position didn't match his vision of a large business. He wasn't burning with passion to help young men necessarily but was trying to be obedient to the call on his life, which he felt was to business.

Bobby used the valet at the restaurant as a networking opportunity to learn and gain wisdom. He also used it to grow his network and influence, thus landing him future opportunities. Although things moved forward for him, it wasn't until he had an epiphany about his customers that things began to move more quickly. After valeting for a brief season at the restaurant, Bobby got an opportunity to valet for an exclusive country club in Atlanta. "At this point, I thought all the country club people were stuck up rich people born with silver spoons in their mouths." He quickly realized, however, that country club members were humans too. Bobby found out that many had worked several jobs when they were young, including valeting. This was a eureka moment for Bobby to understand that his opportunity wasn't just to provide work for an underserved group of men but also to serve his customers.

It's important to note that during this time, Bobby was very clear about his purpose. He was okay with his purpose being centered around helping just one person. Meaning, he was humble enough to not want a platform or to already be thinking of impact in terms of "headcount." Eventually, Bobby went from an employee of the valet company that serviced the country club to owning the company that serviced this country club. He was still thinking of ways to help young men, and during the downtime in between cars, he'd be investing in the young men that worked with him. He would tell you that he'd have loved to hire men to give them a second chance, but this was still not the opportunity yet. The country club's hiring standards prevented that.

One unique thing that also happened during this season at the country club is that Bobby rarely worked on Sunday. The two busiest days at the country club by far are Saturday and Sunday. No other day comes close. Just like Chick-fil-a shocks the world by being closed on Sunday and outperforming every peer in fast-food; Bobby's company was outperforming everyone in Atlanta and doing so while being closed on one of the busiest days of the week. If you're reading this far, you're probably waiting for, "then it happened." Keep waiting. This isn't that kind of story.

As Bobby continued to work as a valet, his business opportunities continued to expand slowly. One day one of the golfers said to Bobby, "It'd sure be nice if you guys could wash my car while I'm playing golf." That was all that was needed for Bobby's business gears to get turning, so he began to introduce this wash and detail service to the members of the club. "Mind you, I didn't know anything about detailing cars at the time, so I had to research it." In other words, Bobby is a king who prepares. The service was a hit, and before long, Bobby had to hire more men. As the owner of the business and by offering this new detailing service, Bobby was finally able to hire the kind of men that might not have been allowed to valet. The business grew and became a full-fledged business. Bobby left UPS to do this full-time. The business continued to grow and grow.

Around this time, Bobby noticed a woman carrying garbage at an apartment complex one day and wondered if that could be a business. Another new business was born. Clubhouse Services was launched with a trash valet service. The business was simple. A landlord or property manager would hire Bobby's company to come to pick up the trash from the doors of the apartment residents and carry it to the dumpster. Given the type of business it is, where you are only needed for a few hours at night to pick up the trash, it's the perfect side gig. It became a great opportunity to hire men that might need a second chance or help with finances. He already had a workforce to pull from and the know-how of how to find men willing to work, as they did at the valet and detailing, so naturally, this business took off as well. For the purposes of this book, I asked Bobby what he was passionate about? What makes him have "holy discontent." Bobby said, "It's not like that. I try to follow God as closely as I can. I get an idea, and then I start to strategize around that, but God is always part of the process. Should I take this job or not? Should I hire this person or not? He's never out of the equation." When a man works for Bobby's company, they get roughly 10 hours of work, Sunday through Thursday, working from 8 to 10 PM. Just enough time to eat dinner with the family, do a few hours of work, and be home in time before everyone is asleep. With a consistent income, it's a safer bet than driving a taxi or delivering pizzas. Of course, Bobby doesn't just train them to be efficient trash collectors. They need to be "valets." In other words, they need to be professional. During their employment, he mentors the men. As the company continues to grow, he leads the managers and leaders in the organization in leading the men. Godly men leading men to be leaders of men! Powerful!

As Bobby puts it, "My best ministry opportunity with my men is my example. I try to live my life in a way that they can follow." At the time of this writing, Bobby currently owns a multi-state company that is in the process of franchising. His entire business model was built on the idea of helping young men in need of a break or a second chance. When I asked him more specifically about how he came to choose his cause, Bobby said, "You know, honestly, when I saw those young men in prison, I was reminded of my life as a young man, a young husband, and a young father. I wish I had someone that would have mentored me and at the same time had an opportunity to provide that took my life into account." As you might guess, Bobby is a giver. He gave his time and money while he worked at UPS, and that has grown as his income and business have grown. With his wife, he formed CFAA (Christian Family Adoption Aid), a non-profit designed to help Christian families with the exorbitant cost of adoption. If you're anything like me, you might ask, what does this have to do with young men? It doesn't. Bobby saw a need, prayed about it, and used his funds to help families in this situation. Through CFAA, he's been able to assist families as well as help a Jamaican Orphanage. Most recently, Bobby funded an entire mission trip to Bristol, England.

Bobby believes that "kings" are blessed to be a blessing. If you ask Bobby what a "king" is, he'll tell you, "A king is there to gather resources for the purposes of the priest. Sometimes a king hears directly from God, and other times a king will fund the priests' work." Bobby has advice for other kingdom driven leaders: Listen to God, listen to your spouse, and pray about everything. Bobby even suggests that it's just as important for a kingdom driven leader to pray about not hiring someone or not giving money. Often as leaders, it's easy to say yes when it comes to money. Yet, that might not be in God's plan. There were no burning bushes or Red Seas in Bobby's story. He simply followed the breadcrumbs and was humble and intentionally submitted to God through the entire process. With God's help, he was able to build the relationships and resources to truly go from success to significance.

Bobby's holy discontentment wasn't something that he could easily describe. However, he had enough experience serving others to know that serving young men was different to him. Later, when he started his charity, it became a bit clearer. By helping families, he could help raise up leaders in impoverished areas. The key takeaway from Bobby's story is that he was constantly serving and, in that process, discovered his holy discontentment around certain causes.

JOSIAH

Some of the characteristics in this book are harder to see because of the way the lives of the kings are presented in the Bible. They might get a chapter or two to describe their entire reign. If they were particularly faithful, the Bible will tell us they were good and tell us of a few of their good deeds. Finding a Biblical king that had a holy discontent for anything, in particular, is a challenge except for one king, Josiah.

From the age of eight years old, Josiah ruled Judah. Thrust into leadership after his father was assassinated, Josiah was wise beyond his years. The Bible tells us that at age eighteen, Josiah began to seek God. He wanted to start rebuilding the temple. When the priest found God's word and brought it to him, he had a moment of holy discontentment (2 Kings 22-23).

> "When the king heard the words of the Book of the Law, he tore his robes"
> **— 2 Kings 22:11 NIV**

After hearing this, Josiah could not sit still. He had to take action. Josiah's actions give us the kingdom driven leader playbook. Josiah immediately humbled himself by tearing his clothes, and he sought God's voice to follow His will. His response was so profound that God noticed and decided to postpone impending destruction.

> "Because your heart was responsive and you humbled yourself before the Lord when you heard what I have spoken against this place and its people—that they would become a curse and be laid waste—and because you tore your robes and wept in my presence, I also have heard you, declares the Lord."
> **—2 Kings 22:19 NIV**

Josiah went on to reconsecrate his covenant with the Lord by tearing down idols, removing strongholds, and instituting a new kingdom culture. If a lot of those items sound familiar, they should; they are all chapters in this book.

Josiah led with humility and served his people. However, his life and his kingdom were changed when he encountered God's word and found his holy discontentment.

JESUS' HOLY DISCONTENTMENT

> "When it was almost time for the Jewish Passover, Jesus went up to Jerusalem. In the temple courts he found people selling cattle, sheep and doves, and others sitting at tables exchanging money. So, he made a whip out of cords, and drove all from the temple courts, both sheep and cattle; he scattered the coins of the   money changers and overturned their tables. To those who sold doves he said, "Get these out of here! Stop turning my Father's house into a market!" His disciples remembered that it is written: "Zeal for your house will consume me."
> **— John 2:13-17 NIV**

One of my favorite stories in the Bible is when Jesus cleared out the temple. He saw His Father's house being used as a place to profit instead of a place of worship. Vendors had set up shop around the temple to sell sacrificial animals. To make matters worse, they were taking advantage of the people that came to worship.

When Jesus saw this, He got angry. He made a whip and drove everyone out of there. I love this story because it goes counter to many of the soft images that I saw of Jesus growing up. This story reveals Jesus' passion or holy discontentment for His Father's will.

If you keep reading, he challenged the religious leaders who allowed the vendors in to tear down the temple and see if it wouldn't be rebuilt. All the while, He was referring to himself. The whole context of this story could just sound like the Messiah being upset, throwing a fit, and then talking in riddles to the religious leaders. However, it reveals the heart of the holy discontentment. He wasn't just upset that the temple was being misused. He knew the greater truth to what was happening. The people, the ones He was sent to save, were being robbed of the opportunity to have a relationship with God.

Before Jesus, the only way to be righteous enough to talk with God was to make an animal sacrifice as prescribed. This was the very system that Jesus came to abolish.

The sacrifice of animals was not arbitrary. God had chosen those animals because they were valuable to the people. Even more so than mere money, animals represented an investment of time as well. And in addition to time, the owner of the animal often hoped for a future return from something the animal produced, whether that be milk, clothing, food, or more animals. This made the process of sacrifice deep and meaningful. It caused introspection and often repentance.

When the vendors came to sell sacrificial animals, it allowed the people to have a convenient way of sinning and then purchasing their item of atonement to go about their life. The temple goers no longer had to worry about selecting animals from their own. They could simply pay for one at the temple. They turned what was meant as an act of repentance and cleansing into a transaction.

Doing away with this process was Jesus' mission. Jesus came to save everyone, but the people at the temple were the representatives. The combination of the eternal damage done by these vendors on the temple goers' lives and Jesus' love for His Father's house caused something to rise in Him.

Holy discontentment doesn't always have to be a feeling of burning anger, though. If you study Jesus' life, you can see He was also passionate about spending time with the Father and about serving the people. If you're wondering what your special calling is, you'll only find it by doing what Jesus did (spending time with God and serving others).

Kingdom driven leaders are intentional. It's that intentionality in every aspect of life that makes leaders more effective. If you're like Bobby, it could just be a feeling while you're serving about a specific people group. It could be "coincidental" opportunities or connections in your life. The point is that you won't find this holy discontentment by doing nothing; you'll find it by serving others.

One area that I think gets overlooked is our spiritual journey. I think God wants us to discover this specific mission because it will bring us the most fulfillment of our purpose. Often as leaders, we can spend our time searching for purpose in the things we do, and yet God often has rewarding, purposeful work hidden behind something as basic as simply serving one person. It's not hidden because God is playing games. Instead, it's hidden because God's idea of purpose looks different than what we're often looking for, which is often shaped by the world's view of purpose.

In addition, when you discover your holy discontentment, you'll begin to realize that for you to do anything, you'll need God. Apart from God, we can do nothing, and that's incredibly evident when we examine the causes we are passionate about. Finding your holy discontentment is about two things. Finding something that you can focus on and realizing that you must be humble to accomplish anything toward that focus.

Once you have thought about this, start asking questions of yourself and your leadership:

- What can my team, sphere of influence, or company do for this cause beyond giving money?
- If I'm righteously disturbed by this situation, what am I willing to do? What am I willing to inspire others to do?
- What would I be willing to lose to accomplish a major goal for this cause?

Adding your holy discontentment to your organization will bring an entirely different, difference-making dynamic to your work. The truth is that the higher up in an organization you are, the harder this will be. Sure, moving your entire organization toward this cause will be difficult. However, the greater difficulty will be potentially giving up your position in order to serve. Bobby, Josiah, and Jesus all shared one thing in common that every leader must learn. Often, in your pursuit of making a positive change in a cause, you'll discover you're on a leadership journey to humility.

9

Be Humble

Humility: Freedom from Pride or Arrogance
— **Webster's Dictionary** [18]

It's pretty hard for me to imagine there being humble kings in the Old Testament. The factual tone doesn't reveal too much about their character. Luckily, when David is anointed as king, the Bible says he was a man after God's own heart (1 Samuel 13:14, Acts 13:22). Whether you interpret that to mean that his heart is similar to God or that his heart chased God's heart still reveals humility.

Throughout each of the kings depicted in Scripture, we see glimpses of humility, from the most evil Ahab humbling himself after committing murder to Josiah humbling himself after finding how far off the kingdom was from following God's word. But to find these examples of humility in the Old Testament, you have to intentionally look.

Humility gets a really bad wrap. The word humble is often used to describe someone who is quiet or meek. In other words, "weak." Webster's dictionary gets the definition right, so why do we get it wrong? Do a quick google on the word, and you'll find full-length articles on what that author thinks humility is. There's even an example of when NFL players say they were humbled to win a Super Bowl. It's a bit amusing to me when a player who just won a contest on the world's largest stage says he is "humbled" when he is out doing interviews and knows he just won one of the most highly esteemed honors in professional sports. The player could be correctly humbled by seeing the vastness of the stage he is on and how insignificant he really is when compared to the effort needed by his team to propel him to victory. This is part of the world's definition of being "humbled," but it's still not close to what we seek as kingdom driven leaders. More often, as Christians, we're familiar with a pastor preaching from the pulpit about humility as a desired weakness. Let's set the record straight.

> **Humility is anything but weak.**

I think what we've been taught of Jesus and humility is that it's the weaker feminine trait. As my pastor would say, "why is every picture of Jesus like a Revlon commercial with Jesus petting a cute sheep?" Humility is not being subservient. Humility is not passiveness. It's actually the opposite. It's a display of power.

> **Humility is power under control AND taking 100% responsibility.**

> "Jesus, **knowing that** the Father had given all things into His hands, and that He had come from God and was going to God, rose from supper and laid aside His garments, took a towel and girded Himself." — **John 13:3 NIV**

Knowing that. Jesus KNEW the power he had and chose to serve His disciples. He did not lose His authority; He chose where His authority was represented. He didn't lose authority, He established it.

Picture the setting. This is the last meal Jesus would eat, Judas was ready to betray Jesus, and the disciples were talking about which one of them was the greatest. He could have easily performed some miracle to stop the arguing. Instead, He chose to serve. The most humble person on the planet was Jesus. The God of the universe put flesh on and walked with us. Jesus is 100% God and 100% man. He was tutored by humans, baptized by humans, taunted, tortured, and killed by humans. This was not because he was so weak or passive that it happened to him. Rather, the ultimate power of the universe decided that he would *choose* not to use His infinite world-crushing power to save Himself. In an act that saved mankind, God chose to restrain himself for the perfect salvation of our lives.

We see in the comics and movies where this supremely powerful being tries to operate by Earth's rules. In doing so, he limits the exercise of his powers to become more human. This is exactly what Jesus did. He came to play the same game we are playing with the same set of rules and left us an example of what humility looks like and how, we too, can walk in humility. He wasn't brought low as the wordplay suggests. No one humbled Him. No, He *chose* to go low. It's the first lesson of a king.

"With great power comes great responsibility," Uncle Ben[19] had it right. On your journey to live like a kingdom driven leader, you will need to master your heart and grab the reins. You were already given power and authority when you accepted Christ. As you become more and more aware of this power, you need humility. The more power you realize, the bigger the chance pride can creep in and destroy you.

For leaders, this can mean waiting on God to direct you instead of acting out on your own. However, for driven people waiting could feel like an eternity. It did for Saul. His impatience caused him to lose his kingship.

Slow down and help those in the company with life. Take time to listen to their stories and be willing to pray for them.

Being humble as a kingdom driven leader means being willing to serve and give up your rights. We only need to look at our example, Jesus, to see the model. Jesus, the greatest King of all time, the one who had the greatest impact on our world, came to serve (Mark 10:45).

On the contrary, society often portrays leaders as the ones in the front with people serving them. It doesn't help that our worldly examples of CEOs and political leaders abuse their power and seemingly get rewarded for this. However, the Bible is clear on this point as well. We are not to concern ourselves when others succeed with worldly success (Psalm 37:7). Instead, we must focus 100 percent on what Christ has called us to, and He's called us to serve.

This is especially tough for leaders who fight their way up to the top serving everyone to get there and then expecting that life will be different at the top. The reality is that leaders that have gotten to the top in this manner are simply better prepared to serve.

Humility says, "I have the power to compel you to action. However, I'm choosing to serve you because I serve someone greater." If you understand what humility truly is - power under control - then you can effectively lead out of your humility. This frees you from being offended when people don't receive your service or what you do for them. You're serving God by serving them. The better you serve them, the better you serve God, and ultimately, the better you'll end up leading.

For a leader, service does not mean doing tasks that seem the lowest. Instead, it means valuing people the highest. You value people when you notice them and when you listen to them. When you serve others, they will naturally want to follow you.

TAKE ACTION

Take the next three to six months and begin to listen to the needs of your direct reports. If you have a multi-tiered organization, do this with your top leaders. If you have a team of five, do this with them. Then, as you listen to the needs of your people, try to apply what they have shared by serving them in new ways. Be proactive and creative.

Additionally, when you hire someone, look at them through a new humility lens. Ask yourself, would you enjoy serving this person, and if this person would be capable of ultimately serving others on the team.

BUT WHAT ABOUT... THEM

Whenever I talk about humility, the response usually is, "Okay, this sounds great, but what about them?" "Them" is the affectionate name for the people in your life that might take advantage of you. Inevitably, when leaders hear about humility and serving, there is a resistance to the idea. They feel like they might appear weak or give up their position. In most organizations, the resistance to humility is that it leaves the humble vulnerable to be taken advantage of. Nowhere is this put more to the test than in marriage. If you're married, you're married to "them." I think God designed marriage to be a training ground for humility.

A pastor that helped my marriage was Jimmy Evans from Marriage Today. He says spouses often worry about serving the other for fear of being taken advantage of. Fear and lack of confidence say, "I wonder who the greatest is," "what if I do this and it doesn't work," "what if they take advantage of me," and the like. What humility says is, "I'm confident in the Power that lives in me to accomplish what I am doing and that I can kneel and wash your feet as an act of that power instead of using my own power to change the outcome."[20]

Serving your spouse is a great place to practice humility. Marriage has the potential to hurt you more deeply than your work ever would. However, you should also be humble at work as well. In doing so, you will please God and likely build influence in your workplace for the Kingdom.

Humility creates an atmosphere of love in full service to others. As you begin to intentionally take action to serve others and show them that you value them, you inevitably start to value them more. I also believe that as you start to value people more by serving them, you'll start to see people more as God sees them.

When we struggle with humility, we are struggling with control. It's hard to be completely humble without some modicum of power. If you are powerless, you don't have any control over what happens. However, God's given each of us control over our choices. We all have an opportunity to be humble. You have to choose to serve someone, and it doesn't come naturally for most of us. It's that choice that begins to make a change in your heart, and ultimately it shapes your attitude.

Power could be translated as a combination of influence and authority. If you live in the United States, then you have an opportunity to exercise this power. Go to any restaurant, and you'll see that you, the customer, have enormous power. For example, let's say a restaurant is running behind on your order. You have two choices; you can make demands and complain, or you can remain humble and offer grace. You would be well within your rights to complain. However, which choice best reflects Christ's love for the staff at the restaurant?

It's the tension between controlling your power by submitting to God's plan and accepting the lack of control in your life that produces humility. At the beginning of this chapter, we looked at Jesus washing His disciple's feet. He had all authority and deep influence in the lives of the disciples. He could have commanded them to do anything. Instead, He chose to wash their feet. And in doing so, He gave us an amazing example of humility.

Humility is a hard thing to describe because words like power and serving rarely go together. It's also easy to get humility confused with false humility. This quote from C. S. Lewis captures the definition of what humility is and isn't.

> "Do not imagine that if you meet a really humble man he will be what most people call 'humble' nowadays: he will not be a sort of greasy, smarmy person, who is always telling you that, of course, he is nobody. Probably all you will think about him is that he seemed a cheerful, intelligent chap who took a real interest in what you said to him. If you do dislike him, it will be because you feel a little envious of anyone who seems to enjoy life so easily. He will not be thinking about humility: he will not be thinking about himself at all.
>
> If anyone would like to acquire humility, I can, I think, tell him the first step. The first step is to realize that one is proud. And a biggish step, too. At least, nothing whatever can be done before it. If you think you are not conceited, it means you are very conceited indeed."
> **— C.S. Lewis, Mere Christianity** [21]

This is where the quote comes from, thanks to Rick Warren.[22] "Humility isn't thinking less of yourself, but rather thinking of yourself less."

HUMBLED THEMSELVES

The Bible has many examples of how kings humbled themselves. In most instances, this meant they would fast from eating, wear sackcloth, and even cover themselves in ashes. This outward expression often mirrored the most marginalized of their kingdom. In other words, the kings acted as if they were poor.

Even though the Bible references many good kings, the one that stands out to me is one that was the most evil, Ahab. At the time, Ahab was one of the evilest kings ever to rule. 1 Kings 16:33 says, "He did more to provoke the anger of the LORD, the God of Israel, than any of the other kings of Israel before him" (NLT). He and his wife Jezebel built temples for other gods and made sacrifices to them, killed their subjects to take their land, and did evil in God's sight.

However, in one instance, Ahab humbled himself before God. Ahab and Jezebel killed a man for his vineyard, and God sent a prophet to condemn Ahab and his descendants for it. Normally not a repentant man, Ahab was shaken by this.

> "But when Ahab heard this message, he tore his clothing, dressed in burlap, and fasted. He even slept in burlap and went about in deep mourning.
>
> Then another message from the LORD came to Elijah: "Do you see how Ahab has humbled himself before me? Because he has done this, I will not do what I promised during his lifetime. It will happen to his sons; I will destroy his dynasty."
> — 1 Kings 21-28 NLT

Ahab's example shows us that humility is choosing to lower your position to accept God's authority over your circumstances. It wasn't the sackcloth or the ashes that got God's attention. It was the mourning. His outward actions reflected what was going on in his heart.

Humility is acknowledging that God's ways are better than our ways (Isaiah 55:8) and choosing to submit to His authority. A kingdom driven leader doesn't need to fast or dress as if they are poor. They need to humble their heart. A kingdom driven leader can give up their rights to serve others because they've built their relationship through communicating with God. This relationship gives a new kind of power, power through humility.

Humility is giving up your rights and choosing to serve others. It requires confidence in who you are in Christ and being submitted to His authority. Nowhere is this tougher than in the area of finances. Friendships have been ruined, marriages have ended, and wars have been fought over money. How we handle money can often give us clues to things going on in our hearts. However, money is not evil. The *love* of money is (1 Timothy 6:10). One practice that requires humility and helps defeat this evil love is tithing which we will discuss in the next chapter.

10

Tithe

Nothing says humility better in my mind than acknowledging that God is our provider and that nothing we own is really ours. Taking that attitude acknowledges God's provision but also our finite lives and legacy.

As the topic of humility in the chapter before, you don't see tithing in Scripture unless you dig deeper than the factual account. When you read Kings and Chronicles, it's easy to miss tithing. Kings often gave sacrifices and humbled themselves, but there is very little mention of the tithe itself.

We'll dive into more about the tithe, but for the sake of brevity, we won't cover the entire history of tithing or have a discussion about the church and state government of Israel. What is worth noting is that both David and Solomon gave extravagantly to build God's temple (1 Chronicles 29). In addition, Hezekiah, one of the last good kings, leads Judah in giving tithes and offerings.

> "Hezekiah gave orders to prepare storerooms in the temple of the Lord, and this was done. Then they faithfully brought in the contributions, tithes and dedicated gifts. Konaniah, a Levite, was the overseer in charge of these things, and his brother Shimei was next in rank."
> **— 2 Chronicles 31:11**

From this, we can see that tithing was a big part of good kings' lives, and we can see that the tithes went to the Levites or the "pastors" of that time. If you start to dig and study the kings solely looking for the tithe, you'll uncover that tithing was commonplace and sometimes as common as paying taxes.

For the most part, this entire book is kind of a Biblical self-help book, but we must leave no stone unturned. Money is often cited as the cause of divorces and corporate dissolutions and is often credited as the reason for many crimes. For many, the topic of money is a sore subject when it comes to the church, as there is no shortage of examples of a church misappropriating funds or church leaders leading lavish lifestyles.

Ultimately, to live like a kingdom driven leader, you are to live as God called you to, not necessarily to do what you want. Thus, tithing is one of the main areas that need to be addressed. Tithing is about stewarding the financial resources that God has given you, and it's about humbling yourself. It's about being 100 percent submitted to Christ. This is why this is in this section and not set apart as a financial stewardship chapter.

WHAT'S THE TITHE?

It's just a tenth. That's all it means. Ten percent. It refers to the mandate God has for His people to give back ten percent of their earnings to the storehouse. It started with Abraham. Abraham was one of the first kingdom driven leaders in the Bible. He was fully submitted to God and humbly followed God into new territory (Genesis 12). A while before Lot's wife was ever turned to salt or flaming meteors crushed Sodom and Gomorrah, there was a war where five kings ganged up on four smaller kingdoms. These smaller kingdoms included the kings of Sodom and Gomorrah.

In Abraham's day, it was common for cities to join forces with neighbors to conquer the land. When the lead king got too prideful or showed some weaknesses, new challengers would come to fight for territory. We see this in modern-day gang warfare, politics, and business.

As you can imagine, five kings had far more manpower and weaponry available than the four small kingdoms did. It should be pretty easy to imagine what happened. To make matters worse, as the four kings retreated from their defeat, many of their armies fell into tar pits. As these battles would go, the winner would get the spoils. If they were lucky, the losers would end up paying taxes or as slaves.

Among the captured was Lot, the same nephew that picked the greener valley where Sodom was and later would leave that city.

Abraham got wind of Lot's capture and took just 318 men from his security detail to go and rescue Lot. God provided, and Abraham was able to defeat the same five kings that routed four kingdoms and rescue Lot and his family. Following the successful battle, Abraham met up with another king, King Melchizedek. The writer of Hebrews wrote this about Melchizedek, "Melchizedek was king of Salem and priest of God Most High. He met Abraham returning from the victory over the kings and blessed him, and Abraham gave him a tenth of everything" (Hebrews 7:1-2 NIV).

Melchizedek was a high priest of the highest order and had no mother or father, "resembling the Son of God." Melchizedek was then both a king and a priest. Abraham decides to give him a tenth of everything. The tithe begins here with Abraham.

NEW COVENANT

You might wonder about the legitimacy of the tithe. I know that I did. You might say that the old covenant and Levitical law passed away with the new covenant with Christ. Here is what Jesus said,

> "Do not think that I have come to abolish the Law or the Prophets; I have not come to abolish them but to fulfill them."
> — **Matthew 5:17 NIV**

Now, look at the book of Acts. They didn't have to mention the tithe at all because everyone gave so freely. They gave *all* their possessions. If you'd like to be a full new covenant Christian, give it all away. This is exactly what the first church did.

> "All the believers were one in heart and mind. **No one claimed that any of their possessions was their own, but they shared everything they had.** With great power the apostles continued to testify to the resurrection of the Lord Jesus. And God's grace was so powerfully at work in them all that there were no needy persons among them. **For from time to time those who owned land or houses sold them, brought the money from the sales and put it at the apostles' feet, and it was distributed to anyone who had need.**"
> — **Acts 4:32-35 NIV**

During Jesus' ministry, religious leaders would often try to trick Him with questions. One such man asked Jesus about the commandments. When Jesus answered the man about the commandments, he didn't say that they were invalid, but rather that they could be summed up in two statements (Matthew 22:36-40).

In fact, in the next chapter, Jesus confirms the need for the tithe while confronting the teachers of the religious law and the Pharisees about their priorities.

> "Hypocrites! For you are careful to tithe even the tiniest income from your herb gardens, but you ignore the more important

> aspects of the law—justice, mercy, and faith. **You should tithe**, yes, but do not neglect the more important things."
> — **Matthew 23:23 NLT**

According to Jesus' answer to the man, the Levitical laws have been fulfilled, and yet the commandments remain. This also means that God's promises still stand. One such promise is one about tithing. This promise was given through the prophet Malachi.

> "'Bring the whole tithe into the storehouse, that there may be food in my house. Test me in this,' says the LORD Almighty, 'and see if I will not throw open the floodgates of heaven and pour out so much blessing that there will not be room enough to store it.'"
> — **Malachi 3:10 NIV**

This one scripture is usually the basis of most tithing sermons, and for a good reason. It shows the promise God has made about it as well as answers the question about what happens if our "storehouse" is unfaithful.

I think we can all think of religious leaders that have used their position to profit themselves. This is a battle for me as well. When I learned how much money is spent on smoke machines and lighting at my own church, it made me question whether I should tithe or not. However, our responsibility is to give the tithe, and it's God's responsibility to judge the stewardship of it.

Tithing is a heart issue. We don't own anything. God has given it all to us. We can then return the tithe to Him without worry. Tithing isn't some religious thing. It's a test of your heart's trust in God's ability to provide what you need and that He will help you do more with 90 percent than 100 percent. Holding onto the tithe then becomes an issue of pride. Pride says, "I know better than God," and nowhere is more present than in our finances. Matthew 6:21 tells us, "For where your treasure is, there your heart will be also" (NIV).

When my family decided to start tithing, we were a bit skeptical at first. We believed in giving but thought our church didn't need the money. We thought that we should give to ministries that were actually in need.

When we heard Biblical teaching about tithing and how Old Testament heroes of the faith practiced this and Jesus reaffirmed it, we decided on that day, for we'd tithe to honor God. This wasn't because it is a salvation issue because it isn't. We decided to do this because we wanted everything God has for us – from the fruit of obedience to the blessing of it. Since that time, we've been incredibly blessed.

It's been such a life change for us that when I consult with other business leaders that are in financial trouble, I often ask if they are tithing. Tithing won't make up for poor choices, and life is not always perfect for tithers, but I have never seen a tither that stewards his possessions without the necessities of life. Like the scripture says,

> "I was young and now I am old, yet I have never seen the righteous forsaken or their children begging bread. They are always generous and lend freely; their children will be a blessing."
> **— Psalm 37:24-25 NIV**

As a kingdom driven leader, one of your biggest battles will be with pride. As your influence grows and as you become more conscientious of your influence, you'll naturally want more control. Tithing is one practice that will help you remain humble because you're giving up control. If you're 100 percent submitted to Christ, then you're also trusting Him for everything. Tithing builds trust. Malachi 3:10 is one of the few scriptures that encourages you to test God and see what He will do.

Matthew 13 starts with Jesus' famous parable of the sower and the seeds. The farmer spreads his seeds, and some fell on hard soil, some were eaten by birds, and still, others were choked by weeds. Only the seeds that fell on fertile soil were received and produced fruit.

In this book, I started with a lot of heart work to encourage you to prepare your soil (and soul) to receive wisdom. Without this preparation, much of the wisdom you receive might fall on hard soil.

Our world is flooded with information, and it's becoming harder to decipher what is wisdom and what is foolishness. These first few chapters were dedicated to creating a lens through which you can view information and answer the question, "Is this wisdom?"

With the previous chapters in mind, let's look forward to growing in wisdom.

11

Gain Wisdom

"The beginning of wisdom is this: Get wisdom. Though it cost all you have, get understanding." — **Proverbs 4:7 NIV**

When I sold real estate, I had the opportunity to work with several investment groups. These groups managed their real estate portfolio in the same way a stockbroker might manage stocks. What impressed me was the amount of wisdom they had in their dealings.

Over 30 years ago, one such group bought a few run-down buildings during a recession in a future up-and-coming neighborhood. Years went by, and the group did nothing with these buildings. The real estate market soared again to its greatest heights ever and then crashed again. Again, this group bought a few of the foreclosed or run-down buildings. When the market rebounded, they didn't sell.

Then in 2007, the market climbed again to amazing new heights. Again, the group did nothing to sell their property. In 2008, the greatest real estate crash we have ever seen happened, and this group bought more real estate in this same neighborhood. Now, over ten years later, the market is climbing again, and this investment group owns almost the entire block for one of the most desirable pieces of real estate in Atlanta.

Unfortunately, I can't reveal too many details at their request, but what I can tell you is that in one instance, they bought a vacant lot for

$50,000, and it's now worth over $5 million. When I talked to members of this group, they told me the secret to their success. They buy low and wait for real estate appreciation to compound, which only happens when the market goes down and up repeatedly. I quickly realized they were operating with a completely different level of wisdom.

These investors were willing to make unpopular decisions to buy property no one wanted at the time because they had a long-term vision. They decided not to sell when the market was up and to continue to wait for an even better opportunity.

While this is an example of worldly wisdom, I think it mirrors the view a kingdom driven leader needs to have. A kingdom driven leader needs an eternal vision of what they are here to do. They need this clarity of vision to make correct decisions – the kind that leads them to pursue and grow in wisdom and character.

Leadership is often measured as influence, but what is influence if there is no action behind it? It's these decisions that are measured. Did followers join, and did it make a lasting impact? Ultimately, decisions can be measured by one asking one question: "Is it wise?"

A kingdom driven leader is driven by God's mission. A leader can be humble, full of integrity, and totally submitted to God but make really poor decisions. It's through wise decisions and choices that a leader can truly make a great impact.

First and foremost, the Bible is clear about the source and value of wisdom. James tells us true wisdom is from God (James 3:13-18). While we will cover some practical ways to increase in wisdom later in this chapter, you must never forget where true wisdom comes from. But before we dive into how and where to get wisdom, it makes sense that we know what it is. After all, how do we know we have it?

> "...Wisdom from above is first of all pure. It is also peace loving, gentle at all times, and willing to yield to others. It is full of mercy and the fruit of good deeds. It shows no favoritism and is always sincere."
> **— James 3:17 NLT**

PROVERBIAL WISDOM

1 Kings 3 opens with the story of Solomon choosing wisdom. In true kingdom leader fashion, Solomon has a conversation with God after humbling himself and offering sacrifices. When God offers him anything he wishes, Solomon chooses wisdom.

If you research the Proverbs, you'll notice a pattern emerging from the advice that Solomon gave. The pattern you see will be one of three possibilities: proverbs that mirror the Ten Commandments, proverbs that call us to gain wisdom, or specific advice around whom you should spend your time.

When you realize that many of the proverbs are paraphrases of the Ten Commandments, they start to read more like Jesus than commandments. For example, Proverbs 5 discusses the adulterous woman. While you certainly could read this as literal advice to avoid adultery, there's another metaphor here. Here the author is telling us to avoid anything that would entice our hearts away from God. To paraphrase, "stay away from the enticement of the world. There will be many distractions that look like fun, but you should avoid them. Instead, spend time with Jesus and learn His approach to life." Proverbs about avoiding adultery are common, but also common are the proverbs about caring for the poor, not being envious of the wicked, and not being prideful in victory.

BE TEACHABLE

When it comes to seeking wisdom, the Proverbs belabors the point that it's more of a posture rather than an item to be obtained. In the humble posture of constantly seeking wisdom, you can keep Jesus and your relationship with Him in the forefront. Being teachable isn't just a "Christian" thing to be. It's not some falsely humble way of backing off and being passive when others are looking. Having a posture that says, "I don't know it all" keeps you away from pride and helps you make better decisions.

Being teachable and willing to learn keeps you in a state of curiosity. Instead of needing to be right, you can look at each situation as an opportunity to learn. The posture of gaining wisdom asks the question, "What can I learn from this?" When someone says or does something offensive, you're able to handle it with more grace. When a situation doesn't turn out as you expected, you're curious as to why.

Research has proven that humility, especially when it comes to being teachable, is key to success. Google's SVP of People Operations, Laszlo Bock, said in a NY Times Article that humility is one of the key traits he's looking for. "Your end goal," explained Bock, "is what can we do together to problem-solve. "Intellectual humility. **Without humility, you are unable to learn.**"[23]

A Harvard Business Review post documented a Catalyst study that shows that this isn't just tied to Google or America, but the world leaders, in general, are better leaders when they are humble and willing to learn.[24] Humble leaders allow their followers to connect on a more personal level because the leader is willing to listen and even learn. When employees feel heard, even if what they say isn't acted on, they feel a greater sense of belonging to the company.

Seeking wisdom is the only way to gain wisdom. You'll have to let your mind be influenced by God by keeping Him first. As you read His word and spend time communicating with God, you'll start to gain wisdom. However, it's the intentionality behind studying His word that really starts to change you. At first reading, many things in the Bible can challenge our thinking.

Whether it's Jesus' parables or understanding the context of something in the Old Testament, the Bible isn't a book you can read once and understand it completely. The wisdom that I would claim to have gotten are all through wrestling with the word and trying to understand its purpose in the context of the entire book.

You'll also have to have an open mind to wise counsel to help you shape your understanding. Sometimes, wise counsel will sting, and sometimes a piece of advice may even appear wrong. However, if you have a humble, teachable spirit, you can examine each piece of advice and get some value out of it.

I once had a mentor tell me that God does not care at all what I do. In my youth, I might have responded to this man rudely or, even worse, allow his words to drive me away from God. However, because I was willing to dive deeper into the conversation and study what this mentor meant, I was able to receive some value from his statement. In this case, my mentor was saying that whether I choose to be in one vocational field or another, it won't limit what God can do in my life. Ensuring that you have the best wise counsel is so important that I've dedicated an entire chapter to it.

I've been processing what wisdom means and how it works, and I would define it like this:

> A revelation your spirit has about something that, when fully realized, passes on actionable knowledge to your mind. From there, your brain can process it further into rules for life, common sense, or an action to be taken.

Essentially, wisdom is a lens with which to make decisions. The challenge in life is that these decisions can often be made based on assumptions. Assumptions help us make reasonable guesses about how the world will play out. However, the ones held most closely are often the ones that are the most wrong.

One of the biggest eye-opening experiences to wrong assumptions I ever had was when I took a behavioral assessment. According to the assessment, I am the kind of person that wants to create a better world through conflict. No, this doesn't mean I thrive on being argumentative, but it does mean I tend to find meaning and extend help to others by having and expressing different thoughts. Consider me the devil's advocate in the room!

An extreme example of this was when I offered a constructive critique to a colleague, hoping to encourage them, and it caused her to run away in tears. I falsely assumed that because I like to think critically about things to get better ideas that other people enjoyed this as well.

For years, I damaged relationships and tried to pray away cynicism and negativity. The results of the assessment shattered my assumptions. Those results revealed to me that not only am I not alone but that there are aspects of the behavior that are productive. The other thing that came from that understanding is that people have different personalities and that most people don't desire conflict in their lives.

Now when I talk with people, I have to ask myself if this person wants to argue about this or are they just telling me about their idea. However, wisdom takes it one step further and forces me to ask even deeper questions like, "Will my comments make this person feel valued, and is this a wise comment or one based on assuming this person is like you?"

And even beyond the interpersonal gains, there are personal gains when we evaluate issues like these against God's Word. This evaluation will often be a battle. We'll be tempted to react to events in life, and we'll have to resist. As mentioned earlier, wisdom will be evaluated by decisions. These decisions start in the battlefield of your mind. Wisdom wars with what the world will say is wise. For example, the world says to punish those that hurt you, and the Bible says to forgive. And the world says to do what makes you happy, but the Bible tells us to serve others.

> "For the weapons of our warfare are not carnal but mighty in God for pulling down strongholds, casting down arguments and every high thing that exalts itself against the knowledge of God, bringing every thought into captivity to the obedience of Christ."
> **— 2 Corinthians 10:4-5 NIV**

A kingdom driven leader is submitted to Christ and teachable. I love the scripture above because although it's talking about the spiritual realm, it's also pretty analogous to the battle in the mind. When our broken world calls something wise, we need a way to evaluate it and, if necessary, fight against it. A kingdom driven leader yearns for wisdom, but the ultimate question this, "How do we know what wisdom is?" Luckily, James 3:17 gives us some great criteria for wisdom and our thought life in general. As you gather ideas and begin to process them in your mind, you must have a filter to test if it's wisdom from God or not. All true wisdom is from God and can pass eight criteria.

THE 8 CRITERIA OF WISDOM

> "Wisdom from above is first of all **pure**. It is also **peace loving, gentle at all times**, and **willing to yield to others**. It is **full of mercy** and the **fruit of good deeds**. It **shows no favoritism** and **is always sincere**."
> **— James 3:17 NLT**

1. WISDOM IS PURE

"Blessed are the pure in heart, for they will see God."
— **Matthew 5:8 NIV**

"How can a young person stay on the path of purity? By living according to your word." — **Psalm 119:9 NIV**

When you hear the word "purity," your mind might go straight to sexual purity. At least Google thinks this is true. Perform any search on Google, and it's full of blog posts on the topic of sexual purity.

Purity in wisdom could pertain to physical relationships. However, as a word, it doesn't always mean that. As mentioned above, the battle to keep our minds pure is ongoing. Purity is pretty simple to define (and hard to live out). The word pure comes from the Greek word *hagios*, which simply means "pure, chaste, holy, sacred, purifying."[25] In other words, pure is something that is 100 percent and set apart.

Did you know that the water we drink is not pure? Even "purified" water can have up to 10 impurities per million gallons of water.[26] Spring water isn't pure either, having naturally occurring minerals. This is why some people have trouble with water when they travel because although the water has been purified, it has minerals or contaminants that your body isn't used to.

In life, we encounter all kinds of advice heralding itself as wisdom. "Just do it, do what feels good, and follow your passion" are very popular sayings in our society. It turns out that these slogans are horrible advice because if we always followed our passions, we'd not only be doing sinful things but also things that often hurt others.

The wisdom of our society often sounds familiar, but it isn't pure. If you look at the shelves and shelves of self-help books, they are filled with similar so-called wisdom. However, most of them borrow ideas from one book, the Bible.

When you encounter something that is calling itself "wisdom," ask, does this "wisdom" contain any other motives? In other words, is it tainted information disguising itself as wisdom? Any thought that is not pure in nature is not from God. I have known people that felt that God told them to leave their wife because they were unhappy (follow your heart). No, He did not. God would never ask you to do anything that does not line up with His Word, and one's happiness is not a Biblical rationale for divorce.

Whether you receive wisdom from reading, advice from another person, or personal reflection, if it doesn't line up with God's word 100 percent, it's not wisdom.

2. WISDOM IS PEACE LOVING

> "Do not let any unwholesome talk come out of your mouths, but only what is helpful for building others up according to their needs, that it may benefit those who listen."
> **— Ephesians 4:29 NIV**

You can know you are making a wise decision that lines up with God's desire when what you are about to say or do is peace loving. Something that is peace loving strives to prefer others' wellbeing over being right. It prefers unity over division, and it values others.

For example, ever notice how often what gets posted on social media is divisive? Sometimes I get a thought about a particular cause or political candidate, but if it doesn't cause unity or glorify God, I'd only be bringing strife, so I abstain from commenting. Every wise thought is one associated with peace and encouragement.

This doesn't mean that you should be silent when you see injustice. Instead, it's a call to be intentional and thoughtful rather than reactive. Capture the reactive thought as suggested in 2 Corinthians 10:4-5. Wrestle with it, and if it's wise, it'll be peace loving in nature.

3. WISDOM IS GENTLE AT ALL TIMES

Normally the Message version of the Bible condenses thought, but here it expounds.

> "Real wisdom, God's wisdom, begins with a holy life and is characterized by getting along with others. It is gentle and reasonable, overflowing with mercy and blessings, not hot one day and cold the next, not two-faced."
> **— James 3:17-18 (MSG)**

In keeping with Ephesians 4:29 and 2 Corinthians, you should be wrestling to expel any thought that is not encouraging or bringing peace. God does not tell us to physically fight with our neighbors or argue with them.

I understand that for some of us, we want to debate someone into heaven, but it'll never happen. It's the love of Jesus that compelled you and me to Him, not His anger. His anger was for the religious debaters of that time, the Pharisees, and it remains so today.

Jesus was 100% truth and love. You must stand on the Word, and you must love others. The thoughts that appear wise to confront will only be truly wise if your approach is gentle.

4. WISDOM IS BEING WILLING TO YIELD TO OTHERS

> "You have heard that it was said, 'Eye for eye, and tooth for tooth.' But I tell you, do not resist an evil person. If anyone slaps you on the right cheek, turn to them the other cheek also. And if anyone wants to sue you and take your shirt, hand over your coat as well."
> **— Matthew 5:38-40 NIV**

For businesspeople, I think this is a tough one to recognize. How do you yield to others without getting walked all over? It requires humility. A kingdom driven leader that is 100 percent submitted to Christ and understands how to operate with humility can yield to others, knowing it may serve another purpose. This is why the topic "Gaining Wisdom" is found later in the book. It's almost impossible to gain wisdom without some humility. It's part of your walk. It's like truth and love.

Ultimately, God is your provider, not man. When someone wrongs you, you might wish to correct the situation. You have the right to correct the situation. However, if you're looking through the lens of wisdom, you have to ask yourself, "Is this a place I can yield?" Sometimes God gives you an opportunity to yield, and it opens a door to someone's heart. Other times you may yield and get no immediate feedback. God's got your back. I can guarantee you that if you are yielding to honor God, you'll be taken care of in His way and in His timing.

Another place I see this popping up is when you receive an opportunity or a blessing. However, something on the inside of you is telling you that this opportunity is for someone else. It's like what is said of Abraham, "blessed to be a blessing." (Genesis 12:2–3).

While immediate profit might seem wise, yielding here and connecting this blessing to the person God intended will often lead to a greater opportunity for you. Hold opportunities with an open hand and be willing to yield because sometimes blessing others might prove more beneficial to God's kingdom than even your own.

I have a recent example of this. I had a friend from church bring a great real estate investment opportunity to me. I thought for sure this was for me. However, I felt like God was telling me to yield to another, but the person I had to yield to was not my favorite person. I wouldn't dare call another brother in Christ a "nemesis," but "frenemy" might be a close approximation. It turned out to be a match made in heaven and worked out better than anything I could have done. The real estate deal blessed far more people because of my "frenemy's" involvement than would have ever happened had I had taken advantage of it. In addition, I earned respect from several people by openly yielding to what I felt like God wanted.

5. WISDOM IS FULL OF MERCY

"Blessed are the merciful, for they will be shown mercy."
— **Matthew 5:7 NIV**

"Since God chose you to be the holy people he loves, you must clothe yourselves with tenderhearted mercy, kindness, humility, gentleness, and patience."
— **Colossians 3:12 NLT**

The entire New Testament speaks of God's mercy. I have been forgiven *much*, so I must be ready with mercy for others. Are you noticing a theme here? Wisdom usually means withholding our natural instincts to fight, argue, protect what's ours, or get revenge.

I don't think this means you keep employees on your team that are not performing. I do think, though, this means you lovingly pull them aside and have a private conversation with them to give them a chance to meet the expectations set for them. And if you do decide to part ways, you do so in a very loving, merciful way.

6. WISDOM BEARS FRUIT

> "Every tree that does not bear good fruit is cut down and thrown into the fire."
> **— Matthew 7:19**

Wisdom acts like a filter through which to view decisions. If you are about to endeavor something, consider the fruit it might produce. If it doesn't add value, then it's likely not wisdom.

As leaders, we can tend to think about efficiencies or profits. In addition to that, we should think about the eternal fruit. If what you do reaches just one person for eternity, it was worth it. However, when we see opportunities through a -short-term view, we often miss the important things.

Early in my real estate business, I would often meet with clients later in the evening and during the weekends. It seems intuitive that people only look for homes after work or on weekends. When I did this, I thought it was the smart move to make more income and provide for the family. However, by doing this, I was missing out on being home with my family. It wasn't wisdom. When I decided to put boundaries around my time and protect my most precious time with my young family, it produced fruit for all of us. I could make that decision because I knew that God was my provider and not me.

Wisdom forces us to think eternally. In the end, all of our efforts to gain something in this world will be burned up. However, what we do for each other, that will last an eternity.

7. WISDOM SHOWS NO FAVORITISM

> "Then Peter began to speak: 'I now realize how true it is that God does not show favoritism.'"
> — **Acts 10:34 NIV**

It's easy to have favorites. You have favorite friends, favorite co-workers, favorite groups of people that share your hobbies. My grandmother used to regularly announce her favorite grandchildren, but we'll save that therapy lesson for another day.

Wisdom asks questions so you can check your motives. "Are you making this decision based on your favorites? What about race, ethnicity, or culture? Do the choices you make show your preference?"

Wisdom can come from all walks of life from every corner. In Heaven, there will be no prejudice against race or cliques in which we belong. We are all His children, and we each have the same value.

Advice or information that steers you away from unity is not wisdom. Going back to our earlier illustration, 90 percent of what you read on social media is not wisdom. Wisdom will bring unity, not division. It is wise to listen to the people you bring to the table as decision-makers. Are they considering others? Are those voices themselves diversified?

8. WISDOM IS SINCERE

> "Unlike so many, we do not peddle the word of God for profit. On the contrary, in Christ we speak before God with sincerity, as those sent from God."
> **— 2 Corinthians 2:17 NIV**

> "Now that you have purified yourselves by obeying the truth so that you have sincere love for each other, love one another deeply, from the heart."
> **— 1 Peter 1:22 NIV**

Sincerity is similar to integrity in that it has to be witnessed to evaluate. When a child gets in trouble and has to face the consequence, they often will say "I'm sorry" almost immediately. A parent's job then becomes evaluating the apology for its sincerity. Are they apologizing to lessen their consequence, or are they truly sincere?

Sincerity comes from a place of confidence. A sincere person is one that knows themselves and their beliefs. What makes this challenging is that many people don't know themselves. To make matters worse, many of us haven't spent enough time thinking about what we truly believe.

This world is dying for authenticity and transparency. Relationships are forged on digital devices. The news reports of trusted leaders failing daily. It's impossible to determine if a news report is true or not. Many of our leaders are afraid to take a stand on what they believe for fear of the backlash. And yet authenticity is the "salt" for this generation.

In Matthew 5:13, Jesus says that His disciples will be salt to this world. They will add the flavor back into a dying world. His disciples will be noticed because they will love differently than what people experience in the world.

A kingdom driven leader has built their beliefs on a rock. They know who they are and can operate in sincerity. They can love others freely that may not reciprocate as Peter calls us to do (1 Peter 1:22). This authentic sincerity stands out from every message our world says.

The pane glass of wisdom will tell you to divest yourself of motives other than His Kingdom. God wouldn't ask you to be fake or insincere. If you have any thoughts that require you to be anything but true to your identity, then it's likely not wisdom.

When you reflect on wisdom, you might start to see a picture of Jesus as well as guidance for how a kingdom driven leader should live. If our thought life is pure, if we keep the peace and remain gentle, if we willingly yield and keep our heart full of mercy, our lives will bear fruit. If we approach our life valuing each person equally and are fully sincere in this approach, we'll truly be a wise leader, like Jesus was.

In this way, being wise is being loving, communicating value to another person. Being wise alone doesn't make a kingdom driven leader, but it is a defining criterion for one. You can't be a kingdom driven leader without gaining wisdom.

On the wise path to growing in wisdom and as a kingdom driven leader, you will need mentors or wise counsel. With the kingdom driven foundation set, you'll be teachable and able to receive the wisdom that only mentors can bring. However, you'll also have the strength of your foundation to evaluate what wisdom truly is. With that in mind, let's discuss one of the most powerful influences in a kingdom driven leader's life, their inner circle.

12

Finding Prophets (Wise Counsel)

> "For lack of guidance a nation falls, but victory is won through many advisers."
> **— Proverbs 11:14 NIV**

Every kingdom driven leader has an inner circle around them. The success of their life and reign often is the result of those closest to them. John C. Maxwell calls this the "Law of the Inner Circle." In his book, the *21 Irrefutable Laws of Leadership*, he says the Law of the Inner Circle is - "A leader's potential is determined by those closest to him or her."[27]

In Biblical times, a king's inner circle included family, scribes or historians, expert advisors, and almost always a prophet. Some of these people were chosen for their excellence in their field, and others, like family, were there by default. The key person in this group is the prophet. Kings loved to have prophets surrounding them.

> "Then the LORD said to Moses, 'Pay close attention to this. I will make you seem like God to Pharaoh, and your brother, Aaron, will be your prophet.'"
> **— Exodus 7:1 NLT**

A simple definition of a prophet is "God's spokesperson." Not all of us are going to be blessed to have personal relationships with a pastor or a person gifted in prophecy in the supernatural sense. However, many times God will use others to speak something to us. That's called "prophecy." It may not be what you imagined but simply put, speaking God's Word or His will to someone is prophecy.

> "A man has joy in giving an appropriate answer, And how good and delightful is a word spoken at the right moment—how good it is!"
> **— Proverbs 15:23 AMP**

The goal for kings should be to build an inner circle of believers that are more spiritually mature than they are. This doesn't mean you dismiss all others. Sometimes when you are struggling to hear God after examining yourself, you may need a fresh outside perspective. Seeking wisdom from others can be dangerous if you don't know much about their values. However, if your inner circle is more mature than you spiritually, they will often be able to nudge you back on the road.

> "A man who isolates himself seeks his own desire [he become self-centered]; He rages against all wise judgment [counsel]. A fool has no delight in understanding [he devalues other's opinions], But in expressing his own heart [values his opinion and emotions over others]."
> **— Proverbs 18:1-2 NKJV [with edits]**

I've been volunteering at our church and in small groups long enough to know that one of the traps the enemy has set is to isolate people. The Bible calls Satan a roaring lion seeking whom he may devour. If you know anything about lions and how they hunt, you know they are looking for stragglers from the pack.

The interesting thing about lions is that they can't really see individuals when grouped together. Their vision is great when it's something small, but when they see a herd or pack, it looks like one big animal. This is why hunters and tourists can feel safe in an open-air jeep. The lion perceives it to be a larger animal than it can take on. However, a lonely antelope or a singular human would be considered fair game.

I imagine Satan has a similar view. Every attack he does seems to cause us to want to isolate ourselves. Guilt and shame are two of his most lethal weapons because they make us want to hide ourselves.

When we isolate ourselves from others, the only input we receive is from ourselves. We get myopic in our views, and we become out of touch. Community is key, and to truly live like a kingdom driven leader, you must be intentional about surrounding yourself with the right people.

When you look at the kings of the Old Testament, there is no doubt that they had counselors. The Bible goes into great detail to explain the advisors and mighty men of David (2 Samuel 23:8-39).

Unfortunately, many of the kings allowed a bad influence to essentially cut their reign short. Israel's history of bad kings has far more examples of kings receiving bad advice such as Rehoboam or not following good advice such as Zedekiah. However, it's clear that all kings had advisors. It makes sense that the kings had strategic and logistical advisors. However, even ungodly kings listened to the prophets. This is why this chapter is an essential characteristic of a king.

God is pretty clear that to accomplish our goals, we'll have to do it with other people. This is one characteristic I saw throughout the Bible. While Jesus didn't necessarily have any known counselors, he could not accomplish his mission without His disciples. No doubt, there were opportunities for Jesus to share His feelings of disappointment when not even His hometown accepted him. He shared His frustrations and successes with them. He did life with them.

Timothy had Paul to mentor him, Joshua had Moses, Esther had

Mordecai, David had Samuel, Saul, Jonathan, Nathan, and his mighty men. If you read the Bible and just look at the relationships, it's easy to see that your closest relationships can often determine whether you succeed or fail.

Find an "iron sharpens iron" tribe that can help you grow in your walk in Christ. In the context of this book, I'm going to ask you to be intentional in your quest for wise counselors or mentors to be a part of your journey, advisors in your kingdom.

SOLOMON'S ADVISORS

As Biblical Kings go, the only King more popular than Solomon was David. David had that whole giant-slaying thing going for him. However, in terms of kingdom, it's arguable that King Solomon had one of the richest kingdoms of all time. An MSN Money post suggested that at his peak, he'd be worth $2.2 Trillion in modern money. Good enough for 5th on this list.[28] This is outstanding when you think about how small his Kingdom was. The other four rulers ahead of him had vast areas. Augustus Caesar and Genghis Khan ruled large parts of the known world at the time, while Solomon had little more than current-day Israel.

Most know about Solomon's request for wisdom and his riches; however, many don't credit him for collecting advisors. Much of the instruction around seeking wise counsel comes from Solomon.

Take a look at what Solomon says about what listening to wise counsel helps you do.

AVOID FOOLISHNESS

> "The way of fools seems right to them, but the wise listen to advice."
> **— Proverbs 12:15 (NIV)**

Have you ever met someone who thought they were right all the time? That is the definition of a fool.

A kingdom driven leader's counsel needs to be able to counsel and not just give opinions. A fool is one who always thinks they are right, while wise counsel carefully considers other points of view. I've taught my kids about foolishness for some time, and I've come to the definition that foolishness is actions taken without wisdom.

Often, we think of a fool as someone who is acting silly or doing something that is, frankly, stupid. However, at the heart of every fool is the belief that they are right, the ignorance of any other possibility, and pride.

AVOID PRIDE

> "Where there is strife, there is pride, -but wisdom is found in those who take advice."
> **— Proverbs 13:10 NIV**

Pride blinds the fool, and they are ignorant of its existence. If we aren't careful, pride can creep into our lives. Having a group of mentors can help us see that often our problems are self-wrought. Proverbs tells us that humbling ourselves to listen to wise counsel is us helping ourselves.

As we'll see later in this book, one of the biggest enemies of the king is pride. Pride causes strife. I've seen this the most prevalent in early marriages where each spouse strives to be right. They are defensive. It's only through humility that they can ever truly survive the ups and downs of marriage.

Often pride is also attached to some hurt which will bring out anger or passive aggressiveness with people—having mentors to whom you can bring problems can often alleviate these issues before they ever fester into strife-causing pride.

PLANS SUCCEED

> "Plans fail for lack of counsel, but with many advisers they succeed."
> **— Proverbs 15:22 NIV**

Chronologically in Proverbs, Solomon gives us advice on how to avoid pride because it'll cause us to do foolish things and create strife in our kingdom - even if that kingdom is simply our household. Solomon knew that we must set our hearts and attitudes right before we could ever really progress and grow.

As you grow in your relationship with Christ and emulate Him, you'll become more humble. This humility translates to teachability. As mentioned in chapter nine, being humble creates opportunities for you to hear opposition without being offended. Humility is a prerequisite to receiving counsel.

If you're seeking wise counsel, you'll need to keep your mind open to not only what counsel is being given but have the humility to try and see it from another point of view. It'll require the humility to accept that your way may not be the best way.

Heeding the advice of your counselors is crucial for your plans to succeed. Practically speaking, they often can see your blind spots. I know from my personal experience that I move fast toward action but often neglect to get any advice. I'd love to blame impatience, but in reality, it's fear that often makes me hasty. I often fear what counselors will say about my plan. I'm fearful they'll see where it will fail, and I'll feel foolish and have wasted my time dreaming. However, what I've found is that other leaders often love to help others with their dreams. Yes, they may see my flaws, but often they will come up with a way to solve an issue before it shuts down the dream altogether.

ACCOUNTABILITY

> "Listen to advice and accept discipline, and at the end you will be counted among the wise."
> **— Proverbs 19:20 NIV**

There is a saying that everyone does better when someone's watching. If you've ever known someone that was addicted to something, then you know one of the very best methods to help them is accountability with someone. Wise counselors can often help us stay accountable.

Most leaders have had direct experience with accountability in the workplace. Leaders have had to answer to someone or have direct reports that answer to them. Nothing is worse as a leader than having to let someone go. In some cases, termination is often the failure of the leader to hold the employee accountable to the standards that have been set for his or her role on the team.

Accountability also often acts as guardrails for our life. When I tell my children that I am watching the internet traffic and that I will examine their history on their phone, it's not because I'm a tyrant or because they have a problem. It's because I know that will help them make better choices. I have the same arrangement for my wife and me to have open access to each other's phones for exactly the same reason.

Accepting accountability will, like much of the last two chapters, require humility. It's allowing another person into your life to question your decisions and call you out. However, having that person in your life can help keep your kingdom driven focus a bit clearer.

CLARITY ON MISSION

> "Plans are established by seeking advice; so, if you wage war, obtain guidance."
> **— Proverbs 20:18 NIV**

Kingdom driven leaders understand that for their missions to be accomplished, they will have to fight in a battle. We've already covered how wise counsel is needed for plans to succeed and how they can often see our blind spots, and how wise advisors can help keep us from making poor decisions.

One area that is often missed is the subtle clarity that wise counsel can bring. I say subtle because usually, we evaluate things as to whether they succeed or fail but often miss those pieces of advice that bring clarity.

I can remember a distinct time when I was under a lot of stress from a business partnership with an unbeliever. He didn't want us to do anything illegal, but it was clear that we did not value the same things. I was already well into this partnership before ever asking for help. When things went wrong, I was completely lost. The partnership was profitable but detrimental to my family's emotional and spiritual health.

I was so lost that I didn't have any clear direction and no good answers. The lack of clarity wasn't just around whether or not to continue the partnership. It was more about how to handle the situation with enough care that I didn't damage the relationship in the process.

Luckily, I had a small group full of leaders and wise counselors. In one meeting, it was revealed through their own experience how they got out of similar situations. This gave me complete clarity on what needed to happen.

Ultimately, I had to buy my way out of the situation and was able to keep the relationship intact. If I had sought wise counsel before agreeing to the partnership, I would have had even greater clarity about what I could have done to improve the situation, or I could have known to avoid it altogether.

Getting wise counsel so your plans can succeed can sound similar to getting clarity, but the difference is in the tense. When you're reviewing your plans with your advisors, you are relying on their experience to help you plan for the future. When you *continue* to rely on these same advisors in the present, it helps create clarity for your vision.

SUCCESSFUL CAMPAIGNS

"Surely you need guidance to wage war, and victory is won through many advisers."
— Proverbs 24:6 NIV

Being surrounded by wise counselors isn't enough. You must be open to being teachable and able to listen. In doing so, you keep yourself from becoming foolish, you maintain your humility, you set yourself up to have your plans succeed, and you're more accountable and able to go to war.

As mentioned, it's not just about the plan. During the war, there will be changes and shifts, and you'll need your band of brothers or sisters to move through it. Make no mistake. We are all at war with Satan and his forces every day. Even though he's been defeated, we must claim our victory. It's best to do this with mentors that help watch your back.

> "A person standing alone can be attacked and defeated, but two can stand back-to-back and conquer. Three are even better, for a triple-braided cord is not easily broken."
> **— Ecclesiastes 4:12 NLT**

WISDOM DOES NOT GUARANTEE RIGHT LIVING

We can see this from Solomon's life very clearly. He was the wisest man to ever have lived, and yet his heart turned from God to idols. You can be "wise" and still be wicked.

> **Wisdom is having the understanding and the ability to know what action to take for the best outcome. True wisdom requires humility to operate fully.**

> "Who among you is wise and intelligent? Let him by his good conduct show his [good] deeds with the gentleness and humility of true wisdom."
> **— James 3:13 AMP**

FINDING PROPHETS (WISE COUNSEL)

REHOBOAM

1 Kings 11 tells of Solomon's demise. Solomon begins to worship other gods, and God intervenes through a prophet to split Israel between Jeroboam and Rehoboam.

Jeroboam was one of Solomon's servants and the head of the labor force. Jeroboam was found to be excellent and continued to rise in the ranks. At this point in the story, God gave him the same promise he gave each king and the same promise he gives you today. Follow Him always, and blessings will follow. Solomon heard about Jeroboam being anointed as the next king and launched a plot to kill him to try and preserve the throne for his son. After his assassination plot failed, Jeroboam escaped to Egypt. Then, after Solomon died, Jeroboam returned to Israel, remembering the promise that was made to him by the prophet.

> "*If* you do whatever I command you and walk in obedience to me and do what is right in my eyes by obeying my decrees and commands, as David my servant did, I will be with you."
> **— 1 Kings 11:38a NIV (emphasis mine)**

Meanwhile, Rehoboam took on the role of King after his father's passing. Rehoboam starts with a really good idea. He asked for advice. He consulted with the trusted advisors of Solomon. He also got counsel from what the Bible calls "young men." And he was even counseled by Jeroboam.

The advice from the elders and Jeroboam was to lighten the load on the people while the young men suggested making it tougher on the people. When you read this, it makes sense. What does a new ruler often does to win the heart of the people...lower taxes! Here's his response,

> "My father laid on you a heavy yoke; I will make it even heavier. My father scourged you with whips; I will scourge you with scorpions."
> **— 1 Kings 12:11 NIV**

When I read that, I was astonished. What I saw was a prideful man so fearful of losing territory and his throne that he crushed the very gift he was given. Rehoboam's kingdom was in turmoil. To compound this, he was so prideful that he only listened to the counsel of his young friends that all agreed with him. He didn't *really* seek counsel. He sought approval. Imagine what would have happened had his young friends agreed with all of the wise counselors there?

This mistake could have been avoided had Rehoboam sought God first and listened to the wise counsel instead of his unwise friends. It reminds us that we are who we surround ourselves with.

It's time to check ourselves. Do the people we let influence our life have a relationship with Jesus at all? Are they wise counsel? Are they there by default, as mentioned at the beginning of this chapter? If not, it's probably not time to unfriend them, but it is time to be intentional about whom you let influence your life. If you have wise counsel, are you letting them influence you even when you don't agree?

EVEN JESUS

While I believe the Old Testament is certainly instructional, the life of Jesus is the perfect model we should follow. Notice that one of the only early accounts of Jesus' life was where He was found in the Temple. As wisdom in the flesh, it's unlikely that He received any deep revelations from studying at the Temple - the very place in traditional Jewish culture you go to receive and discuss wise counsel. Jesus was 100% God and 100% man. It's my opinion that this was recorded for our benefit. Jesus was so submitted to the Father and His mission that He modeled the way for us to be 100% submitted to God and always seeking wisdom while being intentionally focused on the mission.

PRACTICAL WAYS TO GAIN WISDOM

> "Walk with the wise and become wise; associate with fools and get in trouble."
> **— Proverbs 12:20 NLT**

You've likely heard that you are the sum of the five closest people to your life. The easiest way to gain wisdom is to become friends with wise people. Look at the fruit of the lives of the people that you wish to learn from or emulate. Remember, you are looking for wisdom, not just worldly success.

I look for people that are hugely successful in the world's eyes *and* have a relationship with God that I long to have *and* have marriages I want to emulate *and* spend time actually parenting. This narrows the list considerably. However, I've found that when you listen to people's stories that have at least one of these characteristics, you can gain wisdom.

All this preparation is to allow you to reign. Without humility, wisdom, and a submitted heart, you can often allow your kingship to become an idol. I know I am personally guilty of this in my life. I often become obsessed with work or something that feels like a really good thing, like leading a ministry, and miss my family or my time with God. Often, I wonder why something isn't succeeding, and, in the autopsy, I discover that my failure was that I tried to do it all. You can only reign when you're wise enough and humble enough to submit to God and let Him multiply your efforts and resources through you – particularly as you seek wise counsel to help you be everything God has prepared for you to be.

13

Excellence in Everything

"And whatever you do, whether in word or deed, do it all in the name of the Lord Jesus, giving thanks to God the Father through him."
— **Colossians 3:17 NIV**

In theory, this section should be the shortest because if you're reading this, you're already preparing yourself and trying to grow your leadership. The key to really being seen as wise and humble is being excellent in all that you do. You might think that no one sees you, but they do. Yes, God sees you too, but you'd be surprised how many people are watching you. Some of them admire you. Some are hoping you'll slack off to give them an excuse to do the same.

Have you ever been handed a business card that had a fish on it? I can feel you rolling your eyes right now. Why? Because many people will put that on their business card and forget what it represents. Excellence. To be effective salt and light, you must allow people to experience and see you being excellent.

My friend, Beau, is a good financial planner. In fact, at one point during my different entrepreneurial endeavors, I wanted to partner with him. What I found out, though, was that the sales cycle was excruciatingly long. The big reason is that for people to have confidence in you to manage their future, there needs to be real, personal trust.

My friend would tell me stories about how he got new clients. In one story, a new customer had heard him on the radio. Then for six years, he followed him on social media, on the radio, and his website. For those six years, my friend was being stalked by this man. Then it happened, a call was made, and my friend connected with this gentleman.

What's interesting is that in a lot of these things, Beau thought that no one was watching. We'd look at his numbers together to speculate why he wasn't getting engagement on his social media or calls from his show. By all accounts, Beau was a brilliant planner and human being but not a marketer. He had a few things that set him apart. He's humble, one of the humblest people you'll meet. He's also authentic and transparent.

My friend embodies the mantra from one of my favorite authors, Patrick Lencioni, "Humble, Hungry, and Smart."[29] In Lencioni's book, *Ideal Team Player*, he outlines what makes a good foundation for corporate culture is to have people that are humble, hungry, and smart. Isn't it interesting that what works in the corporate world sounds like Biblical principles? My friend is all these things. When you watch him over time, the trust is built because you see excellence.

The point is that to live like a kingdom driven leader; you need to carry yourself like a king. You must start living in excellence. I looked it up and liked this definition.

> "Excellence is a quality that people really appreciate because it's so hard to find. Excellence is the quality of excelling, of being truly the best at something. Getting an A+ shows excellence. Michael Jordan's basketball career was filled with excellence… When you see excellence, you should appreciate the work that went into it. **So much in the world falls short of excellence.**"[30]

This definition nearly nails what I'll call Biblical excellence. What's missing in my mind is humility. It's as Lencioni said, humility, socially smart, and hard work are what make a great team player. Take that and then perform to your absolute best and trust that God is your provider, and you will have no choice but to stand out.

The danger most kings fall into is that many of us are performance driven. We can be too competitive. When you catch yourself wondering when you'll finally "make it," remember Joseph, Daniel, David, Jeroboam, Esther, Ruth, and Nehemiah all were "caught" being excellent. It's easy to gloss over each of these characters and only remember their accomplishments. However, each of them served a "bad king" for a period of time to accomplish God's goals.

SOMETIMES YOU HAVE TO BE THE BLOCKER

I love the game of football. I'm a fan of strategy. Most people get excited about the big-name stars, the quarterbacks, running backs, and receivers. What the average Sunday watcher doesn't see is the blocking needed for their success.

It's the blocking that opens up a hole for the running back to run through. It's the blocking that gives the quarterback time to evaluate where to throw the ball. It's the blocking that allows the receiver to finish his route. In football, everyone on the field is important, even a wide receiver on a running play! I think we can learn a lot from football in this respect.

There are very few moments when I can claim I heard God clearly. I will tell you boldly that we have a relationship, but the clarity of His voice isn't always there for me. One time a few years ago, I asked (ok pleaded) that God would use me. He said, "If you want to be used, you must be usable."

At the time, I had a bad attitude. I was selfish. To an outsider, I looked as if I was doing the right things. However, it was all a show. I was trying to be excellent, but I compared myself to others and was often angry that no one noticed how hard I was trying. I think we often compare ourselves to the players scoring the touchdowns. I don't think we're prideful in this comparison from the standpoint of their greatness. I think more often, it's a comparison of adequacy. I don't want fame. I want to bring fame to the name of Jesus. However, without a measure of success (wins, touchdowns, stats), it's hard to tell how we're doing.

If you remember my story about the event I hosted and how one person was affected, my perception was changed. I see value in being the blocker or the special team's gunner now.

In many ways, the blockers are more important than the runners or the quarterback. Without the blocking, the throw doesn't get made, and the run stops in the backfield. Consider this; no one blocker is more important than the rest. However, if one single blocker misses the play, it is over, it's a sack, a tackle for a loss, or worse.

In 2016, my Atlanta Falcons had a great year. In one particular play, Devonta Freeman, the Falcons running back, took off for a huge run and scored. However, one could argue the most important person on the field wasn't Devonta. It could have been Mohamed Sanu who lined up as a receiver and blocked the very person that should have made the tackle as Devonta got past the first line of defense. It also could have been Alex Mack, the center, who snapped the ball and fired off the line to take out the defensive lineman.

When you're questioning your purpose or your impact, remember that you might be a blocker during this season of your life. The important thing is to remember to be excellent in all that you do and to do it for the glory of God. He sees you; others see you, and He's got you right where you need to be.

JEROBOAM'S EXAMPLE

You might think it is odd for me to list Jeroboam with the likes of Daniel, David, Esther, Ruth, and Nehemiah. All these people did great things for God, while Jeroboam, the king we briefly talked about in the last chapter, is known as the king who made Israel sin. What's up with including him in the excellence chapter? When reading the Bible, it's easy to see the good examples of Daniel or David. The Bible belabors their excellence in their devotion, but what's easily missed is Jeroboam's excellence.

> "Now Jeroboam was a man of standing, and when Solomon saw how well the young man did his work, he put him in charge of the whole labor force of the tribes of Joseph."
> **— 1 Kings 11:28 NIV**

Jeroboam was excellent in all that he did, so much so he caught the eye of the king. He not only caught the eye and favor of Solomon, as time passed, God had His eye on him as well. Solomon began to rebel, and God had a response.

> "So the Lord said to Solomon, "Since this is your attitude and you have not kept my covenant and my decrees, which I commanded you, I will most certainly tear the kingdom away from you and give it to one of your subordinates."
> **— 1 Kings 11:11 NIV**

Solomon's kingdom began to crumble. Enemy forces came against him, and his followers rebelled. He was outside God's hedge of protection. In contrast, by being excellent, Jeroboam had gone from being a simple widow's son to a superintendent to becoming a man with some clout. He was essentially a blocker for Solomon. Finally, he got his opportunity in a meeting with a prophet. Continuing in Kings 11,

> "Then he said to Jeroboam, 'Take ten pieces for yourself, for this is what the Lord, the God of Israel, says: 'See, I am going to tear the kingdom out of Solomon's hand and give you ten tribes. …
>
> I will do this because they have forsaken me and worshiped Ashtoreth the goddess of the Sidonians, Chemosh the god of the Moabites, and Molek the god of the Ammonites, and have not walked in obedience to me, nor done what is right in my eyes, nor kept my decrees and laws as David, Solomon's father, did. …
>
> 'I will take the kingdom from his son's hands and give you ten tribes.
>
> I will give one tribe to his son so that David my servant may always have a lamp before me in Jerusalem, the city where I chose to put my Name.
> However, as for you, I will take you, and you will rule over all that your heart desires; you will be king over Israel.
>
> If you do whatever I command you and walk in obedience to me and do what is right in my eyes by obeying my decrees and commands, as David my servant did, I will be with you. I will build you a dynasty as enduring as the one I built for David and will give Israel to you.
>
> I will humble David's descendants because of this, but not forever.'"
> **— 1 Kings 11:34-39 NIV**

This is the fantasy that a lot of us live in. It's almost as if our heart is waiting for someone to notice us, to discover us, to proclaim value in us. Even Jesus' Father proclaimed, "this is my Son in whom I'm well pleased!" (Matthew 3:17) We all want to hear, "well done, good and faithful servant."(Matthew 25:23) Lucky for us, God loves us and sees all we do, and only remembers the excellent things. Because of this great grace, there needs to be a desire for excellence. This quest for excellence isn't because you can earn anything but rather for His good name. Just as a well-behaved child makes a good reflection on the parents, your excellence will reflect on your Father.

Reminiscent of Samuel anointing David, Jeroboam is foretold to be the king because he was found to be excellent in everything. Jeroboam proves out the scripture that says if you're faithful in little, you'll be trusted with much (Luke 16:10).

HISTORY REPEATS

Just as Saul attempted to kill David, Solomon repeated this pattern and attempted to kill Jeroboam. This forced Jeroboam to flee to Egypt to lay low while the kingdom was in turmoil.

Once Solomon died, Jeroboam returned from Egypt to find Rehoboam as King of Judah, with the people of Israel clamoring for him to take the throne in Israel. We know from 1 Kings 11:28 that Jeroboam was a respected man, a valiant and courageous warrior. He gave wise counsel to Rehoboam about how to handle the people. When Rehoboam arrogantly ignored this advice (and others), the kingdom was in chaos.

Before a civil war ensued, God stepped in and stopped Rehoboam, telling him, "This is my doing" (1 Kings 12:24). Rehoboam returns to rule Jerusalem with two tribes, while Jeroboam steps in to rule the other ten tribes from Samaria.

With the kingdom somewhat stabilized, Jeroboam began to fear a loss of his position. He began to worry that if people traveled to Jerusalem to worship, they would choose Rehoboam to be their king again.

This courageous warrior, who had heard from God's prophet that he'd be king, complete with promises, chooses to believe his fear instead of God's Word. He built golden calves and shrines in Dan and Bethel. While Dan's idolatry went back to Joshua's time, there are still remnants of Jeroboam's high places left in Dan that you can see today in Israel.

"It is too much for you to go up to Jerusalem. Here are your gods, Israel, who brought you up out of Egypt" (1 Kings 12:28). Even with God's spoken word and promises of a dynasty, Jeroboam chose this path. God sent word through Abijah that God would not have it and his kingdom would be taken away. (1 Kings 14).

In almost every instance of reading the Old Testament, there's one enemy that stands out through it all. The enemy is doubt, not doubting yourself but doubting God's Word. I could put this pretty much anywhere in the book, but I chose the section on excellence for a reason.

It's easy for us to doubt God's promises in our daily walk of excellence. Sometimes, there are seasons where there is chaos. Sometimes, there are seasons when you look at the big picture and begin to doubt what God told you in your heart. Maybe God told you that you were going to do big things. Maybe God gave you a dream to travel the world and help people, and yet you look at your life and say, "I don't see it." For entrepreneurs, maybe there was an idea that you had that you thought would be the big breakthrough that God promised.

Let Jeroboam's downfall be a lesson in your mind. When you begin to idolize the promises over the promise maker, you set yourself up to lose those very promises.

> "And without faith it is impossible to please God, because anyone who comes to him must believe that he exists and that he rewards those who earnestly seek him."
> **— Hebrews 11:6 NIV**

Doubt is in direct opposition to faith. Take heart and be excellent in even the smallest things so that God can entrust you with the greater things. Be excellent and know that you're being prepared for something. Be excellent and know that God sees you, and that's all that matters. Take heart and remove the doubt, as the Word says, we are but a vapor, and let your drive be for "heaping up treasures" in eternity.

Excellence, then, to a kingdom driven leader, is working as if God is watching. Not cutting corners and not looking for thanks, but rather doing the very best you can in everything. If you have an eternal kingdom mindset, you know your reward is God's blessing in heaven. Excellence defined this way could be a synonym for serving. In essence, everything you put effort into is in service to God.

Kingdom driven leaders who want to grow as leaders in humility, wisdom, and character do so to be excellent in all they do. Anything less than that diminishes their legacy and impact.

The whole point of this first section of the book is to help leaders get the kingdom mindset - the eternal mindset - so that they can lead more effectively and intentionally. Each of these characteristics are like muscles that need to be worked out.

Accordingly, if you want to be a kingdom driven leader, then it's imperative that you start working out the muscles in these areas. In working out, the core muscles are critical to long-term health. As a kingdom driven leader, your relationship with Christ is that core.

When you submit to Christ 100 percent, you don't stop because time goes on. There will always be new things to bring under submission. You don't read the word and pray once. It's an ongoing relationship. You don't obtain integrity; it's earned over a lifetime. You never stop serving others. It's one of our primary missions.

Being driven by holy discontentment won't make you a perfect leader. However, finding it might give you clarity for the future. Pursuing it might bring you meaningful purpose for a season. When you pursue humility or wisdom, you don't stop. However, it's the intentional pursuit that will open doors to new leading opportunities. And in the same way, tithing won't make you a kingdom driven leader, but starting it will create a work in your heart that will prepare you for something greater.

    The key takeaway is that you have to be extremely intentional about this growth so that you can be intentional in your leadership. The Old Testament kings that were called good were intentional, and no one can argue about how intentional Jesus was. Everyone has some leadership responsibility, and these chapters have been about preparing you to lead well. Now it's time to put these characteristics into action by leading.

SECTION II
LEADING

14

Begin to Reign

"His eyes were like a flame of fire, and on His head were many crowns.

He had a name written that no one knew except Himself.

He was clothed with a robe dipped in blood, and His name is called The Word of God.

And the armies in heaven, clothed in fine linen, white and clean, followed Him on white horses.

Now out of His mouth goes a sharp sword, that with it He should strike the nations.

And He Himself will rule them with a rod of iron.

He Himself treads the winepress of the fierceness and wrath of Almighty God. And He has on His robe and on His thigh a name written:

KING OF KINGS AND LORD OF LORDS."
— **Revelation 19:12-16 NIV**

I'm not sure how you can read this and not be full of fire and anticipation. Every Hollywood story pales in comparison to this triumphant entry. Comic book stories and fantasy don't come close to the God/Man that loves you and me so much that he did all that the Bible says He did and then comes back in this fashion.

Reigning as a king is a process. It's not a destination. You must first understand whose you are and what you are called to be. Once you accept the mantle of leadership, you can be intentional about this process in your preparation and intentional about stewarding your resources of influence, time, and treasure to expand God's kingdom.

When I say expand God's kingdom, I'm simply talking about taking actions that win more souls for Christ. As a businessperson, this can be a one-on-one endeavor. Certainly, there are people that only you can reach, such as your co-workers and others you interact with. However, kings also use strategies and tactics that are multiplicative, not just additive.

Earlier I wrote that I believe businesses can change the world. If you look around the world, what happens to areas where a new business form? Life. People move to be closer to the jobs, and new industries start up as a result, and the area becomes a thriving living thing. A business in and of itself is not Christian. There are no Chick-Fil-A's in heaven. However, businesses can have a culture, vision, and an opportunity to influence through their faith.

My passionate plea to business owners and marketplace leaders is to stop settling for good. Stop settling for a one or two-day-a-week expression of worship and take it to the workplace. If you can turn the corner on this concept, you will be able to leverage the systems that make a business work for the kingdom. Just like Coca-Cola in our previous example could end thirst with just a few tweaks (and a lot of effort), you too can have a multiplicative impact by just grabbing hold of this idea.

If you look at believing businesspeople, most are willing to write checks to a good cause. A few are willing to devote their time to a cause. That's awesome; keep doing that. What I'm really talking about is a complete mindshift from the way you view your business. Instead of pursuing separate endeavors, become one.

Although it's completely possible to have an evangelical outreach business, this is not what I'm talking about. When I explain this concept to most people, they get 90% of the way there but miss that 10% where the exponential impact could be. This is exactly why the example businesses are here and why the process is outlined in this book.

START WITH YOUR WHY

In Simon Sinek's book, "Start With Why [31]", he lays out the principle that people buy *why* you do something versus *what* you do. He then goes on to talk about finding your "why," or your reason or purpose. This is the fundamental purpose of his book. I believe most businesses start to solve a problem, but as kingdom driven leaders, we don't have to stop there.

Your why is what drives you. When you uncover your reason for getting up in the morning, it can be tied to a bunch of different things. It's helpful then to uncover the underlying values that fuel your why. During this exploration exercise, many choose family or achievement as a why. These are great motivators, but often the why is much deeper. The challenge is that we often overload ourselves with busyness that we rarely see a clear picture.

ARE YOU TOO B.U.S.Y.?

It may sound a bit hokey, but my pastor, Dennis Rouse, said that being busy really means "Being Under Satan's Yoke." That's an accurate picture of many of our lives. We're so busy that we miss the important stuff, and we're too far down the road to notice we missed a turn. When this happens, it's important to cut through the mental clutter here and dig deep to find your why.

Once you find your real why it'll change everything. It'll change how you look at your personal life, your home life, spiritual life, and even your work life. The value exercise described later in this book is a great place to start. Once you do it, I suggest taking it to your team and re-examining your company's mission statement and purpose for being here.

If you are concerned that adding in some element of something you are passionate about or holy discontented about will turn off your employees, don't be. Simon Sinek explains, "If you hire people just because they can do a job, they'll work for your money. But if you hire people who believe what you believe, they'll work for you with blood and sweat and tears."[32]

This is why there is no shortage of people that want to work for Chick-Fil-A. This is why the best of the best want to work for companies like Apple. They know why they do what they do, and they could apply their why to pretty much any solution. In Chick-Fil-A's case, it's easy to make sure what you're doing passes the "glorify God" lens of work.

Before we dive into your vocational why we need to look at your personal why. This why shapes who you are and why you do what you do. It influences the culture of your company or shades the influence you make on colleagues.

FINDING YOUR CORE VALUES

If you get this part down, then it makes finding the why of what you do for a living easier. If you remember earlier in the book, I believe that we all have some things for which we have a holy discontent. For Bobby Malone, it was giving young guys more opportunities than he had as a young man.

I have several things that cause a holy discontent in my heart, but family is a big one. Coming from a single-parent home and later discovering a relationship with Jesus in a marriage class, I have a big heart for healthy families. I am also passionate about business, leadership, and systems. With all these things going on, I wondered how I could get clarity on what was driving me.

I learned that if you understand the values you have, you will get a clearer picture of how you operate. One of the best ways to do this is an exercise that I did in a group class put on by the John Maxwell Company. He has a great tool for this, using playing cards if you want to try it. It's a wonderful team building exercise as well. For some, this is a procedural exercise, while others will find this particularly life-changing.

To find your core values, the ones that drive you, you need to write down about 10 to 15 values that you think affect your decision making. Here's a list of words that you can use to come up with the right ones. However, feel free to come up with your own. Some of these words are words that I chose, and others came from others.

Authenticity	Achievement	Adventure	Authority
Autonomy	Balance	Beauty	Boldness
Compassion	Challenge	Community	Competency
Contribution	Creativity	Curiosity	Determination
Fairness	Fame	Friendship	Fun
Growth	Happiness	Honesty	Influence
Integrity	Justice	Kindness	Knowledge
Leadership	Learning	Love	Loyalty

Money	Optimism	Peace	Pleasure
Popularity	Religion	Reputation	Respect
Responsibility	Security	Service	Spirituality
Stability	Success	Trustworthiness	Wealth
Wisdom			

Now that you have your top 10 or 15, it's time to reduce that to your favorite five. If you do this in a group, it can be fun to get words that seem synonymous but can be interpreted differently by other people.

My five were Faith, Family, Growth, Integrity, and Tenacity (notice that's not on the list above). The point of the exercise is to help you find values that shape your "lens."

Next, write down why you picked those five and what they mean to you. Make a self-definition of each word.

With your top five, let's pick just three that you think really define you. Here, it's helpful to consider if there are any values that you selected due to guilt. For me, I had Family and Faith there. They do drive a lot of my decisions, but I also chose them because I'd feel guilty if I didn't. This is why defining what the word means to you is so valuable.

Finally, with your top three selected, choose just one value. This will be the hardest decision yet. However, doing so can bring clarity to your life.

For those that are still struggling with not selecting Faith or Family, think about choosing your third most important value. I know as a Christian, we want God to be first, and not selecting Faith may feel wrong. Go ahead and select faith and family but put them aside so you can find the value that drives the others.

This will be a very difficult choice. Sometimes it can help to consider your top three or top five values and how this one value affects them all.

For me, it was growth. Growth beat tenacity for me because I know that I'm tenacious but only if there is evidence of growth. If I had a longer list, optimism might be on it because I'm optimistic about growth in people and in my endeavors. Growth fuels my quest for wisdom. I always want to grow from reading the Word. I tend to let relationships die if they aren't growing deeper. I tend to abandon projects if they aren't growing or progressing. Growth changes how I interact with my family. It's the sole reason that part of my yearly and 90-day goals include reading a parenting or marriage book. Growth truly defines many of my actions.

JIM'S VALUE

When I did this exercise with a group, there was a man named Jim that sat at our table. When I started talking to Jim, we hit it off. He was serving at the church in the same areas as me and loved his wife and his daughter just as I loved my family. Jim was, by all accounts, a great Christian man. He represents the faith well.

In a group, this exercise can take a few hours. After each round of value selection, the table goes around explaining why they chose what they did and why they cut the ones they did. If you have a good group, then it can be hilarious when someone cuts integrity or honesty. Seriously, how can you be honest with anyone at the table if you just cut honesty?

You get to learn a ton from those at the table when you go through this, including their fears and their loves, along with how they view certain words and what they mean to them. Balance, for instance, could mean creating more time spent doing hobbies or with the family, or it could mean having a more balanced diet.

As the day wore on, Jim made predictable choices like Family, Balance, Fun, and Faith. And like many others doing this exercise, Finances, Wealth, and Money were a part of the mix as well. However, after every round of cuts, most dropped the monetary values in favor of traditional "good" choices.

When you do this exercise in a big group, it's a lot of fun to make everyone pick their singular value and then do a reveal, as a surprise. At this point, we all knew what each person was probably going to pick before they did. Most knew I was going with Faith or Growth. Jim was going with Faith or Family. Another person at the table was going to pick Fun or Authenticity. Still, another was going with Security or Stability.

When the big reveal occurred, there was an uproar in our ballroom of everyone laughing at all the other tables with rounds of "I knew it" bellowing around us. Our table, however, was dead silent. Jim had picked Money. Thoughts whirled in my head. "How could he? How could we be so deceived? This wonderful Christian man was a fraud. All he cares about is Money. I bet his wife is a Doctor. I knew his watch looked expensive. Why would a money-grubbing fraud be here to "improve" himself? I bet he just wanted to gloat."

When it came time to explain our choices, I don't think anyone cared much about what we each shared. We wanted to hear why this despicable man chose money over his own family! We were ready to share a piece of our minds after he shared his. How could he have made such a stupid choice?

"I chose money. It was such a hard decision, but money represents something to me. It's what I can do with money that drives me. Money represents a trip to the ice cream store with my daughter. Money represents the vacation to the beach during the summer. It represents the yearly mission trips with our small group. I feel driven by money, but only because of the experiences I get to have with it. Maybe blessings would be a better value, I'm not sure, but money represents the giving I can do with it. The microloans in Ghana, the church building fund in Thailand, the spread of the gospel that I get to fund. I know many of you might think less of me, but when I think about money, I get excited. I can't wait to get more of it to be that blessing to my family and to grow God's Kingdom."

Before Jim's answer, our mouths were silent, but our minds were yelling at him. Now he had silenced both our heads and our hearts.

This exercise was so powerful that one person who had originally selected authenticity put down that card and picked "fun" instead. She was emboldened by Jim's answer and wanted to be truly authentic.

"Even if I'm authentic, which is a big value in my life, I'd still have to pick fun. Like Jim, fun represents some things in my life that I always gravitate toward. Fun represents experiences for me. I often make decisions based on how fun I think things will be. I don't pick things based on authenticity. I know I'm authentic, and the more authentic I can be without feeling judged, it sometimes affects my fun, but not all the time. I guess what I'm trying to say is that I seem to view life, now with Christ, through a lens of fun. Evangelism, small groups, family time, all of this is very important to me, but I view it as fun. In fact, there are a few things I do that aren't fun, but I have to do them."

Hopefully, you're armed with your key value that drives everything you can do, so you can start applying that value to your life as well. Take a very intentional look at your life and ask, "How do I lean into that?" I ask, in what areas can I affect growth? What areas are not growing and dragging me down? For Jim, he might look at things that are losing money and need to cut them out so he can focus on more profitable endeavors.

FIND YOUR MISSION

Values are great when it comes to determining your personal why or in finding what's driving you, but finding your business or vocation why might be a bit tougher. To make matters worse, you'll have to communicate this to others in an articulate way.

A "mission statement" reminds me of our discussion of the king's quarters. It's also similar to the idea of soul, spirit, and body in the sense that there is something that is at the center, and it emanates out, influencing everything else. Like personal values, it's the filter with which we see the world. In this case, it determines how we see the business world.

Imagine three concentric circles, like a bullseye. At the center of the bullseye is the "why" or mission statement, the next circle is the "how," and the outermost circle is the "what." Most people start with the what. The most popular "getting to know you" question at most cocktail parties is, "*What* do you do?" The reality is that no one cares what you do. They do, however, care *why* you do it.

I spent 15 years as a real estate agent. Early on, when people asked me what I did for a living, I said, "oh, I sell real estate." I was lucky because generally, people like talking about real estate. However, some of my friends had it worse. "Oh, I'm an accountant," no one wanted to be *that* guy. I am halfway kidding here, but you can see how unimpactful that statement is.

It's when you tap into your "why" that it can be powerful. Even a simple exercise of asking yourself why you do what you do is helpful. Let's go through the real estate example because usually, everyone knows at least one real estate agent.

What Do You Do?

I sell real estate.

Why?

I enjoy helping people and making money while doing it.

Why?
I **believe** in real estate as an investment as well as an asset of stability for families. I also need to provide for my family.

Why?
Ultimately, I **believe** God has a design for families, and a stable home can help that. There's something special about moving into a new home and homeownership that can change families for the better and bring them closer. There are also inherent dangers such as overspending or places where home purchasers and sellers can be taken advantage of and need guidance. Statistically, I know that moving is the most stressful thing that families will have to go through, behind death and divorce.

So, what do you do again?
I guide and protect families making a move during one of the most stressful events of their life.

After doing this value and why exercise, I remember going back to my team and spending a day reworking our mission statement. We started first with the values exercise to do two things. First and foremost, I wanted to know what my team valued. Second, I wanted to build trust. We were about to make some big changes in how we operated, and I needed everyone on board
. I found that if you have a team, the values anchor people in such a way that it influences the entire company. I had one agent that valued balance. It was no wonder that in our goal-centric culture (at my company) that he was often uncomfortable. It didn't bother me. I had learned boundaries and was driven by growth. However, for someone driven by balance, the

idea that we weren't balancing performance with family or social activities affected his performance.

Once we established the values, we immediately started to dissect our mission and vision. A mission statement is more than just something you make posters out of and put on the wall. The best mission statements are ones that bring clarity to your purpose. Andy Stanley, a successful author, speaker, and mega-church pastor said that a mission statement needs to be portable.[33] You should be able to remember it and take it with you.

That day we tore apart our company manual. We went from a mission statement of "providing great customer service through leadership and influence in real estate sales" to "moving families forward." We found that all our core values centered around helping people. The light bulb moment was when we started talking about our "I believe" statements. My team believed that homes brought stability to families, were good investments, and ultimately were in the best interest of growing families.

Before this exercise, we would attempt to create culture and mission by saying things like, "we're a leadership company that sells real estate." The challenge was that if you asked what that meant, we all had different versions of that. Moving families forward was a uniting concept. It had the power to create stories that the previous one did not.

You can do this "why" exercise with your family as well. The exercise is simple. Just ask "why?" like a 5-year-old child. Eventually, after about five times, you get to the heart of the matter.

Koch Industries Market-Based Management (MBM) is a great example of this. A company that is usually vilified in the media and even accused of being a part of the Illuminati is simply taking Biblical principles or laws and putting them to work within systems. A Biblical law or promise of God is like gravity. It works whether we want it to or not.

Check out Koch's MBM values list.[34]

- » INTEGRITY — Conduct all affairs with integrity, for which courage is the foundation.

- » COMPLIANCE — Strive for 10,000% compliance with all laws and regulations, which requires 100% of employees fully complying 100% of the time. Stop, think, and ask.

- » VALUE CREATION — Create long-term value by the economic means for customers, the company, and society. Apply MBM® to achieve superior results by making better decisions, pursuing safety and environmental excellence, eliminating waste, optimizing, and innovating.

- » PRINCIPLED ENTREPRENEURSHIP — Apply the judgment, responsibility, initiative, economic and critical thinking skills, and sense of urgency necessary to generate the greatest contribution, consistent with the company's risk philosophy.

- » CUSTOMER FOCUS — Understand and develop relationships with customers to profitably anticipate and satisfy their needs.

- » KNOWLEDGE — Seek and use the best knowledge and proactively share your knowledge while embracing a challenge process. Develop measures that lead to profitable action.

- » CHANGE — Anticipate and embrace change. Envision what could be, challenge the status quo and drive creative destruction through experimental discovery.

- » HUMILITY — Exemplify humility and intellectual honesty. Constantly seek to understand and constructively deal with reality to create value and achieve personal improvement. Hold yourself and others accountable.

» RESPECT — Treat others with honesty, dignity, respect, and sensitivity. Appreciate the value of diversity. Encourage and practice teamwork.

» FULFILLMENT — Find fulfillment and meaning in your work by fully developing your capabilities to produce results that create the greatest value.

The values of integrity, customer focus, and respect sound like chapters in this book. When you look at these values, you can almost see a Biblical influence. These values work for Koch because they are timeless, and values impact culture.

Cultural values influence the way employees interact with each other. With most employees spending over a third of their adult life working, values influence their home life as well.

When I initially wrote this, I wrote that Jesus can't save your business, but that's not true. I've seen where Jesus has provided for businesses that were failing and where His redemptive power changed the business as well. Sure, there might not be any Chick-fil-A's or Hobby Lobby's in heaven, but your business could be responsible for getting souls there.

MORE THAN PASSION

When people get asked what makes a great leader, they often think of someone who is passionate about what they are doing. It's this belief that often attracts people to them. It's that powerful "why." I heard it said once that strong-willed, driven people will only follow someone with a bigger, more powerful "why" or vision than theirs.

Let's look at an earlier statement I made in the context of this why. Below, this statement is the basis for the book. It's why I love businesses. It's also why I spent more than a year studying the Biblical lessons of kings.

I believe (have faith) that missional businesses (if run/influenced by intentional Christian leaders) can change the world (due to their leverage, resources, supply chains, and opportunities).

When we understand our values and our why, it's easier to identify the areas in our life that are incongruent with them. In some cases, these can be what are known as strongholds. Lucky for us, the Old Testament kings and Jesus both attacked strongholds and gave us a blueprint to follow.

15

Tear Down Strongholds

When the Israelites crossed the Jordan, their mission was to completely conquer the land, taking no prisoners. This meant no peace treaties, no wives, no additional slaves. In other words, God wanted no outside influence in the lives of the Israelites. We have the benefit of hindsight to see this clearly.

God knew that the practices of the people of Canaan could detrimentally influence the Jewish people. As history tells it, that's exactly what happened. Israel did not completely clear the land. They intermarried with surrounding "countries," and eventually, idol worship came to be part of life.

> "Otherwise, they will teach you to follow all the detestable things they do in worshiping their gods, and you will sin against the Lord your God."
> **— Deuteronomy 20:18 NIV**

Modern-day Christians aren't the only ones to question God's command. Even in the story of Joshua, we see this. Joshua and his armies didn't completely cleanse the area and stay clear of the influences in the area. The very strongholds and idols that needed to be removed king after king for generations after this were Canaanite influences. You almost wonder whether or not there would have been a book of Judges if the Israelites completely removed all the Canaanites.

For me, it was helpful to understand what was actually being removed when the Bible referenced them. It helped me understand that although these places were physical, they represented spiritual strongholds.

ASHERAH POLES

Asherim were either trees that were likely carved in feminine shape or a pole with a similar shape. This idol was usually placed in the community centers or near homes and was an act of worship to a Canaanite fertility goddess. Often, if the families were too poor to be able to afford a pole, they used a tree or planted a tree for that purpose. Also, they usually had one inside their home. These were the same poles that God commanded against in Exodus, the same ones that Gideon cut down. The same that Asa, Hezekiah, and Josiah all removed.

Because the poles were often in and around the homes, it made me think of the bad influences that we let inside our own homes and what we look at. TV shows and music that glamourize promiscuity are an example of this. We're foolish if we don't think that these things don't influence us. Our unwillingness to remove these influences on a screen (internet or otherwise) might be a kind of modern-day Asherah pole. The question we should ask ourselves as kingdom driven leaders is, "What, outside of God, is influencing me?"

HIGH PLACES

High places were the mounds, hills, and mountains throughout modern-day Israel. The Canaanite people would put their temples and places of worship in these areas for all to see. People would gather there to socialize and engage in orgies or worship of their deities using sacrifice - even child sacrifice.

This led me to think about the social influences that we allow into our life. The question we should ask ourselves as kingdom driven leaders is, "Who, outside of God, is influencing me?"

IDOLS

Most of us know an idol is an object that is made to represent a god. However, the context of that time is that an idol is the physical representation of a god. The yearning for a god was so great that many needed something physical to touch. Even the great philosopher Aristotle said that an idol or an image is the connection between the "inner world of the mind and the outer world of reality."[35] Clearly, the secular world understands this connection. We'd do well to not dismiss it.

Idols are different. You could say that they are like Asherah poles, but to me, idols are those things deep in your life like an addiction, except not just a substance abuse addiction. **This is an abuse of your substance.** Idols are lies that you believe and hold higher than God's truth. A kingdom driven leader asks, "what lies are influencing me?"

Kingdom driven leaders should approach removing strongholds with the same care that old testament kings did. The kings that the Bible labels as good took down not only the obvious Asherah poles but also removed anything that was influencing the culture. The toughest of these strongholds to remove were the people's personal idols. In this case, the king's reinstated religious customs.

Two of the kings that the Bible calls good are Asa and previously mentioned Josiah. Their reigns are similar in that they came to power and had the task of changing the culture of their country. As you read their brief account, notice some keys to their reign. We first assume that God is first in their priority.

- » They sought the Lord.
- » They kept their heart toward God.
- » They removed physical idols, poles, and high places to address the "outside."
- » They instituted mandatory worship and instituted the Law to address the "inside."

ASA

After Solomon's reign, Judah became the remnant of David's legacy. Kings and Chronicles reads like a "who's who" for the despicable but scattered amongst the dictators and tyrants are some kings whom God calls "good." In almost every case, the first action they took was to tear down the high places that were built to serve other gods.

Asa, the grandson of Rehoboam, was one of the good ones. He comes to the throne after his father, Abijah, dies. The Bible is unclear as to the reason for his father's death and short three-year reign. One of the first things Asa does is set about to completely reform his kingdom.

"Asa **did what was good and right in the eyes of the Lord his God.**

He removed the **foreign altars and the high places**, smashed the sacred stones and cut down the Asherah poles.

He **commanded** Judah to seek the Lord, the God of their ancestors, and to obey his laws and commands.

He **removed the high places and incense altars in every town** in Judah, and the <u>kingdom was at peace under him</u>.

He built up the fortified cities of Judah, since the land was at peace. No one was at war with him during those years, for the Lord gave him rest."
— 2 Chronicles 14: 2-6 NIV

1 Kings puts it like this:

"Asa **did what was right in the eyes of the Lord**, as his father David had done.

He expelled the male shrine prostitutes from the land and **got rid of all the idols his ancestors had made.**

He even deposed his grandmother Maakah from her position as queen mother, because she had made a repulsive image for the worship of Asherah. Asa **cut it down and burned it** in the Kidron Valley.

Although he did not remove the high places, Asa's heart was fully committed to the Lord all his life."
— 1 Kings 15:11-14 NIV [36]

What I love here is that God shows us what's important is Asa's heart. Early in his reign, he wanted to be completely devoted to God. He set about tearing down the enemy's strongholds. He removed influence from his inner circle, including his grandmother, as well as the external physical idols. He did this throughout his household, his inner-kingdom, and throughout the land.

Then he commanded his kingdom to worship the Lord. As the head of your household, whether you are male or female, it's your responsibility to remove outside influences from your home. That's the key to tearing down strongholds in our life!

JOSIAH

> "So, Josiah **removed all detestable idols** from the entire land of Israel and required everyone to worship the Lord their God. And throughout the rest of his lifetime, they did not turn away from the Lord, the God of their ancestors."
> **— 2 Chronicles 34:33 (NLT)**

Previously we read that Josiah found God's word, and it changed his world. He became passionate about putting God back on the throne of his people's hearts. Josiah brought down idols and wicked places. He also removed the more insidious of the strongholds, which were the practices of the religious habits. While those actions removed physical structures and creations, they also represented mental and spiritual strongholds and a culture of idolatry. This was not a culture in an ethnic sense but a culture in a corporate sense.

To combat this, Josiah instituted worship and God's Law back into the culture and at the same time removed the physical representations of the strongholds in people's lives. His reign was characterized as good by the Bible. It's said he followed the ways of his forefather David.

What Asa and Josiah understood is easy to miss a few thousand years later. They both knew that it wasn't enough to remove easily seen sins but that they must replace an idolatrous culture with one that honors and worships God. They led by leading the way with worship to create a new culture.

RELIGION AS A CORPORATE CULTURE

The dictionary defines religion as:

> "the service and worship of God or the supernatural: **commitment or devotion to religious faith or observance**
>
> a personal set or institutionalized system of religious attitudes, beliefs, and **practices**"
> — **Merriam-Webster Dictionary**[37]

Culture and religion are almost synonymous in this sense. Check out the definition from Merriam-Webster:

> "the customary beliefs, social forms, and material traits of a racial, religious, or social group.
>
> "the set of **shared** attitudes, values, goals, and **practices** that characterizes an institution or organization a corporate culture focused on the bottom line"[38]

The point is that in order to institute change, Asa and Josiah had to completely change everything, including the habits of the people. From top to bottom, change was instituted in everything from the symbols used to the meetings and social interactions.

Most of us reading this won't immediately believe we have physical, visible strongholds. However, I think it is worth looking at anyway. There are physical ailments that might be strongholds, but maybe even worse are the physical totems disguised as busyness or perhaps masquerading as a hobby. Most of us battle with hidden high places and spiritual influences and don't realize it.

> "For our struggle is not against flesh and blood [contending only with physical opponents], but against the rulers, against the powers, against the world forces of this [present] darkness, against the spiritual forces of wickedness in the heavenly (supernatural) places."
> **— Ephesians 6:12 AMP**

Satan isn't all-knowing, but he does know our biological design and our desires. He can see what's going on in our life, whether it be physical, mental, or spiritual. The Bible calls him a "lion seeking whom he may devour" (1 Peter 5:8) and calls him the "god of the air" (Ephesians 2:2). He's the ultimate spy. He has all the inside information about our Lord and us. He knows more than we do and uses it against us.

To see how he uses our own design against us, we need to understand how easily we are influenced. If we understand these patterns in our life, we can then have the tools to tear down the strongholds, heal our hurts, and begin living truly like a king, all through the power of Christ.

THE HABIT LOOP

Simon Sinek, mentioned in the previous chapter, explains in his book that our response to a *why* is part of our neural wiring. If you think about this spiritually for a second, it makes sense. It's a heart, mind, and body conversation. Look at the what, how, and why. *What* we do is the flesh.

The *how* we do is the battle between the mind and the flesh, but the *why* we do something is at the heart.

> "The things that come out of a person's mouth come from the heart, and these defile them."
> **— Matthew 15:18 NIV**

When you study Kings and Chronicles, you don't necessarily get that emotional deepness, but when you look at the life of Absalom or Rehoboam, you can almost feel the hurt. Their fathers were these great men for sure, but were they present? History is not too kind to fathers when it comes to kings. Rarely did a good king have a son that carried on the "good" title. Often, they acted in a manner different than their father. I propose that it was a way of proving themselves because they had an emotional stronghold in their life – one that only God could pull down.

Researched over and over again and made popular by Charles Duhigg in his book, "Power of Habit,"[39] we know that our brains like routines. Our brains are kind of like pathfinders. Once we do something and receive some positive stimuli, we tend to seek out that experience again. The more we have this particular experience, it creates a path like a well-worn trail through the woods.

How many times have you driven home and been unaware of the turns you make? Every move, from your first steps to riding a bike, is part of these neural pathways, or if you prefer, habits. Some are more subtle muscle memory "habits," while others are psychological habits. Rarely are these two "habits" grouped together.

God wired us this way to be able to do amazing things. Our brains are wired to make everything more efficient, ultimately so we can focus on creative processes. God created us to create, but we'd never be creators if we were bogged down remembering where to step and when to take a breath.

What an amazing metaphor! God gave us an amazing brain that turns everything into a habit so we can spend more time with Him and be like Him. While all this happens biologically, it should be happening spiritually, and it can. Habits are changeable and not set in stone.

To understand how to break and tear down strongholds, we need to know how they work physically and spiritually. Ultimately, the spiritual is the most important aspect of getting free. However, understanding how the physical process works helps us grasp the importance of avoiding certain activities.

In the "Power of Habit," it's explained that we all process habits in virtually the same way. There's the set of tasks or an event for which the brain is assessing, "can this be automated?" The event is often tied to a person, time, location, or emotion. This set of tasks or events in and of itself won't create a habit, but it does influence its creation.

Second, there is often a trigger or cue associated with this event. This cue is often some sort of physical, mental, or emotional stimuli. Take specific note of the emotional point because it's the key to strongholds. Often habits formed emotionally can be the most powerful, and unfortunately, they are often negative habits.

Finally, there is the result. In some cases, the result is called the reward. This result tells the brain this is something to automate. The result doesn't always have to be a "reward" in the most general sense of the word. A reward could be a slight alleviation of anxiety. It could be replacing one pain with another. It could be a feeling of comfort in the form of depression.

The habit part of our brain doesn't have a moral compass. It doesn't know if the habit is good or evil. Let's say you are anxious about a deadline. You have a deadline, and it starts to cause you a great amount of stress. To alleviate this stress, you go to your favorite social media site, where you find out that you have some new "updates" to see. You examine these updates so that the highlighted notification number no long hovers over your account.

Every time you see a personal notification and interact with it, a small amount of dopamine, the feel-good hormone, hits your brain. This reinforces this activity as a habit for you. In addition, not only did you alleviate your stress by escaping for a minute, but you also accomplished some tasks rewarding your time wasting. Unfortunately, because you wasted 30 minutes, you have higher stress overall than when you started. As your day goes on, you'll likely find yourself checking every new notification.

Social media sites know this and are designed with this in mind. They know that your internal wiring sometimes says, "busy equals good." If busy equals good, then clearing email or checking notifications equals good.

Let's examine this loop. Your trigger is the feeling of anxiety about the deadline and an increase in pressure. Your solution, to check your social media, relieves the stress. The reward is a moderate reduction in anxiety and a false perception of productivity. Note that these rewards are almost instant.

If you look at your habits, you'll start to see why some are easily formed, like escaping to social media, and others aren't, like working out. Working out gives you no immediate reward other than a small feeling of accomplishment. Once you start seeing the physical changes, you get a bigger reward. This explains why some people become fanatical about health. They are getting huge payoffs after committing to the habit long term.

BUILDING A STRONGHOLD

Let's shift our focus from the psychological to the spiritual for a moment and connect habits to strongholds. Strongholds are formed when we replace God's truth with a lie. Strongholds are built in the same way a habit is formed. Just like a habit, strongholds start off in life, particularly when there is a traumatic event. These events can be long-term as well. An event could even be a genetic inheritance that affects your physical appearance. Often, a hurt or trauma event will have occurred early in life.

The second part of a stronghold is a lie, which is the trigger. This is the cornerstone or foundation of this huge, sun-darkening tower in our life. This is the cue and the glue that keeps this thing erect in your life. The lie is a misinterpretation of the event. The reason so many strongholds are built during our youth is that we've got cloudy and immature perceptions at that age.

For years I was sarcastic. I thought I was the funniest guy at school, and in reality, I was a huge jerk. I was also angry. I managed to avoid any life-threatening fights, but my so-called witty humor left me pretty much friendless until I met my spouse.

It wasn't until I fully submitted my life to Christ in a Marriage Class that I ever discovered *why* I was sarcastic. The process went with the first realization that I was destroying everyone around me emotionally by tearing them down. If you're sarcastic, then hear me on this. Stop. Sarcasm's root word, "sarc," means to tear. You're essentially cutting people with your words.

The sarcasm wasn't the root of my problem, though. The problem was really why I was using it. I was angry, hurt, and depressed. I would act out in sarcasm because that made me feel like I was in control, and the laughter that often happened at someone else's expense made me feel accepted.

I had to go back to my childhood to discover why this was the case. When I was two, my parents got a divorce. My mom had to work overtime to make ends meet for me. This meant that I was often left alone. I started to resent not having a dad at home. Like many men around the world, I incorrectly responded to this absence as an indication that I was not valued. I set out to prove to the world that I was valuable and built up a defense with sarcasm so that I'd never be hurt by anyone.

Lies in a stronghold are often internalized or placed on God. My thoughts went from "dad doesn't want to be with me" to "no one wants to be with me." Then they went from "I'm not loved" to "I'm not worthy of love." And ultimately, they slipped from "I'm not lovable" to "God doesn't love me" to believing "a loving God isn't real."

While serving in the marriage ministry, we would see this pattern over and over again. As part of the 12-week curriculum, each person had to write their "life story" and explore the causes of some of the behavior they brought to the marriage. We did this for a few years and heard every horrific childhood story you could think of. Whatever you are thinking of right now, we've likely heard it. The good news is that there is a solution... SPOILER ALERT, it's Christ!

What we'd see time and time again was a wound from a parent or loved one that started the lie. What was very interesting was that over the years, the hurts were just as deep, no matter how horrific the event was. The pain was the same! Take some solace in that. Most of the participants in our group felt like they could never recover, whether they suffered physical abuse or absentee parents.

In each case, the event, like a horrific car accident, left them emotionally mangled and damaged. We would typically see two responses similar to the flight or fight. Either the person would remain believing a lie that would cause them to be victimized by doubting what God says about them, or the person would become angry and say "never again," blocking out the truth from their heart about what God says. In both cases, these individuals believed a lie that started with a misinterpretation of an event or "trigger."

The third part of the stronghold is the result or reward. An event occurs which we incorrectly interpret, creating a lie that we internalize that causes us to act out in different ways. Often, it causes us to act out to seek attention or do something to numb the pain.

What makes the stronghold so tough to pull down is the response you receive from others. It creates a cycle of self-fulfilling prophecies.[40] You're creating a habit that constantly reinforces the lie that you believe. To put it another way, your belief is so strong that you are literally creating the very thing you fear.

The clinical term is pseudo feedback or circular causality[41]. If you search for what this means, you'll find very spiritual examples of generational curses. An example might be a child seeking attention from their parents that acts out in some disturbing way and gets in trouble at school. The parents are called in and are visibly upset with the child and begin to discipline him. The child receives this discipline as rejection and seeks to gain more attention by acting out again.

A less obvious example might be our previous social media example. For example, let's say your work is incredibly stressful, and you have a deadline to meet. You turn to social media to relieve the anxiety. In the process, you're wasting time making the stress level rise. As the stress increases, so do your social media visits, making it worse and worse.

Most people fail to free themselves from this cycle because they address the symptoms rather than dealing with the cause. Well-meaning friends will tell people who are smoking to stop smoking or stop overeating for those dealing with obesity. The problem isn't necessarily what we are doing but rather what we are thinking.

We're born with the world's lens on how to process life. When we accept Jesus, He gives us a new lens to see the world through His reality. We need to use this view to tear down the strongholds in our life. We must see the world through the lens of knowing that God's Word is the truth and that every other voice is a lie. In order to break free, you'll have to acknowledge that God's Word is your source of truth and comfort.

Tearing down strongholds is the one thing that separated the kings that God called good and those that He didn't. It's what many of the judges did. It's even what Jesus did. He didn't tear down any physical idols, but you see Him throughout the gospels speaking out against the self-righteous religious influence (the Pharisees) as well as casting out demons.

The Pharisees of that time had valued their religious habits over the re-lationship that God wanted to create for them. They were so caught up in this loop that they missed the Messiah. When He didn't match what they thought He should be, they had Him killed.

It's worth pointing out that I'm in no way trying to diminish what anyone went through. It's very easy for me to sit here and write about how to free yourself in a somewhat sterile way. I'm not laying out steps like this is as easy as one, two, three. It's not. Tearing strongholds down is likely the biggest challenge you'll face in life. For some, it may be a lifelong battle. But it's one that you can win.

> "For though we live in the world, we do not wage war as the world does.
>
> The weapons we fight with are not the weapons of the world. On the contrary, they have divine power to demolish strongholds.
>
> We demolish arguments and every pretension that sets itself up against the knowledge of God, and we take captive every thought to make it obedient to Christ."
> **— 2 Corinthians 10:3-5 NIV**

DEMOLITION DAY

We have a missing piece of our puzzle that only a relationship with God can fill. God knows this. He knew that we'd look for anything to fill that hole. Most of the time, we'd take the easy route if we're honest.

It's much easier to worship a carved statue, a job, a spouse, a form of entertainment over an unseen God that we must work to get to know.

In America, we don't really heal anyone. We medicate them. We treat symptoms, not causes. We tend to do this spiritually as well. That's why it's much easier to watch YouTube or stream Netflix than get before the Lord and wait on Him. I'm guilty of this. It's much easier for me to feed my mind entertainment to numb the pain than it is to do the heart-wrenching work of healing. We often choose the temporary relief of a placebo versus the life-giving heart surgery God needs to do.

God knew all of this. In every instance, it was the leader's job to remove all temptations and all idols. When Joshua crossed the Jordan, his job was to completely remove all potential influences. Yes, all.

This is why when you read the king's account of Asa, Jehoshaphat, Josiah, or Joash, you get a very detailed description of their level of commitment to removing these strongholds in the land. To say it another way, their kingdom prospered only to the level of their submission and commitment to remove the lies. Asa's rule started as one of deep commitment, and his kingdom lived in peace.

Unfortunately, the Old Testament doesn't have a perfect king for us to examine how to tear down strongholds. However, fortunately for us, we have the King of kings, Jesus. Ultimately, to be free and finally demolish this lie, we'll have to trust Him completely.

For you to allow God to tear down this fortress in your life, you will have to take some action. I recommend getting a journal and going somewhere where you can be alone for a while. This could take a few hours for some. While I believe counseling can help, I also know God wants to speak with you and heal you. It's best to at least attempt this time alone with God before seeking outside help.

Start by examining the source of your pain. What are the thoughts in your head about yourself? Ask the Lord, "who is the source of my truth?" or "what is the source of my truth?" Ask the Lord, "what is my source of comfort and security?" I know of a few people that would carry around index cards to record their feelings throughout the day as a way to take them "captive."

> "We demolish arguments and every pretension that sets itself up against the knowledge of God, and we take captive every thought to make it obedient to Christ."
> **— 2 Corinthians 10:5 NIV**

A stronghold typically exists when you've tried to protect yourself instead of letting God be your protector. If you're struggling here, ask God to reveal the lie that you are believing. Ask Him to show you His feelings toward you during that event. In many cases, feeling His response can offer healing. However, it's important to note that He will speak to you uniquely.

Every act of breakthrough starts with a repentant heart. Repentance simply means a change of decision; it's not some religious thing where you have to get on your knees and act any sort of way. That could be your response, but the key is that you have to make a steadfast decision that you will not believe this lie anymore.

Now ask God to reveal the solution, the response to that lie. Get the TRUTH from The Source. Often, He may direct you to scripture. For some things, He may tell you a word that will mean something for you.

For me, I can remember very recently that I was starting back down a depression loop and felt worthless. I remember being in prayer and exclaiming, "the best thing I've done with my life is to be a father. Those children are my greatest accomplishments." I can remember His response very clearly. "That's how I feel about you." And that is how He feels about you, too. You are His greatest creation and masterpiece.

> **"For we are God's masterpiece.** He has created us anew in Christ Jesus, so we can do the good things **he planned for us long ago."**
> **— Ephesians 2:10 NLT**

He has a plan for each of us, and He wants us healed. I could list several scriptures here about God's truth, but He will give you what you need without me spoon-feeding you here. Not everyone will hear a scripture here, but I strongly advise you to get in the Word and get at least one scripture that speaks to you.

> "I will be a Father to you, and you will be my sons and daughters, says the Lord Almighty."
> **— 2 Corinthians 6:18 NIV**

Early on in my life, this scripture reminded me of God's love.

More recently, the Psalm, "For you created my inmost being you knit me together in my mother's womb. I praise you because I am fearfully and wonderfully made; your works are wonderful; I know that full well" (Psalm 139:13-14), speaks to me. It reminds me that He thought about me when He made me. There's something special that I feel here that God thought about me in advance, made me unique, and has an adventurous mission for me... and for you too!

The point is that the scripture is one of your best weapons with which to battle the enemy when he comes back to try to rebuild this stronghold.

> "We are human, but we don't wage war as humans do. We use God's mighty weapons, not worldly weapons, to knock down the strongholds of human reasoning and to destroy false arguments. We destroy every proud obstacle that keeps people from knowing God. We capture their rebellious thoughts and teach them to obey Christ."
> **— 2 Corinthians 10:3-5 NLT**

Just like Asa and Josiah, even after tearing down the monumental strongholds, there are still remnants and influences you have to remove or repair. He wants to help you remove every piece of these strongholds from your heart.

Examine how you learned to protect yourself. What are some of the bad habit loops that you formed? What areas of this hurt did you block out God and take His rightful place as your protector and defender? Ask God to seek your heart and reveal any areas where you might have tried to take His place or replace Him with something or someone else. You may need to confess before the Lord your role in this stronghold. This is different from turning away or repentance. It's important to take responsibility for your portion.

Finally, ask Him to show you what it looks like to completely trust Him. Make a part of your daily walk to ask Him to reveal lies that you might be believing and to help you refute them.

If you go through this process, you might not immediately be free. How-ever, each battle becomes easier because you will have a reminder of who the real source of truth is.[42]

JESUS

As with any of the king's characteristics, we need to see Jesus doing them. When Jesus starts His ministry, He immediately went after strongholds. In fact, Jesus is much more contemporary than Old Testament kings. His ministry went after ideological strongholds, cultural high places, and even idols.

At this point, I'm sure we're all familiar with Jesus' story. It's easy to miss the fact that before attempting to turn the world upside down, Jesus fasted and prayed for 40 days. This time of temptation and refinement was preparing the way for The Way. As you embark on this journey, you may find it hard to complete without doing the same.

RELIGIOUS STRONGHOLD

The way the Bible reads, it's as if Jesus walked right out the desert and right into the synagogues. In every gospel account, the first thing Jesus did was get right to preaching. Each gospel account differs in the way His first actions are presented, but throughout Jesus' life, it's clear he came against the Pharisees in particular. In this way, He mirrored the good kings of the past by going after the most powerful religious and cultural stronghold in Israel.

While this is a great oversimplification of what the Pharisees were, it's worth noting what they represent as well. The Pharisees were a group that separated themselves to become authorities on the law - the same law that was given to Moses. They spent a great deal of time understanding, expounding, teaching, and using this law for their own means. What could have started as a movement to honor God's word changed into a lifeless tool for judging others.

The most prolific writer of the New Testament, Paul, was said to be a Pharisee. We see him in Acts holding the coats of those that are stoning Stephen. Pharisees had a violent history of manipulating politics to eliminate opposition, whether that be Sadducees or Jesus. During Jesus' time, the Pharisees controlled the high places of Jerusalem. Their tenets were focused on purity, in particular, Jewish purity as it related to the law. Can you think of an institution that seems to mirror this very thing? I wonder if I described a Pharisee to an unsaved person if they would mistake that person for a Christian. I love the saying, "Jesus didn't come to make bad people good, but rather dead people alive!"[43]

We learned earlier that a stronghold is simply a lie that has been believed and reinforced into a habit. The Pharisees believed the lie that their interpretations and additions to the law were more valuable than what God gave them. This created a dead religion. Let's be clear, we live in a time with many religious strongholds. Humans use religion to control others, and this abuse is nothing new.

Like a great king, Jesus prepared himself, surrounded himself with followers, and attacked the strongholds of that day. He went to the homes of the Pharisees (the synagogue) and began preaching against them.

> "For I tell you that unless your righteousness surpasses that of the Pharisees and the teachers of the law, you will certainly not enter the kingdom of heaven."
> **— Matthew 5:20 NIV**

Jesus' most famous sermon begins to talk about how God's love is radical and that we can only really show our love by loving others. People can only know we're followers of Christ through our actions.

Several scriptures refer to Jesus' distaste for pharisaical "culture. To me, Jesus' sermon was a hint of what's to come. Luke 11:37-54 makes it blatantly obvious.

> "...'Now then, you Pharisees clean the outside of the cup and dish, but inside you are full of greed and wickedness.'
>
> And they respond, 'Hey wait a minute...'
>
> One of the experts in the law answered him, 'Teacher, when you say these things, you insult us also.'
>
> Jesus replied, 'And you experts in the law, woe to you, because you load people down with burdens they can hardly carry, and

you yourselves will not lift one finger to help them.

Woe to you, because you build tombs for the prophets, and it was your ancestors who killed them!'" **(NIV)**

After being invited to eat at the home of a Pharisee, Jesus purposely avoids their rituals for the purpose of calling them out. If you live in the US, you'd probably consider Jesus to be rude. Not only did He not clean His hands, but He insulted His host. However, if you were ever to travel to Israel or commune with Jewish friends, you'd probably know them as being authentic and direct in their conversation. It's a wonderful cultural holdover.

What's the point of this? Jesus was stirring their hearts by attacking their belief system. He didn't bring a wrecking ball. He set up explosives around this stronghold and set the fuse on Calvary.

This religious spirit is still alive today, and it's one we need to be aware of. The great news is that we can battle it the same way Jesus did: directly and with love.

KILL THE SACRED COWS

If you're like me, you might have picked this book up, hoping for more business insight than I'm giving. As I said before, the key to living like a kingdom driven leader is in the preparation. You'll never achieve the eternal victories without defeating your inner strongholds first and foremost. Your key responsibility is to God first, then your family. Your vocation, whether you are a marketplace leader or a CEO, is a distant third.

However, I do believe there is a business application to this as well. After all, the saying, "Kill the sacred cows," is a religious connotative term for removing the high places in the workplace. I liken this step or characteristic to riding in an airplane. You can't help anyone with their oxygen mask until you have your mask on first.

Assuming you're ready for the next steps, you need to look around your workplace. Ask yourself, "what lies do we believe at work?" This isn't just a nice cap to a chapter; this is a legitimate question. Most of our underachievement in the business realm often comes from believing a lie that we cannot achieve something.

Look at your organization and start with the area you influence the most. Your team. This is your own personal cultural influence. To start this process, you might have to be like Queen Esther or Joseph and influence from within. Others will need to be like Josiah and, after finding the Law, set to turn the entire kingdom around.

From top to bottom, take the lens of this chapter and say, "what do we believe about this?" Then ask, "what if that's not true?" Look at the processes in place and ask, "why do we do this?"

When I was running my real estate company, I went through several changes. At first, it was a simple mission statement, then an adoption of identified values. At first, this affected our sales team and the way we treated customers. However, it spilled into how we hired people, not just from what we looked for in an employee or independent contractor but also in how we held our interviews.

One particular stronghold for me was based around competitiveness. It originated out of a lie that I believed had become an idol. I brought this into my company as well. Once I started to attack the strongholds in my personal life, the ones in my business began to fall as well.

One way this manifested was believing we needed to be the best in technology, my own personal business stronghold. In the pursuit to be the best here, we would examine every new piece of technology service that came out. Every beta test and new platform had to be examined. In some cases, we would switch from provider to provider to be the "best" in this space.

Trying to be known as a leader, at least in one category, was supposed to solve the value equation for me. However, chasing technology cost us a lot of money and time. Each change to the system slowed down the team as a new learning curve was introduced.

Technology was the one thing I understood better than many of my peers, and I believed that if I was a leader in technology, then that would make me a valuable leader – a leader that would be noticed and appreciated by others. I was hoping that by being the absolute best in this area, I'd be appreciated by others.

This thought process was completely outside of my relationship with God. My prayers were about Him blessing my direction. I believed my value came from the approval of others instead of the value that God placed on my life.

I can still remember how freeing the feeling was when I let go of that and embraced what was best for the team – that I turn over my desire to be valued by people to Him. I had to give up the things that I thought were important. It wasn't easy. I had to realize that it wasn't just a business advantage I was pursuing but rather a selfish desire. Once I let go of this and focused on simply trying to add value to my team, there was an immediate boost in momentum.

As with your strongholds, it's worth getting rid of every stone and looking at the details. I'm not here saying that any of these examples are ones you should choose. Rather look at your own business and processes and evaluate them. Then make a conscious decision to tear down the stronghold. If you at least go through this exercise, you'll understand *why* you do certain things in your organization.

A NEW KINGDOM

Removing the strongholds requires a strong foundation in knowing who you are in Christ. This is why the first few chapters were focused on getting that built. When a kingdom driven leader is committed and in communication with God, strongholds crumble. Where wisdom and humility grow, a stronghold's influence diminishes.

As your remove the strongholds from your company and personal life, you will resist the influence of the world and be able to influence people for the kingdom. A kingdom driven leader takes influence to a different level by networking with intention!

16

Build A Network

Before we jump in, I'll warn you that this is going to be a very practical chapter. It's going to feel different than the rest. It's extremely actionable and a key to success for business as well as life. If I ever wrote an autobiography, it would likely be about networking. I'd be tempted to name it "It Just So Happens." In my life, because I've been open to connections and connecting others, it just so happens I've had opportunities that I never even knew existed.

You may have heard it said that it's all about who you know. Intentional networking is one of the hidden factors responsible for success. For the unaware, networking is simply an exchange of information. Whether you're talking about computers or people, networking is all about connections.

Previously, I mentioned that our church has a group of businessmen that meet called the "kings" group. From time to time, there is a guest speaker who usually teaches business and Biblical principles. If I can, I always try to muster up the courage to talk to the speaker before they leave and invite them to coffee. One such event helped shape this book.

During one of those guest speaker days, there was this one speaker who was charismatic, passionate, and funny. When he spoke, the vernacular of leadership just flowed out. He was polished. It was as if he'd not only read every leadership book I did but that he most likely memorized them.

He told stories of organizational leadership and his efforts to help businesses make a bigger impact. In one instance, he helped an organization reach every country on the planet. His topic of kingdom leadership was one that I enjoyed. At the end of his talk, he told us all he'd hang around if anyone wanted to connect. I thought this was my opportunity to gain even more wisdom.

While standing around waiting to talk with him, I overheard him say the word Cambodia. Cambodia is a trigger word for me, and our family had just booked a trip over there. When I got to talk to Dr. Rob, I mentioned my trip. Dr. Rob, forever the connector, connected me to an organization there in Cambodia that I was able to meet face to face.

When I came back from the trip, I immediately set up coffee with "The Robster," as he likes to be called. Equal parts mentor and goofy uncle Dr. Rob and I started to have several meetings over coffees. When I told him I was writing this book and needed some help with the writing process, he pulled out his phone and connected me to his best connection in the world of writing.

At the time of the connection, this book was a haphazard outline and around 20,000 words. Every connection I've had feels God-ordained, and this one was particularly special to me. Charlie is a ghostwriter for one of the most famous non-fiction writers of our time. Hearing about his background created one of those moments in life when your mind rushes through a seemingly endless list of questions. Of course, I didn't want to mess up the meeting by showing up unprepared or with silly questions. It was like I was sitting down with the Michael Jordan of writing, and I didn't want to ask him how to dribble.

Charlie is one of the most humble people I know now. I'm so grateful he was willing to sit down with some random person and talk about God and writing and the business of writing. I can honestly say, along with God, Charlie is one of the few who has shaped this book the most. However, none of that would have happened for me if I had not been willing to invite Rob to coffee, have an open mind, and be ready to connect.

BUILD A NETWORK

Networking isn't a new concept. Throughout Israel's history, there have been connections, networking, and business dealings. In the Old Testament, these networks allowed Israel to flourish. We've mentioned it before, but it's clear God wants to accomplish His mission through us WITH others. Israel has many examples of this. If you pay attention to these examples, the Old Testament reads like a manual of how to handle your business dealings. From Solomon and David's advice on how to approach other Kings (with gifts and respect) to Jesus summing up the entire Biblical commandments (to love God and love others), there are numerous lessons and principles to adopt as a leader who networks well.

Unfortunately, networking sometimes gets a bad name. We've all been invited to a "network marketing" company pitch. A "party" with a friend where a must-have makeup product, state-of-the-art Tupperware, or a miraculous diet pill is pitched. These companies, as you know, encourage the seller to leverage the power of their network, group of friends, and family to sell their products. The hope is that you'll buy from your friend and even decide to throw your own party.

A more fun example of networking is found in the music industry. They call these "collaborations." You might not have thought of Toby Mac and Jamie Grace's song, "Hold Me," as networking, but their work shows off the power of networking. Toby Mac has a huge network available to him, given his platform. Most listeners of Christian Pop know who he is, and even people who don't tend to be familiar with his influence on Christian music. When he collaborates, he's purposefully sharing his network with whomever he collaborates with. It's no wonder now that Jamie Grace's singing career is taking off. She's wonderfully talented and might have had the same level of success due to her God-given talent. However, because of the power of the network she had with Toby, her career got a boost.

The goal of this chapter is to show that God wants you to be intentional around your relationships and intentional around connecting, too. Ultimately, you must trust that God is the provider and not the connection. Otherwise, when the fear of man sets in, the network effect is reversed, and the good fortune ends. In other words, you begin to focus too much on networking and not enough on serving your network.

KING HIRAM OF TYRE

When you read 2 Samuel, you see David's successful campaign to expand the kingdom and gain control of an area. Word of his victories spread throughout the region.

So widespread was his reputation that other nations began to send emissaries to David bringing gifts. This practice of kings sharing resources to gain support among other kings is a key point not to be missed. While it's not the sole purpose of networking, as kings, we are blessed to be a blessing. Proverbs says, "a sinner's wealth is stored up for the righteous (Proverbs 13:22)" and our job is to seize that and use it for His Kingdom.

As David expands his kingdom north, he begins to surround a small patch of coast that belonged to the Phoenicians. In what is now modern-day Lebanon, Tyre sat as an island fortress city that ruled the seas and had control of almost every sea trade route in the Mediterranean.

> "Now Hiram king of Tyre sent envoys to David, along with cedar logs and carpenters and stonemasons, and they built a palace for David. Then David knew that the Lord had established him as king over Israel and had exalted his kingdom for the sake of his people Israel."
> **— 2 Samuel 5:10 NIV**

1 Kings 5 - 10 tells us about this business relationship that lends us what we might need to understand how God can use our connections to grow his Kingdom. During King Hiram's reign, Tyre was the most important Phoenician city, a center of a trading empire. Historians would

call King Hiram one of the wealthiest kings in the world.[44][45]

Hiram was the ultimate connector. Controlling a small island in the Mediterranean, Hiram was the go-to person for pretty much anything. He had connections with Indian gold, spices, and skilled labor. With every new connection he made, new trade routes were established, and all parties usually flourished.

Hiram's success came from his intentionality. History tells us that prior to King Hiram's reign, Tyre was simply an empty island.[46] Hiram turned it into a hub, making it the center of trade in this area. When David became king and began to expand his territory, Hiram intentionally built the connection between them, not just to protect his assets but to create opportunities. Notice what Hiram did. He didn't simply bring gifts but rather sought to fulfill David's desires to build a temple or house for the Lord. While God forbade David from acting on this himself, He did not stop at providing resources for which to build the temple. This should remind us that our mission is often bigger than our lifetime! Without the connection to King Hiram, the temple might not have been built. Hiram's relationship with David continued to thrive throughout both of David's and Solomon's reigns.

As King David aged, he had materials and plans for the temple itself. When the time came for Solomon to rule, David's trusted business associate, King Hiram, was the one he chose to do the construction project. This business deal proved to be very fruitful. King Hiram would provide the materials and the skilled labor, while Solomon would provide the lower-skilled labor as well as food and olive oil.

It is interesting to note the influence that David and Solomon had on Hiram. History regards him as a pagan who worshiped Melqart, the god of Tyre. Hiram knew how to build temples for gods. However, he may very well have been converted by his interactions with those that worshipped the one true God.

> "Hiram king of Tyre replied by letter to Solomon: 'Because the Lord loves his people, he has made you their king.'"
> **— 2 Chronicles 2:11 NIV**

> "Praise be to the Lord today, for he has given David a wise son to rule over this great nation."
> **— 1 Kings 5:7 NIV**

Did his acknowledgment of the God of Israel save him? We won't ever know until we get to heaven. But while we're discussing building your own network, it's worth noting that you're here to be an influence but not to be influenced. Your influence for Christ in your network could very well cause someone else to be open to the truth.

Hiram and Solomon had a long-lasting business relationship, from building the temple to allowing the Jews to participate in the trade on the Mediterranean. Hiram placed trusted ship captains within Jewish fleets to allow them to get gold from India. Solomon gave King Hiram 20 cities, and Hiram gave him his daughter in marriage.

Both men go down as some of the wealthiest kings ever to walk the earth. It's also clear that neither would have had the success they had without their connection to one another. God will sometimes use others, both believers and non-believers, to benefit our mission. If you fail to be intentional about this, then you could very well miss out on the opportunity of your lifetime.

UNEQUALLY YOKED

As you are reading this, you might think back to where the Bible says in 2 Corinthians 6:14 not to be "unequally yoked" with unbelievers. Newer translations use the word "team-up" (NLT) or "bound" (AMP) to make it clearer. However, the image of a yoke is actually more descriptive.

A yoke is a device that binds animals together to do work, usually farming work. When two animals are yoked together, they are bound to one another. The stronger of the two animals leads, and the smaller animal is forced to follow the others' lead and help or be dragged along for the ride.

In my interpretation, yoking isn't simply working together; it's being bound in partnership with one another. In the business world, this would be called co-founding. I believe this arrangement represents a far more serious investment than choosing to co-labor with someone of a different faith background. After all, if God didn't want us to work together with unbelievers, then how would we influence them where they are?

I recognize, however, that the line is so thin you might wonder how to distinguish the difference. I suggest you ask yourself if the partnership you are considering entering could potentially drag you into situations you don't want to be in. Could it force you to overlook your convictions, ethics, or Christian values to partner with this person or in this context? If so, I would say this is what Paul meant when he said not to be yoked with unbelievers, and it will only cause you problems when you run into situations in which you differ on your values and ethos.

The good news is working with others is a choice you get to make. As I stated at the beginning of this book, preparation is key to being a kingdom driven leader. Take the time to prepare yourself before forging any binding partnerships by considering whether you are yoking yourself to a person that does not espouse your same faith in Christ.

Remember, when you're yoked, the one with the strongest influence is going to lead, so choose wisely.

NETWORKING WITH INTENTION

> "Jesus told his disciples: 'There was a rich man whose manager was accused of wasting his possessions. So, he called him in and asked him, 'What is this I hear about you? Give an account of your management, because you cannot be manager any longer.' The manager said to himself, 'What shall I do now? My master is taking away my job. I'm not strong enough to dig, and I'm ashamed to beg— I know what I'll do so that, when I lose my job here, people will welcome me into their houses.' So he called in each one of his master's debtors. He asked the first, 'How much do you owe my master?' 'Nine hundred gallons of olive oil,' he replied. The manager told him, 'Take your bill, sit down quickly, and make it four hundred and fifty.' Then he asked the second, 'And how much do you owe?' 'A thousand bushels of wheat,' he replied. He told him, 'Take your bill and make it eight hundred.' The master commended the dishonest manager because he had acted shrewdly. For the people of this world are more shrewd in dealing with their own kind than are the people of the light. I tell you, use worldly wealth to gain friends for yourselves, so that when it is gone, you will be welcomed into eternal dwellings."
> — **Luke 16:1-9 NIV**

What might be one of the most curious parables that Jesus ever taught is a lesson on networking. It might seem that He's condoning the dishonest behavior, but I believe He's commending the thought process, not the execution. The dishonest manager isn't doing a good thing, but he's leveraging his network for his own personal gain. This is like a politician who makes a few key votes for corporations so that he can continue his career as a lobbyist after he's no longer in power. What would happen if we, as believers, intentionally leverage our network for God's glory! That's the whole point of this chapter!

I have a friend who says, "networking is the key to life." I fully believe that to achieve our calling, God wants us to do that through our relationships with other people. In more than one instance, I've been contacted about an opportunity. Instead of taking advantage of the opportunity for myself, I connected the opportunity to someone in my sphere of influence. The impact of the opportunity would have been nice for me, but for the individuals I've connected, it's been truly impactful. Personally, I never feel more fulfilled than when I'm connecting two people that can help solve each other's problems.

When I look at some of the most successful kings, they had a strong inner circle, and they networked. David, Solomon, and Hiram are all documented networkers. However, Jesus mirrored this, and this parable (above) reminds us of some very practical ways we can network with intention.

THE VALUE OF A NETWORK

The best networkers understand that their database of contacts is their greatest asset. When businesses go to sell, it's the customer database that helps them get the value they want. When online companies get funded, they get big payouts based on the number of users they have or the size of their database.

In the *Power of Habit*, Charles Duhigg shows us the value of our network is more than just a list of contacts in our phone. Our network is where we will get inside information on new jobs, new opportunities and rely on when we need help to do something.[47]

The dishonest manager in the parable above was scrambling with no job and no real future. If it weren't for his network, he'd be out on the streets. Instead, he built a network of friends that gave him a place to stay.

Likewise, your network is likely where many of your opportunities will come from.

I DON'T CARE ABOUT YOU

There was a time when I ran a formalized networking meeting at a popular golf club. We routinely would have 40 or more guests in attendance. The concept was pretty simple. You show up to meet other people who were predisposed to give you business. It was a referral network.

If you have ever been in this environment, you've likely encountered the different personalities in the room. There's the guy that gives you a business card but doesn't even ask for your name or what you do. There are the wallflowers who stick to the sides of the room with little engagement. There all kinds of people approaching these events in different ways.

Usually, the light bulb goes off for these professional networkers when they realize that they shouldn't be trying to make sales because connections lead to greater opportunities than isolated sales. I remember one person said something that will always stick with me.

"Joshua, I don't care about you. I care about who you know."

While that's not the most eloquent way to put it, it encapsulates the whole idea I'm trying to make. This gentleman didn't want to sell me anything. He wanted to get to that point in our relationship where we could pass referrals to each other. He had a half-step in the right direction. Networking is at its best when both parties seek to add value to each other's lives, not just pass on referrals.

In my estimation, it's worth being repetitive here, so I'll say it again. Your Christian values of loving others first are absolutely the key to success in this arena. Be a giver here, and you'll see your network flourish. Be a connector, and you'll see the improvements in your kingdom. Seek first to understand people, always coming from a place of desiring to hear their

BUILD A NETWORK

story. Doing this will allow you to have deeper conversations and open up opportunities for you to minister to them.

Evaluate your network right now. Pull out your mobile device and look at your contact list. It's likely family, friends, coworkers, and a few people from church. That list is likely built by proximity. Chances are good if we polled every reader of this book and forced them to dig deep on those contacts, we'd all average around 150 contacts.

British anthropologist Robin Dunbar proposed in 1990 that the average person can comfortably maintain only 150 stable relationships. Even after 30 years, multiple iterations of phones and social media, this number still holds up.

Dunbar explained, "the number of people you would not feel embarrassed about joining uninvited for a drink if you happened to bump into them in a bar." The point here is that the number of people in your network is finite. Maybe for you, it's 100, and for someone else, it's 160, but it's not thousands. It's a relatively small number.

Over the years, Dunbar's research has been debated.[48] While some could argue that you can have a much larger network now with technology or based on personality, you inevitably have more shallow relationships the more you try to maintain them. The important thing isn't the exact number but realizing that this number is small. If you want to influence people, you may even have to go smaller.

With a number this small, you can apply the same principles you might in your business network to your personal network. Great salespeople top-grade their network. Because great salespeople don't sell to their network but rather their network's network, they see their connections as their "team." Top performers in sales continue to add power players to their network while diminishing the time they spend with those that don't open up their network.

This is a book about growing yourself, your leadership, and your network so you can grow the kingdom. Kingdom growth only comes from intentionality. This area of our lives is one of the most overlooked. I think one reason is that we'd never want to think so judgmentally about people. It feels cold to treat your friends and acquaintances as some reality tv game show. I'm not talking about a robotic approach to friendships, but rather an approach that says, "Yes, you should choose your friends." Despite the many things you can't control, you can control who you are in a relationship with (aside from family).

As you improve your network, we must remind ourselves that we represent Christ and that each person is valuable and worth whatever time or effort you spend with them. At the same time, you should evaluate your current network and decide who should stay and who should go so you can maximize your effort and time with people well.

It's simple math. There are four types of people in your life, and you can define them based on quadrants. There will be people that add tremendous value and those that take or subtract your energy. There will be those that multiply your efforts and those that divide your resources. When you evaluate your network, you should be on the lookout for these different types of people so that you can be intentional about surrounding yourself with more value adders and multipliers rather than subtractors or dividers.

- » **Adders** - People who add to your life are the vast majority of people. They are great people to know and do life with, and they add something special to your life in one area or another. When you spend time with them, you don't feel drained.
- » **Subtractors** – Anyone can be a subtractor on a given day, but what should concern you is if they are subtracting daily. Subtractors often have negative attitudes and complain about life. We all have bad days or even bad seasons, but subtractors often have bad years and decades. Often subtractors aren't intentionally trying to drag anyone down.

- » **Multipliers** – People who multiply change your life. This could be financial, but more often, these people lift your life in other ways. People who multiply your life are people that you marry and try to do life with. You feel energized with them, and when you think of that person that brings you the most joy, you're likely thinking of a multiplier.
- » **Dividers** – People who bring division to your life should be removed. As Christians, we're called to love all people, and dividers require extra grace to do so. Unless you're actively ministering to someone in this category, you should actively try to limit your time with them. When I talk about people who divide, you might think of angry, abusive people, but that's not always the case. A divider is someone who stresses you out, the person that you just feel tired after talking with.

The point of these classifications isn't to cast judgment. Instead, it's a shorthand way of classifying your sphere of influence. As I went through the different groups, names probably came to mind. Write those down. This isn't a game of *Survivor*. In other words, I'm not suggesting that you walk up to people that drain you and subtract from your life and say, "The tribe has spoken. It's time for you to go." I'm saying be intentional about your relational equity. Intentionally spend less time with those that drag you down and invest your energy in those that add the most value.

Like David and the King of Tyre, kingdom driven leaders need partners. Christ calls us to love all and yet not be unequally yoked. This is a challenge because we often like our relationship to be organic. In order to achieve this level of intentionality, you need a system. A system will help you with boundaries and give you direction for what is one of your most valuable assets, your relationships. Once mastered, a system frees you to focus on the individual and gives you the confidence of what to expect.

Most people recoil at the idea of systematizing relationships. They may think it feels robotic and inauthentic. A system can feel fake and forced if you don't value people first. Systems are all around us. You can see them easily in business and also in your church. If systems work well in these environments, why wouldn't they work in relationships too?

The interesting thing is that even with the right mindset, I've found it takes time to grow the relationship. This likely means getting together one on one with someone over lunch or coffee. I will help as many people as I can when I'm in a group, but when it comes to helping others through connections, I must go deeper one-on-one.

To go back to the big picture, we want to grow as kingdom driven leaders. Jesus tells us to be the greatest, we need to be the biggest servant. The key then to networking with intention is to intentionally evaluate the relationship based on the biggest impact you can bring them. Because you have finite time and energy, you have to evaluate your contacts.

Jesus didn't pick just anyone to be his disciples; He picked a certain kind of man that had an element of hardiness and grit to him. He selected hard-working fishermen, a crafty tax collector, and a passionate zealot with hopes of overthrowing the Roman rule, just to name a few. He was gracious with the masses and everyone who called on Him, but notice He was also intentional about spending time with a select few.

Some of you reading this might be inclined to be very systematic with it. You'll set the coffee dates like a business appointment, and you'll go to lunch with something to achieve. For those of you that need it, here's a little agenda help for creating a systematic approach to networking or, as I like to call it, connecting on purpose.

CONNECT ON PURPOSE

When creating a system for building relationships, I suggest you start by focusing on connecting with others on purpose. Talk about what their big goals are. Be accountability partners for one another. Get them talking about their "why." Your goal for the relationship should be to help them move forward with their own goals. As a kingdom driven leader, you want to impact people for the kingdom. This doesn't have to only happen in a church setting. Helping people achieve their professional and personal goals often helps them in their spiritual life as well.

As you are meeting with people, you should take notes. Not only will this show that you are listening to them, but it will help you keep track of the progress you are making in your relationship as well as the progress that you are making together. Hopefully, at some point, you'll know their hopes and dreams.

It'd be easy to read this section and forget this is all based on Biblical principles. These networking connections work best when there is a directive in which you both feel led to serve, whether you tackle a mission together or simply help each other with independent missions by sharing wisdom and contacts.

I tend to gravitate toward practical and logical thinking, and I resist the urge to go into CRM (Client Relationship Manager) analysis and reviews and simply tell you to find something that works. Whether it's notes on your phone, an app, or paper, you should track your progress.

REVIEW YOUR PROGRESS

In business, we say, "inspect what you expect." The reason you should take notes and track your progress is to see if you are helping each other move toward the relational goals you set. I like to ask these questions listed in order of importance.

1. Is our relationship helping us get closer to God?

2. Is our relationship helping us expand God's Kingdom?
3. Is our relationship helping us be better spouses, parents, and/or friends to others?
4. Is our relationship helping us personally?
5. Is our relationship helping us professionally?

If you can answer yes to these questions, you'll find yourself living out the Great Commission. You'll be growing your network, your kingdom, and your influence in people's lives. While you may make deeper overall connections with like-minded Christians, mastering networking can often allow you to influence someone that isn't a believer for the kingdom as well.

Let's pause for a brief moment. Think of the business leaders you know or wish to know. Do they love Jesus? Are they passionately on fire for God? Most of the ones I know are passionate, but not about the things of God. We sometimes have to remind ourselves that our number one mission is to share the Good News of the love of God through the death of His Son (Matthew 28:16-20). While systematic networking may seem like a strange thing to include in this book, I believe that if you apply these, you will find yourself with opportunities to share your faith.

To my surprise, I regularly find myself sitting with an unbeliever discussing a deal we might make together when they ask me, "Do you really believe the Bible?" Something struck them as different about the way I live my life. Although it might be somewhat boring to them, they see how I prioritize God and serve my family.

The world has popularized the idea of an entrepreneurial hustle that suggests success is measured by the effort you put in and your bank account. The combination of being passionate about business and family seems incompatible due to the perception that you have to choose one or the other but that you cannot have both.

It's surprising because I never intentionally bring it up. I'm guilty of using "church-ease" or "Christian vocabulary," but I've never intentionally asked anyone where they stand with Jesus. It's something I'm working to be more intentional about because I want to expand the kingdom. However, it's my example of conviction and faith that causes them to ask me questions, and it's your example that will cause the same thing to happen to you.

THREE KEY CHARACTERISTICS OF YOUR NETWORK

When we started this section, I wrote about the different groups of people and how you should be intentional around those with whom you spend your time. Just like Jesus had twelve disciples he spent more time with than the rest, you too should handpick the key people in your network.

Every kingdom driven leader needs to have at least three characteristics among the people in their network. Unfortunately, for most, that means separate groups, but not always. You need a group of believing friends, much like Jesus had, that could support you in a time of anguish. This is crucial for the road ahead. You should always seek God first, yet there are times when a "friend sticks closer than a brother," and you need someone to talk to or do life with. This is the same group that has the right to hold you in check if you start trusting yourself or your connections too much.

You also need a group of friends that understand the marketplace and the business world. This can be the same group, but it rarely is. The fact is that business owners have a unique set of problems to solve that an employee does not have. Leaders with direct reports also have a different set of problems. Having people around you that understand these leadership dynamics and challenges are going to be crucial.

Finally, you need wise counsel. Again, this can be the same group of people, but it's rare for you to have friends that can be all three to you. I have found that my best business and wise counsel friends tend to be less sympathetic to general problems. I'm very guilty of this myself. I tend to see life as a problem to be solved versus a relationship to be had. Business mentors, like the aforementioned King Hiram, could be used by God to help you solve a big business problem. However, those same mentors often aren't the ones to go to for family advice or spiritual counsel.

The point is that it's rare for people to be intentional about finding good fits for their network. Most people choose friends based on proximity because that's what is natural and easy. Your personal friends are from school or work. Your church friends from the small group that's closest to your church or home. Any other friends that you count on might be considered family members.

It turns out that you can truly formalize the process of growing your network. Some may be naturally gifted "schmoozers," but for others, the process can be learned. As someone who experiences high anxiety around individuals, I can attest to this. You simply need to know what to do and how to do it, and I believe it starts with making sure you have the right kind of people in your network.

WHO DO YOU KNOW THAT I SHOULD KNOW?

One easy way to begin being intentional about growing your network is by adding this question to your conversational repertoire. This question is super practical because its focus is on building your network. Having a canned question might feel awkward. I know it did to me at first. However, the question takes the pressure off the person answering because it's transparent. After you've built some rapport with a new contact in a business setting, try this question out. The idea for this question comes from a good source.

This is a question I learned from John C. Maxwell. To get a bigger picture of this, you could elaborate. "Now that you know what I'm trying to accomplish, who do you know that I should know?" Most people genuinely want to help you if they have the time, see the value and have the ability to do so.

The research will tell us that when you ask generic questions like "what do you do?" the brain literally shuts off. In fact, both party's brains go to sleep for this conversation. Your brain treats it exactly like a habit. You've heard these questions so often, and often, they aren't meaningful interactions. The science says that your brain is attempting to conserve energy for more meaningful interactions! If you want to grow your network purposefully, you must start now by asking better questions.

To do this, first, spend some time asking yourself what type of person you need in your life. You might think of a few types of people, such as referral sources if you are in sales or wise parents if you're struggling in a particular area of raising your children. Perhaps you think about your dream of writing a book and know you need a mentor in that area. Use the previous section as a guide as well. Are you missing that business mentor or maybe just a brother or sister with whom you can do life?

Being intentional here means not relying on proximity for your network. Imagine if you conducted all of your life and every choice you made based purely on convenience. The danger is that you would likely miss out on some great relationships. Most times, I've experienced the best parts of life when I have intentionally pushed myself outside my comfort zone.

As a believer, I am convinced you can have "divine connections." Sometimes in prayer, I'll be reminded of a name to connect with. At least initially, I would pursue any thought that comes to mind. Often, I'll meet with people to see where it takes me. Many times, I'll connect the two individuals (the one I'm meeting with and the one whose name came to mind) and find out later it was a great connection to move something in their life forward.

THEY DIDN'T ASK

I'll never forget what one business leader told me. At the time, he was the largest real estate franchise owner with businesses all over Atlanta and in Florida. This leader is a savvy salesperson that understands business systems and people, and it's very rare to be a master of both. He and his wife are king and queen in their own right. They've also launched several charitable giving initiatives to benefit the less fortunate children all over Atlanta.

He said he would hear people say, "I wish I could have coffee with you" or "I wish I had someone like you to mentor me." He told me that he doesn't have coffee with them or spend time with those people for only one reason.

They didn't ask.

When he said this, I was surprised. I know I assumed he would be too busy to have time for me. I think the perception that high-quality contacts are too busy is one that causes a lot of would-be networkers to miss out on great opportunities. There are people right now that want to share their wisdom with you, but it's up to you to ask. The wonderful news for both of you is that now you have a plan that will guide you through that relationship.

EVERY KING NEEDS A PRIEST

Every kingdom driven leader needs a priest who has a clear mission and vision for the church Body as a whole. This is different from a prophet. Your inner circle should be full of prophets that can speak God's Word over you.

It's not a requirement for salvation, and I'm not even talking about being in a church. A priest isn't someone who is a replacement for your effort to hear from God either. A priest or prophet is that friend, mentor, or pastor that spends their life in God's presence. Typically, although not always, the priest is tied to your mission.

Every kingdom leader needs a priest for accountability, encouragement, and wisdom. In a traditional sense, a "priest" is like your pastor. The pastor can offer an eternal perspective if you get lost in the weeds. Because a priest's occupation is to spend time with God, they often can see things that you might not. This is especially true if you're early on this journey. Their position often lets them see the big picture of many people's lives.

Many times, a Pastor's vision can help shape a king's own vision. If the pastor has a big enough vision, it will often inspire the kings of his church to not only increase their resource involvement but also volunteer their time, which is a kingdom driven leader's most precious commodity. You can often see this during building campaigns or special projects. For example, if your heart is for the homeless and the pastor already has a vision for the homeless in the city, then it could be a match made in heaven.

The submission to authority, to the truth with love, is what a king needs and why a king needs a priest. For many kings, they are accountable to no one other than God. While that accountability always takes priority, it's the pastor that kings should submit to. I'm not suggesting submitting blindly or following a leader that isn't following Christ. I'm suggesting that every king needs that person that is chasing God and can challenge them to do the same.

Kingdom driven leaders don't need help thinking bigger for business strategy. However, many times leaders don't think big enough when it comes to ministry. That's a great opportunity for the pastor here. The key for the leader is not feeling envious that the pastor is more significant in God's Kingdom. That's pretty much the point of this book. Your role as a kingdom driven leader most likely is bigger than just helping a pastor achieve their vision. Your personal "king" vision might be to help others achieve their missions with your resources. Just like Solomon could not build the temple without Hiram, a pastor's vision will likely require the aid of kingdom driven leaders.

In the business world, when you want to accomplish a project, you assemble a team together. You don't just hire people who are the closest to you, rather you pick individuals based on their talents. If the project is particularly difficult, you might bring in a subject matter expert. A kingdom driven leader must take that same deliberateness of project management and apply it in their spiritual walk. The biggest difference here is that while the business world is often about to give and take, the kingdom driven world is measured only by how much you can give and serve.

17

Grow Your Giving

When I meet with businesspeople giving is the one principle of being a kingdom driven leader that they understand without much explanation. Most professing Christians give to some organization or a charity. As discussed before, most of us have some holy discontent around injustices around the world. Just like every other aspect of being a kingdom driven leader, you must be intentional around this area as well. I'm not talking about the kind of giving where you write a check because you felt compelled by an emotional commercial. I'm talking specifically about making an internal decision of the cause's importance to your values and adding it as a line item on your budget.

Giving is anything over and above the tithe. Here's a great way to intentionally grow your giving. Add 1% to your budget. You'd have your tithe at 10% and 1% for a "giving account." The trick to this is that you grow this percentage year over year. So that 20 years from now, you're giving 20% away. You might think my math is funny here. Tithing isn't giving; it's returning to God what He gave you. Because of that, I don't even count it when I think of giving, however for accounting purposes, yes, you're giving 30%.

People fail in this area because they have a someday attitude. They say to themselves, "someday, I'll give more." How much better would it be if you did this intentionally? What if you had a budget set aside for giving and could give as the need arose? As someone who loves to debate,

I know some might say that when you budget this way, it takes faith out of the equation. I would counter to say that it requires faith to set aside the money in the first place, and it takes faith to know when God wants you to give and how much.

Just because you budget the giving doesn't mean you have to stop there. Every year that we've added 1% to our budget, we have felt like God asked us for more. Almost inevitably, there was an opportunity to give that required a little bit more than what we had set aside. Here's the thing about the budget. Had we not had budgeted, then we wouldn't have been able to stretch our faith and give. For example, one year, we were able to give to two projects in Cambodia while also giving to a project locally. If we didn't budget, we simply wouldn't have had the funds to do all three.

I also know that you might be uncomfortable with this thought process. It's only natural, after all, because I'm talking about your money – perhaps one of the most controversial topics. However, the tithe protects your provision and opens up the windows of heaven. It is the starting line for giving. It's great if you've never tithed to see what happens in your life afterward. All of the sudden, you're living off less and doing more. As Robert Morris says in *The Blessed Life*,[51] "tithing isn't giving, it's returning."

With giving (above the tithe), there's a different kind of blessing that comes. It's not giving to receive, but rather an experience of expectation of wondering what God will do next with your life. It could be that through your giving, something else opens up for you to use your gifts and talents to reach others for Christ.

I could easily spend the next 100 pages talking about what giving can do in the spiritual realm and how it might change your life here on Earth, but let me break it down into two things that every kingdom driven leader needs to understand about giving.

GIVING BREAKS DOWN PRIDE

Giving is often the only tangible caring I might do each month. I give because I care. Time spent leading should look like caring. Many leaders are leaders because they can execute efficiently. Pride is an enemy of every person and every king. Giving is one thing that keeps me humble when I get to be part of something bigger than myself.

GIVING IS ETERNAL

Long after your accolades are dust or littering the junkyard, your giving will still reap dividends. Whether it's a church building where you get to participate in souls being saved, water for impoverished nations, or simply giving to the local food bank, God sees what we give, and it's one of the only things that is counting in our heavenly scoreboard.

ANOTHER CIRCLE

When you're consumed with anything other than God, you miss your true purpose. What's required is a value transformation, the realization that He owns it all and has given it to you to distribute. The value transformation is the turning point. It's the ah-ha moment when Christians go from just giving out of compulsion to understanding and embracing the privilege of giving to a mission.

One of the best messages I've ever heard[52] on how to truly become a master at giving comes from the concept of the circle. In this case, it's the circle of blessing. You put everything you could ever want inside the circle. This idea is powerful because you are deciding ahead of time where to draw the line. The concept is like a budget. However, instead of a monthly or yearly budget, you create a life budget. We'll go into more detail below, but it's deciding today about your strategy for giving so that tomorrow you can defeat the "wanting" in your life.

You can't care for the vulnerable if you're trying to figure out how to get more for yourself. You could argue that you could give to a cause. That would be true. However, if you don't settle now what you want financially, then when money comes, you might be limited with what you can truly do with it. To me, this is what's needed to go from really good to *great*.

The best way to teach your children about temptation and prepare them for it is to set up boundaries and role-play the events. The best way to train people who work for you is to set up boundaries and role play with them. You decide beforehand what you will do before it happens so that you're more likely to get the result you desire, even when you might be weak or unskilled. It makes sense that the best way to carry out our mission as kings is to set boundaries and role-play the concepts.

The circle of blessing isn't just a clever marketing word for "budget." It's also extremely practical for other areas of our life. Dave Ramsey, the popular Radio Host Entertainer and creator of "Financial Peace University," says a budget is you telling your money where to go before it ever gets there[53]. Budgeting doesn't have to be a scary word. Thankfully, the circle of blessing doesn't have to be as detailed as a budget to be effective.

DRAW THE CIRCLE

This exercise is fun. You get to dream as big as you possibly want. You could even say, "I'm not dreaming big enough," and then multiply your dream by a factor of ten. Then you draw your circle. You can put your beach house, your Lamborghini in there, and yearly trips to Paris if you want. The point of the circle isn't to stop you from having luxury in life, it's for you to know when to stop growing your lifestyle so that you can be free to give. Thinking about these things in advance helps you create a vision for your finances as a resource to be used to expand the kingdom. There are practical resources for budgeting. Our family didn't find any that fit how we received income, which can fluctuate wildly from one month to the next. Using percentages and "rules" for accounts helped us far more, so we designated a percentage for giving. When we do this, our giving continues to grow as our income does. The takeaway is that the circle of blessing encapsulates a lens through which you now view possessions and giving through. How does this beach home impact our giving? How does this new car, vacation, tv, subscription, eating out, or anything else affect our mission?

It's interesting, but the actions here spill over as well. Not only do we want to give more money, but more time and more energy to things that glorify God. Truly, where your treasure is, your heart will follow (Matthew 6:21).

No one should be judged for "only" tithing. All things being equal, it's clear that if I can give my time, talent and treasure, I'll make a greater kingdom impact than I would if I simply gave only my time or my time and talent and some of my treasure. Decide today how you want to give.

My last point on this subject is to decide today. Not just decide today what you will do when you make it, but rather decide to start giving today. Make this plan, then execute it today. Someday means never.

> "Whoever can be trusted with very little can also be trusted with much"
> **— Luke 16:10 NIV**

Start today and create a habit of giving. You can't wait until you're successful enough or "made it." That's because no one ever "makes it." Behind every success is often years of hard work. I heard a funny saying that Jack Canfield, author of *Chicken Soup for the Soul*, said, "I'm a 40-year overnight success story."[54] If you were to google overnight success quotes, you'd see a page full of people that are immensely successful that worked their tail off, and you only just learned about them.

The point is, giving intentionally is work, so you must make it a habit. Then as you're stewarding what God has given you, He can trust you to expand your responsibility and know that giving will be a big part of what you're doing. We're blessed to be a blessing.

With the foundations we talked about previously, giving with a clear vision is like leveling up your faith and humility as a kingdom driven leader. However, when you tap into what giving has to offer, you'll truly be making an impact for His kingdom and begin reigning with Christ.

SECTION III
REIGNING WITH CHRIST

18

Reigning with Christ

Every Christian is familiar with the story of Jesus' resurrection. We hear this story every Easter. However, in all the years of hearing this story, I had never heard it shared where Jesus is being depicted as a warrior king until I heard a message shared by Pastor Robert Morris of Gateway Church[55].

He explained that before Jesus came, the Devil had dominion over the earth. This is evidenced by Jesus' non-response when Satan tempted Him.

> "The devil led him up to a high place and showed him in an instant all the kingdoms of the world. And he said to him, 'I will give you all their authority and splendor; it has been given to me, and I can give it to anyone I want to. If you worship me, it will all be yours.'"
> **— Luke 4:5-7 NIV**

Jesus didn't argue with Satan about this point at all. I am confident that if Satan had been lying about this, Jesus would have called him out on it. Jesus was preparing Himself to take the authority back by force.

When Jesus went to the cross for our sake, He not only paid for us but during those three days, He was busy defeating Satan and taking the authority back. His first words to His disciples when He came back from the grave announced this fact.

> "Then Jesus came to them and said, 'All authority in heaven and on earth has been given to me.'"
> — **Matthew 28:18 NIV**

I had never really thought about it in this way. Jesus, the King, came and gave up His life for us. He also went to hell and defeated Satan and brought back with Him the authority to have dominion (through Him) over the world. Let that sink in for a moment.

This is the authority that we have through Christ to reign and rule with Him!

GROW IN INFLUENCE

As a kingdom driven leader in the world's marketplace, you need to grow your level of influence to grow your impact on the kingdom. This can and likely will happen naturally, but as we've seen in previous chapters, you'll need to be intentional about growing your influence if you want to make a greater kingdom impact. As you start to lead yourself and be intentional in valuing others, people will naturally gravitate towards your leadership.

If you read the account of King David's son, Absalom, you might be in such shock at how he overthrew his dad in 2 Samuel 15 that you miss the details of what he did. He was very intentional about growing his influence, albeit with the desire to overthrow his father, the king. However, it shows the key to growing your influence is being deliberate about growing relationships.

> "Whenever anyone approached him to bow down before him, Absalom would reach out his hand, take hold of him, and kiss him. Absalom behaved in this way toward all the Israelites who

> came to the king asking for justice, and so he stole the hearts of the people of Israel."
> **— 2 Samuel 15:5-6 NIV**

He was sitting at the city gates and intentionally built influence to undermine his dad's kingdom. This is particularly significant because usually, only the King would be at the city gates. In Biblical times, Kings throughout history judged the people from the city gates. In addition, anything of importance usually occurred at the gates. From marriage contracts to judicial hearings, all of this was done by the gates.

Absalom didn't just whisper to the people; he went where the King should be and started building his kingdom by assuming responsibility. What better way to overthrow the king than by doing what the king was supposed to do? This is the exact strategy that you, as King, need to have. While the story of Absalom is one of deceit, your story is one of destiny. Assume your rightful place in the Kingdom and begin to win the hearts of the people.

Absalom's strategy was twofold, to win the hearts of the people and to create doubt in their minds about David's leadership. We'll get a closer look at the enemies of the king in later chapters but watch how Absalom wins the hearts of the people.

The passage we read earlier says Absalom would reach for those kneeling to honor him, and he would kiss them. He was fully engaged with them as individuals. He wasn't preoccupied or aloof. He touched them, held them, looked them in the eye, listened to their complaints, and kissed them. This was akin to greeting them as family members whom he cared for and loved.

Absalom's plan worked because it satisfied the people's need for belonging. He managed to convince "David's subjects" to join/become "Absalom's friends" by showing that he cared. He was seen as being approachable, which was not a common characteristic for a King.

This tactic eventually helped him unseat King David, who was heralded as the greatest king to ever rule Israel because he listened to the people and valued them, which grew his influence every day.

As you network through life, you must fully engage with the people you want to influence. Influence is something that someone gives you when you've earned their trust. You can only earn trust by showing that you care. It happens through actions. However, it's not often accomplished through grandiose actions; rather, it's the little things like focusing your attention on the other person and intentionally listening. Be approachable and always listen, and your influence will grow.

JESUS VALUES PEOPLE

The most influential person to ever walk the earth has a lot to teach us about growing our influence. It might be easy to dismiss what Jesus did because, well, He's Jesus. However, the methods He used were the same that work today.

Jesus saw people for who they were to Him. He was sent to save them, so He looked at them through eternal lenses that were set ablaze with a deep love for them. He didn't just listen to their needs, but He actively listened.

Any couple can tell you there is a difference between reading your texts while listening to your spouse versus looking them in the eye and setting aside other distractions. The difference between the two is engagement. Jesus was engaged with others.

Jesus didn't just make people feel valuable by being a great conversationalist. He was willing to hold people accountable for their sins. I've heard of grace and truth being coined as "the velvet hammer." When you correct someone in love, it doesn't carry the same kind of sting it does when it's just truth.

In John 8, we see Jesus' response to the woman caught in adultery. The crowd of accusers was ready to kill her, and they ask Jesus what they should do. It's here that Jesus' famous words, "let the one who has never sinned throw the first stone," left everyone speechless. After the accusers go away, He speaks to the woman.

> "Has no one condemned you?"
>
> "No one, sir," she said.
>
> "Then neither do I condemn you," Jesus declared. "Go now and leave your life of sin."
> **— John 8:11 NIV**

Jesus acknowledged her sin and told her to sin no more. He didn't condemn her or make her feel bad about what she did. Instead, He spoke the truth in love and extended grace. He did the same for us so that we can value others.

JESUS SAW THE INDIVIDUAL

Whether it's little Zacchaeus, the woman at the well, or the tax collector, you get a sense that Jesus "saw" them. The only thing that I can compare this to is when you first see your spouse walking down the aisle. There is something special about that walk where everything fades, and there is just you and your spouse. It's no wonder the Bible is full of wedding language. We are called "His Bride," after all. God loves us so passionately, so intentionally, and so intimately. It's not hard to draw the conclusion that He also loved the people this way when He walked the Earth.

What Jesus did with each one of the people He interacted with was "see" them for who they were and how valuable they were to Him. He did this by seeing, touching, and listening. Much like our Absalom example, Jesus was 100 percent present in the moment. While He did not have the technological distractions we do today, no generation is exempt from their own form of distraction. And the Bible was clear that He had to make a special effort to get solitude. Jesus was constantly around people and being pulled in every direction.

Great politicians understand this better than most. They are constantly being asked questions, they are often found on both sides of an issue, and yet, the most effective politicians can grab your hand, look you in the eye and communicate value. Take that same thought and multiply it when it comes to the Savior of the world. He came for the one, and He loved the one.

JESUS PRACTICED ACTIVE LISTENING

If you want to grow your influence in the lives of others around you, you'll have to grow your ability to actively listen. If you were to research listening, you'd find study after study on it. The writings on listening in the last decade might reveal it's a bit of a lost art. If you google it, you'll find pretty much the same advice. To listen well, you should make eye contact, affirm the person with some encouraging words, parrot back what the person says, and ask questions.

One study conducted by Jack Zenger and Joseph Folkman at the Harvard Business Review studied almost 3,500 participant leaders and managers.[56] Of that group, they took the top 5 percent considered to be the best listeners to discover what great listeners do. Their premise was to ask, "How do you listen so that the other person is 'heard?'"

Their study found that there is some distinct characteristic of good liste-ners. Although most of these traits are familiar, they are different enough that it's worth looking into, as they are often attributed to the difference between being a good listener and a great listener.

Contrary to the "be silent and listen" approach, active listeners engage in the dialog creating a two-way connection. While the silent approach is much better than the "waiting to speak" approach, to be a great listener, you need to engage in the conversation without interrupting.

The only way you can do that is by creating a sense of safety in the conversation by seeing it as cooperative rather than competitive. Many helpful leaders tend to look for errors in reasoning and prepare to communicate opposing views or arguments. When you want to be an active listener, you don't have to agree with the person speaking, but you can't approach it like you are trying to win a debate. You can disagree. However, you must do it in a way that conveys value as if you are truly helping and not merely trying to "win."

As I mentioned earlier, safety to be heard includes being free of distractions of things like a phone or looking around. Experts also agree eye contact is a fundamental key to being a great listener.

Up to 80 percent of our communication is nonverbal. The expression on our face, the tone of our voice, and our overall body language communicates far more than just the words we say. To be an effective active listener, you need to be able to observe these cues. While observing the speaker, look out for emotional ranges in which their words get faster, or the volume gets higher as well as the opposite. This is where knowing how to encourage or be supportive will come in. These emotional cues can help you with your response or feedback if needed.

While this is a tough assignment, the research was clear. The best listeners gave feedback that continued the discussion with thoughtful questions. Typically, people complain about someone not listening, especially when they feel like you are trying to solve their problem. However, the research shows that when you are fully engaged and people feel heard, they are open to receiving your opinion.

In other words, when you've heard and valued their opinion, they are open to receiving yours. You've probably heard it said, "People don't care how much you know until they know how much you care."

Zenger and Folkman go on to suggest that active listening done by the top 5 percent of leaders is more like a trampoline than a sponge.

> "While many of us have thought of being a good listener being like a sponge that accurately absorbs what the other person is saying, instead, what these findings show is that good listeners are like trampolines. They are someone you can bounce ideas off of — and rather than absorbing your ideas and energy, they amplify, energize, and clarify your thinking. They make you feel better not merely passively absorbing, but by actively supporting. This lets you gain energy and height, just like someone jumping on a trampoline." [57]

In other words, ask questions that reveal your curiosity about the person. You're not a detective looking trying to solve someone's problem, you're a friend trying to understand the speaker's heart. Active listeners like Jesus asked questions to get a better understanding. When we read the questions, we know He was illustrating a point or bringing enlightenment. The receiver of the question felt heard because of the deep level of the question.

Ultimately, we might not get it right all the time, but if we are striving to become better listeners, we'll grow in our influence. With the right heart and motivation, active listening can make a huge impact.

JESUS CALLED YOU

You are called to be an influencer, not to be influenced. Whether it was the Samaritan woman at the well that Jesus went out of His way to connect with or answering Nicodemus' questions, you get a sense of how intensely Jesus listened. You can only grow your influence through being intentional, and one of the most powerful ways to do that is by actively listening.

Throughout this book, we've been building the foundation so that you can begin to not just walk with Christ but reign with Him. To actively listen and serve another person, you have to be humble. You have to approach the interaction without any expectations about what you might get. Having a teachable spirit and understanding that God is your provider frees you up to focus on others.

As a kingdom driven leader, you are strategic and eternally focused on growing the kingdom. You understand in your humility that you cannot accomplish anything without Christ, but if you are submitted and driving after Christ, you can reign with Him and grow your influence. As your influence grows, so will your impact. All this work from this book doesn't just build your character but creates a launching pad for you to launch an offensive, an offensive action to take back territory from the enemy for the kingdom.

19

Launch Offensives

Biblical kings launched offensives to take territory back from their ene-mies. The warrior King David might be the most prolific, but there were other kings that left their mark on the battlefield as well. King Uzziah most notably not only took back cities but built strong towers and war machines that the Bible describes as early catapults. Amazingly, this predates the Greek invention of the catapult.

However, we are not fighting a physical battle any longer. One king that launched spiritual offensives with his relationship with God was Hezekiah. Few kings are honored the way he is in Israel's history. Even today, you can visit Israel and see the care that Israel has taken to preserve his tunnels firsthand.

Hezekiah reigned over Judah at a time when Israel fell to the Assyrians. Chaos surrounded Judah at that time. Turmoil with allies in Egypt and new empires rising up made matters worse, but the Bible says there were none like Hezekiah before or after him.

> "Hezekiah trusted in the Lord, the God of Israel. There was no one like him among all the kings of Judah, either before him or after him. He held fast to the Lord and did not stop following him; he kept the commands the Lord had given Moses. And the Lord was with him; he was successful in whatever he undertook. He rebelled against the king of Assyria and did not serve him. From

watchtower to fortified city, he defeated the Philistines, as far as Gaza and its territory."
— **2 Kings 18: 5-8**

Hezekiah is a great example of a kingdom driven leader. When I originally started writing, he was the king's story I opened with. His rule reminds me so much of what it's like to run a company. He was running the kingdom in the middle of chaos, with threats of a hostile takeover were looming.

He trusted completely in God, as evidenced by his work to remove high places and purify the temple. During his reign, war was all around, and he made strategic moves to protect Israel that are still visible there today. He built the broad wall and the famous "Hezekiah Tunnels," which brought fresh water from the Kedron Valley springs to the city.

Hezekiah grew his influence and network. Because of his leadership, Jerusalem had a time of prosperity in the middle of chaos. Prophets like Isaiah, Amos, and Micah flourished during this time as well.

The business metaphors are just too prevalent for me, not to mention them. While the world said, "You will fail," Hezekiah trusted God. Instead of running from the problem, he did things to strengthen his position to allow him the ability to withstand a "shift in the market."

The Assyrian army had just defeated Israel. The Assyrians were known for their warrior nature. All males were required to serve in the military, and history records them as brutal when it came to dealing with women and slaves. When they came to conquer you, they didn't just come with swords drawn. They bullied you first. Their reputations were such that death or becoming a willing slave was better than the alternative defeat on the battlefield.

When they threatened a nation, one of their tactics wasn't just to communicate with the king and messengers. No, they would use ancient loudspeakers to threaten the people, casting doubt on the leadership and the protection that a kingdom's god offered.

This is exactly what happened in Judah. It's even recorded biblically where Hezekiah complained to the Assyrians about talking to his people. Although threatened, Hezekiah didn't rely on his allies, such as Egypt. He relied on the Lord.

> "When King Hezekiah heard this, he tore his clothes and put on sackcloth and went into the temple of the Lord."
> **— 2 Kings 19:1 NIV**

Tearing clothes and putting on sackcloth was a way to show humility. He then went and sought wisdom from the Prophet Isaiah to get a word from the Lord. The Lord heard his cries.

> "This is what the Lord says: Do not be afraid of what you have heard—those words with which the underlings of the king of Assyria have blasphemed me. Listen! When he hears a certain report, I will make him want to return to his own country, and there I will have him cut down with the sword.'"
> **— 2 Kings 19:6-7 NIV**

Jerusalem was threatened by the reigning world empire of the time, the Assyrian kingdom. Hezekiah humbled himself, and God made them go away. It was almost like a fairy tale – except that's not what happened. Sennacherib continued to threaten Israel. "Do not let the god you depend on deceive you" (2 Kings 19:10). We've all heard that one before in the Garden of Eden. "Did God really say?"

The enemy taunted and threatened, and yet Hezekiah was steadfast, strong, and courageous."

> "It is true, Lord, that the Assyrian kings have laid waste these nations and their lands. They have thrown their gods into the fire and destroyed them, for they were not gods but only wood and stone, fashioned by human hands. Now, Lord our God, deliver us from his hand, so that all the kingdoms of the earth may know that you alone, Lord, are God."
> **— 2 Kings 19:17-19 NIV**

Notice his prayer. He doesn't falsely claim something that's not real. He talks to God like we should. "Lord, here is what I see before me. Here are my circumstances. However, You can deliver us." If you read the verses before that, he basically puts it back on God. "Look, these guys are calling you out, God. Aren't you going to do something about that?"

God's answer through Isaiah is lengthy, almost as if to say, "I've been waiting for this moment." He curses Assyria, reaffirms his ultimate power, then gives a word for Hezekiah about the future, but there seems to be a pause before he gives a real answer to the immediate problem. Verses 21 through 31 talk about God's power, Judah's future, and how despised Assyria is.

We don't know for sure if the answer was provided immediately or if there was a slight delay. However, what we do know is that the answer was given at the end. It reminds me of how often we pray and seek God for an answer. What He gives us is ultimately better long-term, but, in the moment, it doesn't always seem like the answer we're looking for.

I often feel as if I'm praying, "Okay, God, Your promises are amazing, but I'd love some of those promises to be fulfilled right now. Like, literally right now. At this moment. Today."

I know that He often does this for people, but I've never experienced it. Instead, like a loving Father, He does what I need most. He reminds me that He is Lord, that He is in control, and that this present circumstance is just a fleeting moment.

In almost Columbo-esque fashion, God's response to Sennacherib's threat is, "oh and by the way..."

> 'He will not enter this city or shoot an arrow here. He will not come before it with shield or build a siege ramp against it. By the way that he came he will return; he will not enter this city, declares the Lord. I will defend this city and save it, for my sake and for the sake of David my servant."
> **— 2 Kings 19:32-34 NIV**

If Hezekiah was anything like me, he would have said something like, "Well, that's a relief, Isaiah, but how and when is this going to happen?" Lucky for us the Bible paints Hezekiah as a man of stronger faith than I! Notice he had faith in God this entire time. He didn't call on his allies. He didn't surrender. He didn't take matters into his own hands. He let God fight his battles! In this case, God fought his battle for him.

> "That night the angel of the Lord went out and put to death a hundred and eighty-five thousand in the Assyrian camp. When the people got up the next morning—there were all the dead bodies! So, Sennacherib king of Assyria broke camp and withdrew. He returned to Nineveh and stayed there."
> **— 2 Kings 19:35 NIV**

Non-biblical ancient accounts record something about this[58]. Typically, the history of empires is one-sided accounts of their greatness. According to Herodotus, a Greek historian, mice ate the leather equipment of Sennacherib's soldiers, and a plague caused a high number of deaths. Which story requires more faith? Also, Sennacherib's own historical account says, "As to Hezekiah, the Jew, he did not submit to my yoke."[59]

This is not to say that Hezekiah didn't experience losses, but rather that God delivered him right when it was needed. Hezekiah had lost cities and thus retreated to Jerusalem. In the midst of impending defeat and threatening from the enemy, Hezekiah chose to believe the promises of God versus the reality of circumstances.

When I talk of launching offensives, I'm talking about knowing whose you are, what authority you have, and acting on it. It's action in prayer and understanding the promises of God that allow you to defeat the enemy. Before we move on, I'm sure you're curious about what happened to Sennacherib.

> "One day, while he was worshiping in the temple of his god Nisrok, his sons Adrammelek and Sharezer killed him with the sword, and they escaped to the land of Ararat. And Esarhaddon his son succeeded him as king."
> **— 2 Kings 19:37 NIV**

Sennacherib retreated after losing his army and returned home only to be killed by his sons while worshiping a false god. Meanwhile, Hezekiah's rule continued, and as it went on, he became deathly ill. It didn't look like he would recover, and even Isaiah told him to put his house in order (2 Kings 20). It should come as no surprise, though, what he did in the face of this illness. Hezekiah turned and prayed, and before Isaiah was even back home, God told him that He would heal Hezekiah.

Whether we want to conquer spiritual territory for the Lord, take on a new endeavor that might grow us financially or spiritually, or face an enemy of epic proportions such as cancer, the message is clear. Trust God. Kings of ancient times fought with swords, flesh, and blood. Today, we let God's army fight for us while we stand ready with the Word of God in our hearts.

Let that soak in. Life has seasons, and I can be optimistic and still tell you that you will face trials and you will be at mountain tops. When you are in an "up" season, looking to expand, let God fight your battles.

When you're down and out, let God fight your battles. When you get a bad doctor's report, let God fight your battles.

This isn't a message about passivity. Hezekiah wasn't passive. He launched a strategic offensive. He bypassed what he could see in the natural and called on supernatural intervention. If we, as co-leaders with Christ, are going to expand God's territory, we must learn how to access His power.

As I'm writing this, there is one song that epitomizes this section. "Surrounded" by Michael W. Smith. There aren't too many words to this song, but it's exactly the words you need to remember in this battle. "It may look like I'm surrounded, but I'm surrounded by You. This is how I fight my battles."[60]

We must be intentional in our worship, prayer, and actions and let God do what He does.

FALSE EXPECTATIONS

Jesus can bring this metaphor to life. He is the King of kings, in the flesh, sent here to wage war and claim the throne. The problem with many of the people of Jesus' time is they thought literally. They thought the Messiah would come and free them from Roman oppression. However, Jesus' mission wasn't to pursue their physical freedom; He was sent to secure their spiritual freedom.

It was said that Judas was one of these people. I bring this up because Judas was the treasurer. It's very likely that he was a savvy businessperson and was hoping that Jesus' ministry would launch the revolution. When Jesus insisted on talking about His impending death and subsequent resurrection, it was disappointing to everyone, not just Judas.

Every Christian and most non-Christians know the highlights of

Judas' betrayal. I propose that Judas was upset over what his expectations and dreams were of Jesus and the reality of what he saw as the current circumstances. In an effort to fix the circumstances to be closer to his dream, he betrayed Jesus.

I am guilty of this often. As someone who loves to plan, I witness every year how my brilliant plan fails miserably, but God still provides. There have been many times in my life where I've wanted something, dreamed about it, "named it and claimed it," and done just about every other prayer gimmick to make sure it happened. When things didn't turn out as I had envisioned, I would be devastated and depressed.

In some cases, the outcome was better than I imagined, but I couldn't see it at the moment because I let my will become an idol of sorts. In other cases, I became a type of "Judas" or "Saul" trying to create the reality I wanted instead of letting God do it in His timing and in His way through me.

A MAN ON A MISSION

No matter what example I use from the Old Testament, none will be the perfect example that Jesus is the most powerful human to ever walk the Earth and that He did nothing without the Father. He prayed daily to get instruction, and we know He studied the Word because He used it against the Devil, and He taught at the temple in His Father's house.

I might say He not only sought the Father's will and studied His Word, but He also "prepared" for His mission. Jesus' ministry is recorded as if He is indeed on a mission. We see Jesus first going to John the Baptist, getting baptized, and then getting out of the water and going right into the wilderness to fast and prepare. He sounds like a very intense, driven man to me. He trusted God for everything. Further, He was God yet trusted in the Father. Let that sink in for a second.

Here's Jesus, who has the power of the universe in His hands, and yet He chose to trust the Father for everything.

In John 5:19, Jesus gave them this answer: "Very truly I tell you, the Son can do nothing by himself; he can do only what he sees his Father doing, because whatever the Father does the Son also does" (NIV).

He continued in verse 30. "By myself, I can do nothing; I judge only as I hear, and my judgment is just, for I seek not to please myself but him who sent me."

Jesus did nothing without the Father, and yet He accomplished so much in three years. As leadership-minded people, I think we can easily fall into the action trap. We want to take so much action, so we take the wheel while we make Jesus a passenger. If you're like me, you find yourself driving through the woods on a collision course with a tree; and meanwhile, God was telling you to take that next left out of that mess.

The way to achieve this balance is understanding whose you are and what authority you have. Understand that you are a loved son or daughter with a doting Father that only wants what's best for you. You have authority within His will to do anything (Galatians 4:5-7, Romans 8, Luke 12:32).

I have a friend that I am reminded of when I think about this balance. This friend is a gifted entrepreneur and works in the cybersecurity arena. I can remember at one point in his life, he had a startup with offers for funding and buyouts, an offer to work with the Gates Foundation at the C-suite level, and a local job opportunity as the CISO (Chief Information Security Officer) for a city government.

Any outsider looking at his situation would say that the Gates Foundation or the tech money was the way to go. My friend has no lack of drive or initiative. The job offers and his startup are evidence of this. I belabor this point because when I tell you that he waited on the Lord, it may make you think he was being passive. But my friend sought the Lord and showed me what it truly means to be submitted in this way.

Ultimately, he took the local job, much to everyone's surprise. God wanted to use him to influence the city government, send him overseas, and disciple a young person. While some might see this 2-year journey as a detour, my friend will tell you that it was challenging and fulfilling.

As I write this, my friend is still very successful in everything he does. He took action when God told him to and waited when God told him. If you know who your provider is and that everything will work out for the best, you can trust completely in Him.

Our challenge isn't learning when to act and when to wait. It's not deciphering dreams and visions. Our challenge has nothing to do with what we sense as our reality or current circumstances. Our challenge is that if we don't know the Father that well, any mission we attempt on our own is going to be rough.

Luckily, Jesus modeled this for us.

> "Very early in the morning, while it was still dark, Jesus got up, left the house and went off to a solitary place, where he prayed.
> **— Mark 1:35 NIV**

> "But Jesus often withdrew to lonely places and prayed."
> **— Luke 5:16 NIV**

> "One of those days Jesus went out to a mountainside to pray and spent the night praying to God.
> **— Luke 6:12 NIV**

Right now, there is an abundance of great source material on how to cultivate this relationship the way Jesus did. You will only begin to truly know your Heavenly Father by reading His notes to you (the Bible) and talking with him (prayer). Whether you get an idea from the movie "War Room" or perhaps are inspired to study the Bible through Philip Hunter's "The Promise Principle," the important thing is that you move forward.

TRUST AND GO

To launch offensives to claim the territory the enemy is on, we need to know our mission and calling. As kingdom driven leaders, you have to find that balance of being action-oriented and driven while being completely submitted to letting God get the glory.

To be honest, I wanted to write this chapter about how kingdom driven leaders follow God-given missions and change the world. This is true! However, God kept redirecting me to what you're reading now. As kings, we will never be truly satisfied with completing our objectives without getting into our sweet spot.

Just a few years ago, my wife and I felt led to give extravagantly. We gave a large amount of money to ministries God put on our hearts, and it stretched us. I had a sense of pride and ownership in the things I invested in. We even made a trip overseas to Cambodia to see about investing in a particular mission-driven endeavor.

As a result, we changed a bit. We started to look at the endeavors with a more critical eye. I think it was a great season for us, but I'm here to tell you, as a business-minded person, I had one thought after we gave that amount. "What's next?" I thought for sure we were on our way up, that God's blessings would just shower us, and we could continue to give at that rate.

To be clear, I was under the impression that we were on the fast track to potentially launch a business that frankly would be 100 times what I have in the states. I reasoned it was because of our giving and the holy discontent I had for the people of Cambodia. I thought for sure God was greenlighting a dream I've had for a long time to launch businesses that changes the world.

It didn't happen at all like that, though.

We gave an amount that stretched us and made us proud, and we didn't see a financial return on that money immediately. I believe you can't out give God, but you're not dealing with a bank. You're dealing with a foreign exchange. God gives us beauty for ashes, life instead of death. God's commodity is simply different and brilliantly fulfilling, unlike any earthly gift we could receive in return. It's all about how God chooses to bless, but we often don't get to choose how he returns His love.

We didn't give because we were expecting something in return. However, because we gave, we waited expectantly for the return. I have full confidence we'll see the reward, but that wasn't the motivation. However, the point of the story is to notice my attitude. My attitude was, "box checked, goal achieved, let's multiply this by ten, God."

God failed to meet my expectations in this particular instance, and I was upset. And not only that, but my life financially took a turn the following few years, and life became much more difficult. Here's the thing, despite a business imploding, a launch of a new business, and 50 percent less income, God always provided. My family's bills got paid, and somehow, we were able to increase our savings and giving at the same time.

Admittedly though, depression hit me during this time. I kept questioning God. "We gave so much. I invested so much time into this project for what?" The next year or so was brutal. At some points, I was so depressed I spent hours reading the Word and journaling to avoid dealing with my work problems.

It was during this time that the message of this book took shape, and it was during this time that I learned to lean on God and trust Him. I also began to realize this is a lifelong process. While I didn't grow financially in the midst of it all, I did grow spiritually, and I learned how to trust God and keep moving forward.

I love the story of Moses leading the people and arriving at the Red Sea in Exodus 14. He tried to calm the people by saying, "Do not be afraid. Stand firm, and you will see the deliverance the Lord will bring you today.

The Egyptians you see today you will never see again. *The Lord will fight for you; you need only to be still."*

That's an encouraging word. After all, the people had seen the miracles, so why not this time? Unfortunately, when God asks you to be still, He's telling you to spend more time with Him. In this instance, Moses and God are called "friends," and there isn't a communication gap. Moses is operating with authority, and he knows he needs to move.

Then we get the truly LOL moment at verse 14. "Then the Lord said to Moses, "Why are you crying out to me? Tell the Israelites to move on." In other words, what are you waiting for? Get moving!

That's the message in a nutshell. Follow God hard, give Him your all, go after the missions hard, and change the world. You are more than a conqueror! However, never let the mission be more important to you than the Mission Giver. Never let God's promises become more important than the Promise Keeper.

You might be considering a somewhat conflicting message. Hezekiah waited on the Lord to do the work of defeating his enemy, while God told Moses explicitly, 'What are you waiting for? Move!" I firmly believe God has a big mission for you, one that you might not be able to complete in your lifetime. I also know it's going to require waiting and acting. This isn't a binary conversation of wait or move. It's one where you will be doing both and often at the same time.

The only way you'll know how to do either one is by giving everything to Him. You'll have to have peace about doing the little He gives you.

Practically, for me, that means time, taking time out to be with Him, to journal, worship, and pray. Like exercising or eating more vegetables, I don't want to do these things at first, but I love the fruit, and I'm helpless when I don't do those things. For you, it might look like putting a limit on your work hours or intentionally leaving your phone charging at night.

The term "balance" is a misnomer. There is no such thing. We're always constantly counterbalancing work life with family life and our spiritual walk with our engagement in the secular world. Even our relationship requires constant maintenance, and one key relationship might be growing but almost always at the expense of another. The key is that we're always moving, and we're always waiting. We're always in a state of faith and trust while we move forward with His commands to launch offensives and claim territory.

20

Claim Territory

We launch offensives to claim territory in our lives and the lives of others. When David and later Solomon rose to power, they expanded their territory through battle and partnerships. This kingdom expansion sets itself up for a great business metaphor. However, to reign with Christ, we don't start with that mindset. Our King has already won the war. However, the enemy still sits defeated on our land.

Asa and Jehoshaphat show us two lessons from this Father-Son dynasty. The first lesson is how to claim territory through influence and intentionality. The second is that sometimes our missions are bigger than our lifetimes.

Asa was one of the kings that the Bible calls good. He fortified the city, and as we read earlier, he was responsible for instituting the Law into practice. Asa's reign was so peaceful that historians would say that his reign (and later his son's reign) was marked not only by peace but also by a time of philosophy and art.

In the thirty-ninth year of his reign, Asa was afflicted with a disease in his feet (2 Chronicles 16:12 NIV). At this point, Asa's co-regent, his son Jehoshaphat, stepped up. Jehoshaphat was, by all accounts, also a good king. He continued his father's work of removing the idols and worship centers throughout the land.

Jehoshaphat reigned as king of Judah at a time when Elijah and Elisha were prophesying to Israel. At age 35, he had already witnessed his father not trusting God and trying to achieve his agenda and failing. He watched as his father's heart grew cold to God to the point that he didn't even pray for healing when he became ill. The Bible calls Asa a good king, but he died bitter and miserable.

Determined not to finish as his father did, his priorities were set; he was vigilant in his efforts to honor God, and it showed. Jehoshaphat was well known throughout the lands because of his intentional networking and alliances. At one point, he met with the king of Israel, Ahab, one of Israel's most evil kings ever. At this meeting, Elisha showed up and acknowledged the good king that Jehoshaphat is in front of Ahab.

> "If I did not have respect for the presence of Jehoshaphat king of Judah, I would not pay any attention to you."
> **— 2 Kings 3:14 NIV**

In that meeting, Jehoshaphat made an alliance with Ahab to profit his people as well as other kings. While the Bible isn't clear on the specifics, we know that Jehoshaphat was a well-known and respected king that used alliances several times to keep out other nations such as the Moabites.

Like Jehoshaphat, you must be vigilantly intentional about your alliances to claim territory that God's already given you. Every successful king used relationships and alliances to expand their territory. Often this occurred through arranged marriages. Other times, it was more obvious mercantile and economic exchanges such as with David and Hiram.

When I read about the kings in the Bible, I imagine scenes from great war movies. I imagine we're going to battle it out like they do in these movies and claim territory. Viewing spiritual warfare this way is incorrect. Unlike in the movies, machismo isn't needed in this scenario. The enemy is defeated, and we have to claim it.

Territory is likely a poor metaphor for souls because it doesn't communicate the invaluable nature of a soul. However, Jesus uses farming metaphors, and it's easy to translate your farming territory here. Personally, your territory is your family and immediate connections. Those people that salespeople call your sphere of influence or your "Dunbar 150." These are people that you can fertilize, water, and prune individually. Understand that it is God's job to provide the miracle of fruit, but it's your job to shine the Light and sustain the environment as an example.

This personal farm is great and if God's purpose is for you or me to invest in one small plot, then to Him be the glory. Great evangelists like Billy Graham can trace their salvation back to one person being obedient in a one-on-one manner. Most people's salvation stories contain a relationship that helped turn the tide for them. Paul-like miraculous conversions are the exception, not the rule.

However, as a business-minded person, you have a unique opportunity. With God's help, you can create a community farm. A community farm utilizes business systems, supply chains, leadership, and God's infinite power in a multiplicative manner. The purpose isn't so you can reap more fruit personally, but rather so that you can provide more resources for the harvesters.

How you behave matters. While writing this book, I had the opportunity to serve on jury duty. In the questioning of us, the attorneys revealed much about themselves. In one case, it was clear that the individual had a distaste for religion. Other questions pointed out the irony of a lawsuit by a Christian and the sanctity of life as viewed by the legal system. I figured they may have heard of Jesus, but unfortunately, did not know Him.

Regardless, these attorneys were influential, and their job was to influence our opinions. If one person can influence people intentionally, how much more could your business?

To put it a bit more plainly, a business has the opportunity to influence three key areas, its employees, its customers, and the community.

EMPLOYEES

A business has a great impact on the lives of those that work there. It's such a big deal that much research has been given to workplace happiness, creating winning cultures, and even the topic of vacation lengths for optimum rest and rejuvenation. Obviously, the research is all about creating efficiencies in the workplace to increase production.

If you're the leader of your organization, then you must be intentional about these values. It makes a big difference. If you're a leader in an organization but not the decision-maker, then it's your job to bring your values to the workplace and influence from within.

I met with one business owner who told me that when he first started his business, he just wanted to create a business that generated profits so he could give more away. In his mind, the business was a vehicle for generosity. The comment he made was that there were no "Christian businesses" in heaven. Sadly, he misses the greater impact that his business could have with this view.

In his world, there was no place for religion. He would tell me, and so he would focus on giving and doing good but keep his work and religion separate. That's good because I don't want religion in my work. I do want Jesus, though, because that means as a collective team, we're serving each other and adding value to people's lives in a way that we can only do with the Holy Spirit's help.

CUSTOMERS

> "And whatever you do, whether in word or deed, do it all in the name of the Lord Jesus, giving thanks to God the Father through him."
> **— Colossians 3:17 NIV**

Just like your beliefs influence your actions and then influence those around you, your business influences customers. In much of our life, we interact with different businesses. Most times, the experience is neutral, meaning it's neither good nor bad. But many times, there are situations that make the experience less than desirable. For example, you might be tempted to give a restaurant a bad review, or perhaps you've dealt with a cable company recently, and the idea of crafting a negative review comes flooding back.

It's rare when we're "wowed" by a business. It's not necessarily that the business isn't a good one, but rather we've grown so accustomed to a certain level of service that it's rare to see someone exceed it in a way that causes us to notice. Sometimes the wow is how professional the people are you're interacting with. Other times it could be policies that are brought to your knowledge that makes you like this company.

Right now, if you live in the south, you are immediately thinking about Chick-fil-a. Teenagers saying "my pleasure" to every half-said, "thank you" causes you to notice. The fact that, as a fast-food chain, they've subtly added service to their restaurants without drawing attention is notable.

Service professionals such as real estate agents, financial planners, and others interact with people on a very personal level. As a result, for better or worse, their customers have strong opinions about them.

The point is that what we do as people influences others, but also how our business operates can impact someone. As followers of Christ, and now as kingdom driven leaders, we live up to a different standard. It's our job as leaders in our organization to cast a vision of the values and to create systems that train and encourage our teams to deliver the kind of service and to have policies that make people go "wow."

We discussed values previously and said a great litmus test to see if you truly hold to those values is how you treat your worst customers. If Jesus was your CEO, would you truly have these policies? What's your policy on return items if you have a store? Would you ever sue a customer or competitor? What about how you treat those that have different beliefs than you? Will interacting with your business cause a person to see Christians in a new light or reinforce a judgmental view?

I didn't write this book to tackle the complicated decisions you'll have to make in your business. There are often good reasons for every decision. However, too often, those good reasons haven't passed the filter of "How will this impact the kingdom of Heaven?" No, not every decision is a kingdom decision, but many critical ones are or have the potential to be the ones that impact other people in particular.

It matters because your customers will almost always outnumber your employees. Somewhere along your supply chain, one of your people, whether you are a CEO or a team leader, will interact with a customer directly. Business owners are often aware that the business's reputation is at stake with every interaction. However, someone's soul could be at stake in the opportunities afforded you to be a witness of the truth! No, I'm not saying every "king" should be asking their customers for their confession of Jesus Christ as Lord. What I am suggesting, though, is that every interaction has the opportunity to water and nurture a seed that was planted.

If you look back to the beginning, one of the key characteristics of a king is excellence in everything. When you perform your job with excellence, people notice. In Colossians, Paul admonishes us to "Work as unto the Lord." This doesn't just mean how you conduct yourself in your job function, but how you interact with customers as well.

COMMUNITY

When you search for companies with Christian values, you get a full front page of Google with titles such as "18 Extremely Religious Big Businesses in America." Unfortunately, every single post I reviewed had very silly references. Most companies were cited as "religious" because they printed a Bible verse on their products. Some cited God as their source of inspiration and provision. None of the "Christian" companies I read about in these articles were highlighted due to their great community involvement.

> "What good is it, my brothers and sisters, if someone claims to have faith but has no deeds? Can such faith save them? Suppose a brother or a sister is without clothes and daily food. If one of you says to them, 'Go in peace; keep warm and well fed,' but does nothing about their physical needs, what good is it? In the same way, faith by itself, if it is not accompanied by action, is dead."
> **— James 2:14-17 NIV**

We've discussed how you personally, as a kingdom driven leader, can influence the kingdom by giving your time, talent, and treasure to a missional organization. My dream would be that this would also apply to your business and not be something separate or personal. A mission-driven business can change the world because when people unite, nothing can stop them. The Lord Himself even confirms this in Genesis.

> "The Lord said, 'If as one people speaking the same language, they have begun to do this, then nothing they plan to do will be impossible for them.'"
> — **Genesis 11:6 NIV**

We all know the businesses in our community. A few of them will send their employees to do charity work. Even fewer run their own charities and non-profits, but a select few are missional in everything they do.

The business sees a need in the community and leverages its resources to solve the problem. Often the problems that businesses solve in a community benefit the business as well. However, that's not the point of solving the problems, just rather a great byproduct.

> "A good name is more desirable than great riches; to be esteemed is better than silver or gold."
> — **Proverbs 22:1 NIV**

Having a good name is important to any business, and there isn't a better way than making one by doing something for the community. It's the intentionality behind the community effort that makes the impact. The individuals that are affected are the ones that get influenced. In this case, you are directly watering and nurturing the seed, truly shining light. In this case, you can and should be more overt about why you're doing something.

MISSION-DRIVEN JESUS

I love the intentionality of Jesus. To have someone so fiercely driven and full of love is truly inspiring. When Jesus called, people followed. I always wondered why men would leave what they were doing to follow this man. I'm certain Jesus gave off an aura of authority. The Bible is clear on this point.

> "When Jesus had finished saying these things, the crowds were amazed at his teaching, because he taught as one who had authority, and not as their teachers of the law."
> **— Matthew 7:28-29 NIV**

But even further, after studying this topic and weighing it in my mind, I still fall back to the fact that He's Jesus. He is the One who is the Word, the One Who has authority, and the One who truly sees us. I believe if you ever met Jesus in the flesh, you'd never forget Him, not because of His appearance but because of who He is.

Jesus started His ministry with entrepreneurs as His disciples were made up of fishermen, tax collectors, political activists, and other careermen. Jesus intentionally chose this group because of their hardiness and ability to function outside the norm. He knew His mission was going to be tough. There would be naysayers, there would be hard times, and what they were going to do was going to be unpopular. It would be easy to quit and give up. Jesus knew that not only would the social pressure be tough but that what He had to teach could be difficult for them. Therefore, He needed a team that could carry this mission out without faltering.

Jesus even tested His followers' grit. My pastor likes to say, "Whenever Jesus' followers became too many, He'd thin the herd by bringing truth."

> "From this time many of his disciples turned back and no longer followed him."
> **— John 6:66 NIV**

This verse comes to us after Jesus just got done telling the people that they needed to eat His flesh and drink His blood. Even given the context of the Bible, this is a tough statement to understand and accept! With statements like this, He knew he needed disciples that would be willing to listen and learn instead of judging. He knew that He needed a group that was willing to live outside social norms.

The kind of follower He was looking for had to have the work ethic to do the work. Fishermen, in particular, would work during all seasons, and while it was a profitable business, it wasn't seen as a desirable job. Fishing in Biblical times was nothing like what we might imagine now. They didn't use a rod and reel but rather circular nets with weights. It was grueling, hard work.

How's your work ethic? One of the greatest examples of character I ever see in the world are men who go out, do their job well, and come back without complaint. Many so-called blue-collar jobs are thankless, and yet they provide an income for one's family. Fishermen in Biblical times were the epitome of this. However, you don't have to be a blue-collar worker to work hard with excellence. When you look at the qualities of a disciple, I think hard work often goes unnoticed.

Disciples also had to be open-minded and forward-thinking. The first recorded disciple, Andrew, was a follower of John the Baptist. He was known as a wild man preaching repentance while upsetting all the religious leaders.

One of my biggest challenges sometimes is judging other churches. I'll hear a teaching that sounds too soft, and I'll immediately jump to some broad conclusions about whether or not it is false teaching. Often, I'll even find myself using passive-aggressive sarcasm about them in conversations with other believers. I know from experience that this only causes division! I must stop. I need to be open-minded and ask, "How does this line up with the Word?" The Word tells us to judge by the fruit. I'm left with this as my response, "This message does not resonate with me, but people are being saved, and lives are being changed because they met Jesus through this message."

Jesus intentionally picked outliers of religious society that had the grit to grow the Kingdom. The word "apostle" means sent. This is why the Bible says, "all are invited, few are chosen (Matthew 22:14)." Being chosen isn't about saying the prayer of salvation and then going back to your life. Being chosen is 100 percent about your actions. We are all invited to be a part of His Kingdom, but those that lack the integrity of hard work, the willingness to heed His voice, and the open-mindedness to be outside of what the world says is popular are simply not chosen to be kingdom driven leaders.

MISSIONAL INFLUENCE

What does all this have to do with business and leadership? We've already covered how you cannot separate the two walks of your professional and personal life. You are a kingdom driven leader, and Jesus has chosen you to impact those around you and through you in the workplace. Claiming territory for Christ is taking your intentionality behind this kingdom mission and doubling down on it.

It plays itself out in scheduling appointments with people and investing in them. You see it when there is an initiative to do something in the city, and instead of simply writing a check, you decide to make the call and see how you can help grow it. It might be buying that ticket to the nation outside the US that is on your heart and flying there to invest your time, talent, and treasure with other kingdom minded entrepreneurs in the third world.

Business can be the vehicle to reach many people and impact nations. However, claiming territory for Christ is often a one-person-at-a-time initiative. As a kingdom driven leader, you want to be there to support systems of influence. John C. Maxwell says, "leadership is influence,"[61] therefore, I believe influence is leadership. It's your influence and your business's influence that will open the door to connect with people where they are.

Before we close out this thought, let's be real for a second. I acknowledge that doing "stuff" costs money. Traveling to where people are, giving things to them, and doing ministry costs money. Business, at its core, is a system to derive profit from solving problems. I'm merely suggesting you solve consumer problems to make money and use that money to solve God-sized problems in our world.

A kingdom driven leader looks at the big picture. They see not only the resources that they can gather and give to their local church, but they also see that the multiplicative efforts of their influence can impact the kingdom. Accordingly, a kingdom driven leader deliberately leverages their relationship and resources to expand the kingdom.

Throughout this book, I've written about the big stages of kingdom dri-ven leadership. We started with the foundation of every great leader by preparing and growing. With the chapter "beginning to rule," we discussed how to be more intentional around your growth for long-term impact. Finally, reigning with Christ put all those lessons into action for a greater kingdom impact. As you journey to becoming a kingdom driven leader, you'll face enemies along the way.

SECTION IV
ENEMIES OF A KING

21

Enemies of a King

"For everything in the world—the lust of the flesh, the lust of the eyes, and the pride of life—comes not from the Father but from the world."
— **1 John 2:16 NIV**

When you read Kings and Chronicles, it reads like a "here's what *not* to do in life" story. Don't put anyone or anything before God, don't go to war without Him, don't make deals with fools, and don't have more than one spouse. Maybe better stated, those books read like a list of "Here's the things that happen when you break the 10 Commandments."

What's fascinating about the Bible is that there are so many historical accounts for us to learn what to do. The very sins that tripped these kings up are also the same temptations that Satan tried against Jesus and that he will use against us.

The Holy Spirit led Jesus into the wilderness to strengthen His relationship with the Father through prayer and fasting. While that certainly might be the resulting fruit of His trip, the Bible says He was led by the spirit to be tested by the Devil (Matthew 4:1).

I don't want to mess with your theology, but if it's good enough for Jesus to be tested by the Devil, then I'd say God will allow us to be tested as well. Take comfort in that. If you're going through something, "count it all joy" (James 1:2) that you are being tested and refined for some great work. Note that God didn't cause anything to happen that hurt Jesus here, only that He was tested.

Throughout this section of the book, we'll be highlighting the very things that tripped up the kings of Israel, how Jesus was tempted by these same traps and escaped or defeated these enemies. Spoiler Alert! The answer will always be inside a relationship with God and in the Word. In fact, this is how Jesus battled Satan during His temptation.

LUST OF THE FLESH

> "For everything in the world—the lust of the flesh, the lust of the eyes, and the pride of life—comes not from the Father but from the world."
> **— 1 John 2:16 NIV**

What is the lust of the flesh? It's our fleshly desires. When we think of sin, lust is usually the first kind of sin that many men think of. However, lust does not just mean sexual sin. Lust is an unhealthy, passionate desire for more. Even in the dictionary, lust is associated with greed and envy.[62]

The lust of the flesh is a physical type of sin, from sexual sins to overeating. Drug and alcohol abuse could also be included in this list. Apostle Paul gives us a good description.

> "The acts of the flesh are obvious: sexual immorality, impurity and debauchery; idolatry and witchcraft; hatred, discord, jealousy, fits of rage, selfish ambition, dissensions, factions and envy; drunkenness, orgies, and the like. I warn you, as I did before, that those who live like this will not inherit the kingdom of God."
> **— Galatians 5:19-21 NIV**

Fasting is exceptional at breaking the lust of the flesh. It's always worth pointing out that God made food and sex, but they are to be enjoyed in accordance with His Word. When we eat too much or have sex outside of marriage, the Bible is clear it has the power to ravage our lives (Proverbs 6:32, Hebrews 13:4, Proverbs 23:20-21).

My pastor always likes to point out, if your sin isn't on the list in Galatians 5, Paul covers it with "the like." These just account for the sins that are often publicized, and they are easy for people with influence to fall into. As you grow your influence, your relationships and resources will grow as well. This opens up more opportunities for sin as well.

The lust of the flesh is when we try to satisfy a need outside of the will of God. Our needs are to be filled by God and provided for by God. God is our provider, not just for practical needs like finances but for everything we need – practical or immaterial. One of God's names is Jehovah Jireh, "the Lord, Our Provider."

> "Abraham named the place Yahweh-Yireh (also known as 'Jehovah Jireh,' which means 'the Lord will provide'). To this day, people still use that name as a proverb: 'On the mountain of the Lord it will be provided.'"
> **— Genesis 22:14 NLT**

God is called Jehovah Jireh right after Abraham's fateful march up the mountain with his own son, Isaac. God provides for all our needs. The lust of the flesh includes our fleshly desires that are screaming out. God can provide for every one of them. Just because He can and will provide, however, doesn't mean He will always do it in our desired timing. Our job is simply to continue to petition Him through prayer and fasting and wait on Him.

In terms of these sinful traps brought on by the lust of the flesh, Jesus has already defeated and disarmed them.

> "After fasting forty days and forty nights, he was hungry. The tempter came to him and said, 'If you are the Son of God, tell these stones to become bread.' Jesus answered, 'It is written: 'Man shall not live on bread alone, but on every word that comes from the mouth of God.'"
> — **Matthew 2:2-4 NIV**

Most Christians know the story of Christ's temptation. When Jesus was ready to start His mission, he went to John the Baptist, the crazy man dressed in camel skin, eating locusts and baptizing people in the river. John, Jesus' cousin, baptized Jesus and the heavens parted as the Holy Spirit descended, and God said, "This is my son whom I am well pleased" (Matthew 3:17).

Jesus then set the example by heading off to be alone to pray and fast for forty days. Some of us can barely go forty minutes, let alone forty days, without food. Jesus is still part man, so we know that He was hungry. Accordingly, the Devil's first temptation involved His flesh. He tempted Jesus with food. Notice though, he didn't tempt Him with a plate of food, He tempted Him with the thought of producing His *own* food.

When I saw that, the lightbulb in my mind turned on. For leaders, it is easy to be tempted to attempt to fill our perceived needs ourselves. I know I am especially guilty of this one.

I've run a few businesses, and one commonality in each business has been debt. There is a good case for strategic debt, and businesses cost money to start up, so there is an investment that needs to be made. However, what I was doing in each of these businesses was trusting the systems, and frankly, the sales pitches instead of trusting God. The "shiny object" had essentially become an idol.

In one business, I made what I thought to be a good investment in new leads and a database program. My wife was not on board with it. She knew that this was risky and would overleverage the business. When I asked her, I had already decided in my mind. When I prayed about it, it was only to ask God to bless what I was doing. In my mind, my wife didn't get the big picture of what I was doing, and certainly, God brought this to me.

As you might guess, it overextended my business finances to the point that if it didn't work, I'd be in trouble. From the moment I started the program, I was in the red. However, I embraced the mantra "you have to spend money to make money," and so I kept on.

I realized that to make the program work, I needed at least twice the number of salespeople. Instead of re-evaluating the program and getting wise counsel, I pressed on. I thought that this was where our provision would and should come from. I went about trying to hire people. In twelve months, I hired or fired 12 different salespeople. Even with that turnover, I was determined to make this work.

Eventually, the debt got so bad that I had to admit defeat to try to keep my marriage from more damage than what was already done. While this one decision wasn't what ultimately got me out of that business, it certainly sped up the decision-making process. What I've learned from this is that in each of these businesses, I've trusted my credit more than my God to provide. I tried to meet my own needs with the world's tools instead of using God's tools.

The lust of the flesh is only defeated when you are willing to sacrifice everything and live for God's kingdom. You have to be willing to lay down every dream, every goal, and every blessing to follow Him. You have to be willing to accept His vision for your life. You must allow God to provide for you. When you allow these things to happen, this defeated enemy of lust cannot hold you any longer.

LUST OF THE EYES

David is the most heralded king of Israel's history. During his time, he would have been world-famous. Naturally, as his son Solomon comes to the throne, he would have some big shoes to fill. In 1 Kings 1, we learn about how Solomon comes to power. As David's other son, Adonijah, tries to take the throne, Solomon's mother and the prophet Nathan work together to make sure Solomon becomes king. This was always the plan according to 1 Kings 1:29, and Solomon would have been prepared for this moment. I believe that it was during this time that Solomon asked God for wisdom. He was surrounded by a loving family, wise counselors, and prophets and was under godly influence.

Solomon began to multiply what his father did. He was building a new temple, and Israel was growing in prosperity. Like his father before him, he executed every kingly trait covered in this book. He listened to God, gained wisdom every day, and his kingdom expanded. He networked and made deals with other kingdoms to grow his own. It's in this networking that things started to crack and eventually crumble, though.

It's well recorded that Solomon began to marry foreign wives with dif-ferent beliefs than his own. Many of these wives were gifts from other nations to solidify the deals he made. With God's favor, he must have felt invincible. His kingdom was the most wealthy in the world, and he could do whatever pleased him. He would later write Ecclesiastes, in which he laments doing everything he wanted to do because it failed to provide the pleasure he wanted after a while.

Fast forward to the end of the story, and you will find Solomon worshiping other gods and having his kingdom ripped apart. He fell into the trap of access without accountability. Without accountability, it was easy to be tempted by new things for the sake of curiosity. However, when curiosity goes unchecked, it often creates a desire. Unchecked, these desires created a spiral of lust where Solomon wanted more and more, and he was never content. Ultimately, our desires will always have diminishing returns the more we seek them, whereas God's love is the only thing that continues to be better the more we seek it.

If the lust of the flesh is a result of our attempt to provide for ourselves what God has said He would provide, then the lust of the eyes is the sin that comes from wanting things that are outside God's will.

The difference is subtle. Lust of the flesh is an active passion, whereas lust of the eyes is a passive passion. Lust of the flesh is about your pursuit; the lust of the eyes is about your dreams. What do you elevate above God? What are your modern-day idols?

> "Again, the devil took him to a very high mountain and showed him all the kingdoms of the world and their splendor. 'All this I will give you,' he said, 'if you will bow down and worship me.' Jesus said to him, 'Away from me, Satan! For it is written: 'Worship the Lord your God and serve him only.'"
> **— Matthew 4:8-10 NIV**

Hollywood has played this scene out a few times. In the classic scene, the devil shows up, sometimes played by a beautiful woman, who tempts the leading man and succeeds at getting him to promise his soul in return for power and wealth. Of course, the movie plays out what the reality is for anyone who chooses their way instead of following God. The character begins to see that the power and wealth they receive have consequences they weren't ready for, and the Devil wasn't entirely truthful about the deal. Now they wish things were back the way they were.

When Jesus rejects Satan, He made a choice for His chosen mission. He set the example for us. Everyone I've met in leadership has had to confront some version of this temptation. Often for me, it's a sin of comparison that causes me problems. I look at my peers and make a judgment that if they can do it, why can't I. I see their exterior; I see the veneer of their life. I don't see the hard work, inner character, or sacrifices they made to get where they are. I don't know what their family life was or any of their circumstances.

None of it matters. Whether they were handed everything and kissed by God or whether a tumultuous life chiseled out a rock of success, it's not relevant to my story. God has handcrafted us as His work of unique art to accomplish His mission. He uses our circumstances to equip and propel us to accomplish this objective.

> "For we are God's masterpiece. He has created us anew in Christ Jesus, so we can *do the good things he planned for us long ago.*"
> **— Ephesians 2:10 NLT**

Jesus knew His mission. He didn't waver when He was shown it all. I know that if the scene was me up there with Satan, the thought of shortcutting the hard work would have come up. Accomplishing more than maybe I thought I could in delusions of grandeur. Of course, it's all a lie. Jesus sniffed out the liar and rebuked him. Now it's our turn.

When you're tempted to do things outside the will of God, resist the Devil, and he will flee (James 4:7 NLT).

The lust of the eyes isn't just looking at things that God's not called us for. When we dream and desire these things, it's like planting little seeds in our hearts. We start to move toward those things and away from our mission. The mission may seem mundane. In fact, to some, Jesus' life might have seemed that way during that period.

If Jesus wasn't the son of God, then His story might go like this: A carpenter from a small town goes a bit crazy, causes a raucous, and eventually gets himself crucified. The End.

Thank God that Jesus knew the outcome of His mission. Here is the point: your mission is bigger than you could ever imagine. Stop daydreaming about someone else's mission or story and stay focused on your own. Trust that God has a story written about your life, and it's amazing. However, it might take more than your lifetime to accomplish.

> "You saw me before I was born. Every day of my life was recorded in your book. Every moment was laid out before a single day had passed." — **Psalm 139:16 NLT**

God wrote the book; He knows what we can and will do. However, it's up to us to use the gifts He has given us and the power of our free will to execute it, always trusting He's working things out for our good.

> "And we know that in all things God works for the good of those who love him, who have been called according to his purpose."
> — **Romans 8:28 NIV**

As mentioned in the last section, the only way to trample on this defeated enemy is sacrifice. It doesn't mean that your dreams won't come true but rather that you are willing to sacrifice them to follow the life God has for you.

THE PRIDE OF LIFE

> "There is one vice of which no man in the world is free; which everyone in the world loathes when he sees it in someone else; and of which hardly any people, except Christians, ever imagine that they are guilty themselves. [...] There is no fault which makes a man more unpopular, and no fault which we are more unconscious of in ourselves.[...]The vice I am talking of is Pride or Self-Conceit: and the virtue opposite to it, in Christian morals, is called Humility."
> — **C.S. Lewis, Mere Christianity**[63]

Pride is a disease that blinds the eyes and dulls the mind. So often, we think of pride as being braggadocious or being self-centered. We often think of celebrities or politicians as being prideful and arrogant. Certainly, pride can be found in those personalities, but they are not isolated to them.

Pride didn't start with the first king. Pride was present long before that. However, Saul's downfall shows us the insidiousness and destructiveness of pride. As C.S. Lewis, who wrote a great deal on pride, would tell us, "For pride is spiritual cancer: it eats up the very possibility of love, or contentment, or even common sense." It starts with some very subtle things. Pride starts when we declare we are too busy to pray or read the Bible. You start taking small actions without considering what God says about those very actions. You might make a business deal or launch a business and then ask God to bless it. It might start as casual as creating your to-do list or goals for a day before praying. I don't want to be legalistic and suggest that you must ritualistically pray. But how can you possibly have a good day without talking to your Father first?

When my wife and I were only a few years into our marriage, we decided to upgrade our home. It was a huge mistake because it wasn't until we were under contract that we asked for His guidance. Speaking for myself, our prayers were only asking for blessings. Instead, God worked a miracle of sorts. The builder put the wrong brick on the home and made some other mistakes that were so costly they would let us out of the contract easily instead of redoing or discounting the work.

Instead of receiving the message as a gift of God's grace, we decided this home should be ours anyway. Surely, we could make it work. It didn't feel like pride at the time. It felt like the opposite, but looking back, I have zero doubts about what was at work there.

It took us nearly eight years of being house poor until we were able to start truly living in the home. He knew the economy was going to change! He knew that we'd change careers, that one of us would stay home, and that we had no idea how to care for a huge home or furnish it. Pride is insidious this way; it's spiritual cancer.

Business leaders are notorious for their drive. Sometimes though, what drives a business decision that looks like "initiative" is actually driven by fear. That's what happened to Saul. He lost his kingdom because he took the matter into his own hands.

Like an epic movie, Saul was about to lead a battle against the Philistine army with their three thousand chariots and a sea of soldiers "as many as sands on the seashore" (1 Samuel 13:5). Up until this point in the story, God's hand had been on Saul. The Bible says, "the Spirit of the Lord was powerfully upon Saul" (1 Samuel 11:6).

Saul had won many victories with God's power. He was seemingly in-vincible on the battlefield as both a powerful warrior and a cunning strategist. When God works through you, you feel heroic. This feeling should remind you that it's *His* power, not your own, but Saul didn't recognize this.

He had a few missteps before this, yet God stayed with Him. He believed that this battle would be no different. He had so much faith, and even though what he was about to do was disobedient, there is a part of me that admires him for his faith. However, the Bible says that his people lacked this faith. They were "quaking with fear" and hiding in caves.

He was conscious of the power of God. However, there was one problem. He needed to wait on Samuel, but he was growing impatient. He had to wait seven days for Samuel to come and offer sacrifices to God and receive His direction. I'm sure those seven days were agony. Saul was torn between knowing that everything would come out okay but not knowing how it was going to happen. It likely frustrated him not to have any control over the situation.

The Bible doesn't specifically say this, but I think Saul started thinking to himself, "I know how this works, I got this. I just need to do the thing Samuel does, and God will have to bless me."

I also think as we examine this story that there was some serious fear here for Saul. I don't think he was fearful of losing the battle as much as he feared what the people would say if he wasn't victorious.

God's order for Saul's battles was to have the prophet be hand in hand with the king, giving honor and praise to the Lord for a victorious battle. Like a sports athlete who has a tarnished legacy because he got to play with other great players, Saul feared that his legacy might be tied to Samuel forever. The Bible doesn't say this, but as I read it, it seems to me that every disobedient act from Saul was his attempt to make a name for himself with his own power.

In other words, Saul decided to act without God's blessing and against God's will and then asked God to bless him.

Contrast Saul's decision with Hezekiah's. Both were faced with seemingly impossible odds. Both had seen God come through. Saul chose to take actions in his own hands and with his own power while Hezekiah made his prayer for breakthrough a written petition.

> "Saul remained at Gilgal, and all the troops with him were quaking with fear. He waited seven days, the time set by Samuel; but Samuel did not come to Gilgal, and Saul's men began to scatter. So, he said, 'Bring me the burnt offering and the fellowship offerings.' And Saul offered up the burnt offering."
> **— 1 Samuel 13:7-9 NIV**

This is the moment of decision that causes Saul to lose his kingdom, but the pride had been there all along.

> "Pride gets no pleasure out of having something, only out of having more of it than the next man... It is the comparison that makes you proud: the pleasure of being above the rest."
> **— C.S. Lewis, Mere Christianity**[64]

In our society, today pride is a common problem for multiple reasons. At least one of those is related to father wounds. In American culture, the outstanding rate of fatherlessness and parental problems cause children to want to make a name for themselves by proving their value through achievements.

I personally deal with this every day. I question my life's value by compa-ring myself to others. I also fall into the trap of pride when success does happen. Yet, God, in His infinite grace and love, has healed me and continues to remind me that I am His adopted son. Adopted kids are chosen. Let it sink in for a moment that God has chosen you.

Imagine that you are a child sitting on your daddy's lap driving a car. He is driving the car, but your little hands are on the wheel. You're so small that you can barely see over the wheel, and you certainly can't reach the pedals. Your hands are so tiny you can barely grasp the wheel, and you're too weak to turn the wheel on your own.

And yet, when pride rises, we think we're doing the driving. When we try to control our lives, like a child fighting his dad for the wheel, the car swerves into a potentially dangerous situation. Sometimes the dad must stop the car entirely to correct what's happening.

If humility is power under control or knowing that your power comes from God, then pride is the opposite. Pride is uncontrolled fear and a sense of unhealthy confidence that your power comes from you. I say uncontrolled fear because outwardly, pride manifests as a feeling of pleasure about what you accomplished. Inwardly you experience cognitive dissonance to some degree because you can't accomplish anything alone, and you don't have any real control.

> "Then the devil took him to the holy city and had him stand on the highest point of the temple. 'If you are the Son of God,' he said, 'throw yourself down. For it is written: 'He will command his angels concerning you, and they will lift you up in their hands, so

> that you will not strike your foot against a stone.' Jesus answered him, 'It is also written: 'Do not put the Lord your God to the test.'"
> — **Matthew 4:5-7 NIV**

I can remember reading this one and thinking this was the worst temp-tation ever. When I read it, I thought to myself that it was a dare. It was like Satan was telling Jesus, "Jump, I dare you." I didn't think anyone would fall for that one! Yet, everyone jumps!

When we do something outside the will of God, we test Him. Since we've all sinned, we've all jumped. We're jumping and saying, "If this doesn't work out, catch me." Pride says, "I know better than God; I have control."

When it comes to pride, I'm often reminded of my own pride when I see my children. When my son was younger, we wanted him to try out some different activities, one of which was Tae Kwon Do. One day he told us that he didn't want to go that evening. I asked him why, and he told me, "I already know it all." He went on to show me his moves and described himself as a master.

While his moves were impressive, he had only attended one session so far!

When I pressed him to explain why he thought he knew it all already, he said he knew it all from watching his cartoons - all displaying a poorly executed and unrealistic version of martial arts. Most of the time, those cartoons had no foundation of reality. The cartoons he watched were so far removed from anything that could be used as self-defense, it was comical.

How often do we as leaders get a glimpse of what God is doing and think, "I know it all?" or "I got this." We say this after seeing a substitute for the real thing. But just like my son humorously reminded me, I can't even imagine what God is doing in my life, and the closest proximity to it is a poor imitation of the real thing.

> "Remain in me, as I also remain in you. No branch can bear fruit by itself; it must remain in the vine. Neither can you bear fruit unless you remain in me. I am the vine; you are the branches. If you remain in me and I in you, you will bear much fruit; apart from me you can do nothing."
> **— John 15:4-5 NIV**

If the lust of the flesh is about our unhealthy pursuits, and the lust of the eyes is about our unhealthy dreams, then the pride of life is about our unhealthy view of our relationship with God. The only way we can defeat this defeated enemy is to completely surrender.

You have probably figured it out by now, but to defeat pride, you have to sacrifice yourself. To defeat these enemies, you'll have to sacrifice your pursuits, your dreams, and yourself. You have to accept that you can do nothing without God.

22

Traps of The Enemy

In the last chapter, we looked at enemies that every person must face. These enemies were defeated by Jesus, and He showed us the way to defeat them in our own lives. However, there is a set of traps that the enemy uses specifically against kingdom driven leaders. Another way to put it is that while we are all in the crosshairs of the enemy, those lifted up on a platform are easier targets.

Before you read about the traps, I want you to think about all the chapters leading up to this one. Being 100 percent submitted to Christ and being humble will go a long way to helping you avoid these traps. Keeping continual conversation with God and surrounding yourself with wise counsel will give you excellent vision to see these traps before you fall. However, no matter how hard you try, you might end up like David, caught in a trap. The traps of the enemy don't take kingdom driven leaders out. Instead, they expose leaders to vulnerabilities. None of them by themselves are sins. Instead, they open the door for sin to enter our lives in stealthy ways. These traps are famous, and they were exposed in David's life, the man after God's own heart. The man with such faith in God he killed Goliath. The king who had faith even when he was running for his life. The king that wrote Psalms and was likely the greatest king in Israel's history. However, with all of those accolades outlined in Scripture, we also get an eye into David's sin.

What happened to David is a lesson for everyone. We all look at the murder and adultery and wag our finger. The sin didn't start there. It started when David lost his focus. In Samuel 10, David defeated the Arameans. However, in chapter 11, we see him lounging in the palace while his troops went off to battle.

TRAP: LOSS OF VISION

> "In the spring, at the time when kings go off to war, David sent Joab out with the king's men and the whole Israelite army. They destroyed the Ammonites and besieged Rabbah. But David remained in Jerusalem."
> — **2 Samuel 11:1 NIV**

In the spring, when kings went off to war, David stayed home. From the text, it's clear that a King's responsibility was to be with his troops. Kings had seasonal responsibilities, which included time for a vacation. So not only was he not where he should have been, but he was choosing to do things out of season. He lost his vision for the kingdom.

Then there is this line from verse 2 in the New Living translation,

"Late one afternoon, after his midday rest, David got out of bed."

When we unpack this incident with David, it becomes clear that he wasn't simply looking out over his kingdom one day and saw a beautiful woman. This isn't the first time that he's looked out over the kingdom and had a privileged view.

The Bible uses the word "haerev,"[65] which means evening, but in a Jewish context, this could be as early as 6 PM or the start of the sunset. It's unlikely that Bathsheba would want to bathe any later than the beginning of the evening period. She'd likely want the light. There were no streetlights per se, so David would need some light to see a good distance and get a view of a bather.

While the discourse of time is an exercise in futility, it paints a picture of a king that was shirking his responsibility to feed his desires. In other words, he was *really* enjoying his unscheduled vacation. Whether he was sleeping all day because he was over-indulging himself on other things or whether he was restless one night, it matters not. Let's not forget that David had wives and concubines to satisfy any sexual desire he had. Yet, often an appetite left unchecked always wants more.

Pay attention. This is a bit subtle, but it's one of the bigger pitfalls that leaders fall into. After grueling deadlines, long hours, and the success of short-term goals, it's easy for leaders to want to rest. It's common for businesspeople to lose their perspective. In many cases, this is the moment we dread as businesspeople. We've finally made it, and it has no meaning.

There are seasons of rest. However, if we're not vigilant, we can become like David. If we let go of the good habits that keep us faithful, we can lose it all. The more success you have, the more you need to constantly be checking your heart and your nearness to God. As success grows, so do the opportunities to lose it all and worse, to lose things you cannot recover from.

This is such a pitfall for successful people that two professors, Dean Ludwig and Clinton Longenecker, wrote a paper entitled "The Bathsheba Syndrome."[66] In Ludwig's and Longenecker's paper, they reveal key dangers or traps of business success. They suggest that success creates, in their words, "an explosive combination" that can cause leaders to have a propensity to implode. They write that "success is the antecedent to ethical failure,[67]" and an ethical failure is a failure for any kings.

The other lesson here is one of balance. It could be that David had been pushing and pushing so long that he felt a need for a release after the last battle. He had been so out of balance with his life that he needed to correct it. I've seen this dilemma with too many businessmen, myself included.

We can push so hard for so long that we burn ourselves out. Instead of resting in the right seasons, we push through to get to the finish line. God prescribes rest on the seventh day and for Israel in the seventh year. I firmly believe in a day of rest with no work-related activities, but you also need to rest seasonally.

When you're burnt out, your mind and body have to recalibrate. Often you find yourself feeling like you might be free-falling or lost in the fog. Things you used to desire no longer engage you. There is a numbness to the world in general. It's not that something in you has changed. You fried your mind and willpower.

The word "midlife crisis" is often related to two things:

1. overworking to the point of burnout
2. the realization that all that work didn't matter

> "Where there is no vision [no revelation of God and His word], the people are unrestrained; But happy and blessed is he who keeps the law [of God]."
> **— Proverbs 29:18 AMP**

It's in these seasons that we can lose sight or vision of what we're called to do. The Bible warns of this. When there is no revelation from God or when we don't see clearly what our mission is, we become unrestrained. We walk in a fog without a view of the destination or the boundaries. God's Word isn't there to take away our fun. It's quite the opposite. God's Word is there to protect us from the consequence of poor choices and to illuminate the path that will bring us the greatest satisfaction.

As a leader, one component of your job is to cast a vision for the company. "Casting off restraint" is true of companies too. If there isn't a clear vision, the product of the work won't live up to the potential. If there is no vision, the employees won't engage with each other or engage with customers. Vision is so crucial, and yet it's easy to lose it when you've just achieved a major breakthrough or burned yourself out.

TRAP: ACCESS WITHOUT ACCOUNTABILITY

If you look at the table of contents in this book, the longest chapters are about preparing to lead. The reason is that as success grows, so do privileges and access. People that would have never considered talking to you are now interested in what you have to say. As a leader, you have influence. Those in the early days of success often remember the first time they delegated a task or asked for something and had someone else do it for them. An epiphany occurs in the mind of every leader as the realization of what power influence really is.

Unrestrained, this power gets abused, and we have history books full of faulty leaders. In a weekly news cycle, you'll likely see this multiple times with not only CEOs but for all sorts of people, including teachers. This potential for abuse is just as dangerous in your company as it is for political leaders.

To understand privileged access, you only need to look at the internet. We have every piece of information available for us to access. However, without accountability in our lives and a close relationship with God, we may fall into sin. As Uncle Ben said, "with power comes great responsibility."[68]

David had unlimited access to his kingdom. He could have invited any woman to the palace, and no one would have questioned him. With his men out on the battlefront, he had no one to keep him from going over the edge.

This is why community is even more important for a leader. With access to resources and relationships that others might not have, there needs to be accountability. It doesn't have to sound as overbearing as the word accountability sounds, but there needs to be people in your life that can call you out and ask you questions about your life that you allow in. These people aren't there to condemn you but rather to encourage you and redirect you when needed.

TRAP: ISOLATION

Successful people tend to become isolated. In the beginning, it's not their own doing, and it starts with maybe short goal-driven interactions leaving little room for relational growth with peers. Often when they use the word sacrifice, they are thinking of the relationships that might have been sacrificed at the altar of their success.

Few are more isolated than political leaders. As king, David could have you killed, could take your daughter as his wife, or could ask you to dine with him in the palace. With this much power, subjects and even confidants had to choose their words wisely around a king. Authentic relationships were few and far between.

When you start a business, you immediately create a boss-to-employee relationship as you hire. You might not intend to do this. You might do things like call someone a partner to lessen the gap between you. However, unless you are giving them ownership that could overturn your voice, you're still the boss. This leader-to-follower relationship doesn't only happen with founders of companies; it can happen with managers and even interdepartmentally.

When you control someone else's time or their ability to make income, you have a modicum of influence over that person. It creates a wall for those you are in a relationship with. It becomes your responsibility to be humble enough to receive their input as well as to be vigilant enough to see authenticity and transparency in your communication.

This is why a board of directors can be helpful for businesses and why small groups are a must for any kingdom driven leader. Having a small group of believers to do life with can often be the one thing that keeps you from acting on the impulses or exercising the freedom and power at your fingertips.

TRAP: FALSE SENSE OF CONTROL

As we talked about previously, our walk is one where God does things for us and through us. As we reach what the world would consider being a success, we can often lose sight of that fact during the journey. We can fail to recognize that it was God that opened the door. It was God that delivered the success.

Control is often an ongoing battle for leaders. The sense that what you do and say can influence the outcome certainly feels like control. It's just enough of a taste of control that it drives us to want more.

For those in leadership positions, the sense of control is more deliberate. A person in authority can hire and fire and make decisions on the direction of company initiatives. God designed for us to have free will and to make decisions. Making decisions is a good thing. The trap is when we start to make those decisions independent of our walk with God. The bigger the decision, the bigger the reason to seek God's wisdom on it.

As we continue to make decisions without God, we move further and fur-ther away from Him. Every time something goes as planned, it reinforces that thought that we are in control. However, when we make choices and take action to influence things outside of God's will, we fall into the trap. Whether David scrambled after he committed the sin or thought it out to begin with, it remains that he thought he could control the outcome. His plans went awry when he encountered Bathsheba's husband, Uriah, who had more character than he did at that moment. He sensed the complete loss of control of the situation and grabbed hold of what he knew he could control- his people. He knew his generals would never question an order, even if it seemed out of place.

David's problem didn't start an adulterous act; David's problem started when he lost his vision. He already had complete access with no one to hold him accountable, other than Nathan, the prophet. David was already in the snare and exposed. He got into trouble thinking he was in control, and he found out the harder you try to control something outside of the will of God, the worse it gets.

Remember, these traps, in and of themselves, aren't necessarily deadly. Like a spider web, they leave the victim vulnerable to attack. Luckily for us, we have a leader who knows how to disarm the traps we face.

DISARM THE TRAPS

"So, let's keep focused on that goal, those of us who want everything God has for us. If any of you have something else in mind, something less than total commitment, God will clear your blurred vision—you'll see it yet! Now that we're on the right track, let's stay on it. Stick with me, friends. Keep track of those you see running this same course, headed for this same goal. There are many out there taking other paths, choosing other goals, and trying to get you to go along with them. I've warned you of them many times; sadly, I'm having to do it again. All they want is easy street. They hate Christ's Cross. But easy street is a dead-end street. Those who live there make their bellies their gods;

> belches are their praise; all they can think of is their appetites. But there's far more to life for us. We're citizens of high heaven! We're waiting for the arrival of the Savior, the Master, Jesus Christ, who will transform our earthy bodies into glorious bodies like his own. He'll make us beautiful and whole with the same powerful skill by which he is putting everything as it should be, under and around him."
> **— Philippians 3:15-21 MSG**

If David, a good king and a man after God's own heart could fall, then any of us could fall too. Although some of these traps are more common for people in positions of leadership, they are everywhere, and it's important to be aware of them.

This entire book isn't simply a listing of characteristics of good kings, just like Kings and Chronicles in the Bible aren't there for historical purposes. This book is about giving you the tools to grow as an active mission driven disciple of Christ. The best way to disarm these traps is in pursuit of a relationship with Christ. I write pursuit because, like any relationship, you have to be intentional in order to grow it.

The more deliberate you are about working on your relationship, the more the Holy Spirit will begin to change you, your tastes will change. For example, entertainment that you used to engage in won't have the same level of enjoyment. It's not necessarily because the entertainment is bad, but rather because the love you're becoming familiar with is so much greater.

You'll begin to notice other changes, which are sometimes called the fruit of the spirit (Galatians 5:22-23). You might be more patient while driving, or you might respond more lovingly when verbally attacked by others. The point is that the closer you get to Christ, the more like Him you become. Ultimately, the greatest mission in life is to emulate Christ. We first need to experience His love and then, in the overflow of the love, share it with others.

As you have already read, you must prepare in advance to live like a Biblically good king. You must be intentional in your preparation to lead. This maintaining of your vision is crucial for you to take territory for God's kingdom through Christ's power and authority. If this sounds intense, it is! It's this focused intensity and intentionality that will keep you from the traps.

How leaders are remembered and the impact they leave on the world is history's measuring stick for success. The greatest leader who ever walked the Earth left us talking about Him 2,000 years later, and He led us all to be sacrificial in our service to others. From Him, we see 11 followers multiplied into thousands after He leaves. This multiplication created a dynasty of kingdom driven leaders for all of us to follow and aspire to.

23

Leading A Dynasty

I've done my best to show you the patterns that I saw from studying the Old Testament kings. For me, this journey was pretty eye-opening. The "ah-ha!" moment for me was when I saw Jesus doing the same things that the good kings did. What spoke to me was that it all seemed to translate into practical business leadership strategies and tactics that we can use.

The real measure of a great king is their legacy. For Christians, what we do in this life is "training camp" for eternity. My favorite movie line is from Gladiator, "what we do in this life echoes in eternity."[69] It's the absolute truth, and Jesus confirms it.

> Jesus said: "A man of noble birth went to a distant country to have himself appointed king and then to return. So, he called ten of his servants and gave them ten minas. 'Put this money to work,' he said, 'until I come back.' But his subjects hated him and sent a delegation after him to say, 'We don't want this man to be our king.' He was made king, however, and returned home. Then he sent for the servants to whom he had given the money in order to find out what they had gained with it. The first one came and said, 'Sir, your mina has earned ten more.' 'Well done, my good servant!' his master replied. 'Because you have been trustworthy in a very small matter, take charge of ten cities.' The second came and said, 'Sir, your mina has earned five more.' His

master answered, 'You take charge of five cities.' Then another servant came and said, 'Sir, here is your mina; I have kept it laid away in a piece of cloth. I was afraid of you because you are a hard man. You take out what you did not put in and reap what you did not sow.' His master replied, 'I will judge you by your own words, you wicked servant! You knew, did you, that I am a hard man, taking out what I did not put in, and reaping what I did not sow? Why then didn't you put my money on deposit, so that when I came back, I could have collected it with interest?' Then he said to those standing by, 'Take his mina away from him and give it to the one who has ten minas.' 'Sir,' they said, 'he already has ten!' He replied, 'I tell you that to everyone who has, more will be given, but as for the one who has nothing, even what they have will be taken away. But those enemies of mine who did not want me to be king over them—bring them here and kill them in front of me.'"

— Luke 19:12-27 NIV

Relative to eternity with Christ, what you do with your life and your business matter is simply a dress rehearsal. I truly want you to become driven by what eternity holds for you.

As we've mentioned throughout this book, living like a king isn't a 12-step program, it's a process. I'm constantly having to work on pride or re-engaging in seeking wisdom. Strongholds have been torn down, but their remnants are still there. I am cognizant of the traps the enemy has laid out for me, yet I still fall into them.

I believe when you know who you are called to be and you work toward attaining the character of a kingdom driven leader, you will be able to complete your mission.

For the marketplace leader and the CEO, a mission statement emerged from the study of the good kings of Israel. Serve, Give, Lead. These words summarize what it takes to be a true kingdom driven leader.

SERVE

Serving is an attitude. To do it right requires humility. This is not false humility. This is not the false humility that says, "I think less of myself," but rather, thinking of yourself less. You know you are serving in the right spot when you feel truly alive, and the Holy Spirit's presence is sustaining you.

Serving is something that everyone can do. If a young person were made to read this book and they say, "'These characteristics are great, but I'm still in school." I'd tell them to start serving and listening.

Let's be clear. I'm talking about two things—the attitude of helping others and slowing down long enough to hear other people. I'm also talking about literally "volunteering" your time at your local church or cause. Invest your time. When you are physically serving, you can often invest your time and your talent. When you do this with the kingdom mindset, it'll open other avenues in your mind on what you might do as your influence grows.

Going on a mission trip isn't necessarily serving, in my opinion, unless you're there to serve. So many mission trips are experiential. However, I'm still a big, big advocate of these trips because even the ones that are more vacation missions expose you to people in a way that we don't often get to experience in the US. Sometimes just getting outside of the US can give you this perspective.

GIVE

In writing this book, it became abundantly clear that everyone had a different view of what a "kingdom driven leader" was. It became important for me to find a definition that we could all look at and point to and say, "I can't put my finger on it, but that's a kingdom driven leader."

Nowhere was this more apparent than giving. Every business leader that was referenced as a modern-day king was a giver. They often served on non-profit boards, started their own non-profits, and made it their life mission to give as much away as they could.

When I think of the audience this is mostly for, I would think many of them are already giving to something, either a local charity or their church endeavors over and above the tithe. However, as we already covered, I think there is an opportunity to grow that and be more intentionally led in this arena.

If you aren't giving, let this be a challenge to you. You can give three things: your talent, your time, and your treasure. God can use you in immense ways with those first two; however, I think God does something special when we share finances He's given to us.

LEAD

Being a giver and a servant doesn't make you a kingdom driven leader but being intentional in how you serve and give does. This intentional leadership of self, finances and others is another key.

To me, the greatest leadership is leading by example. When you live your life the way God intended, it gives off an aroma (2 Corinthians 2:15) that attracts people to allow you into their lives. This influence is far more powerful than any facade you could manufacture.

> "Therefore, go and make disciples of all nations, baptizing them in the name of the Father and of the Son and of the Holy Spirit, and teaching them to obey everything I have commanded you. And surely, I am with you always, to the very end of the age."
> **— Matthew 28:19-20 NIV**

Ultimately, our greatest calling is to make disciples of Christ. I still believe it's the marketplace leaders, the kingdom driven leaders, who have the biggest opportunity to set up systems so that this can happen in scale. Even with that belief, I know that we should never squander an opportunity to lead one person to Christ or to help one brother move closer to Christ.

I have a friend named Ben who has an amazing testimony of faith. God healed him in a miraculous way and taught him about faith and being patient. I met Ben through being intentional about networking. Ben is a venture capitalist (VC) from my alma mater, Georgia Tech. His job is to evaluate the business to see if they are a good investment. To be good at this, he must understand the systems that make the business work and the financial viability of the business.

When a VC looks at a business, they have to understand what will hap-pen to the business if they invest their money. What happens if they ex-ponentially expand it? In other words, can it scale?

Ben also loves Jesus. Through his non-profit, he leads a team to Africa to teach Africans about business God's way, which means he essentially teaches them how to be a kingdom driven leader. The program not only teaches business principles, but it provides seed money to launch businesses in the form of small loans.

The program itself is divided into three rigorous training sessions. The first session explains kingdom principles and requires the would-be entrepreneur to develop a business plan. Those that do that are taken through the next phase, where they begin to do the research necessary to launch the business. Finally, for the last session, a team walks them through how to launch the business with the funds provided.

What I love about Ben's story is that he's taken his talent and invested his time and money into the lives of the African businesses in a way that will leave a legacy.

When thinking about God's Kingdom and your own legacy, you

may have to shift your thought process. One business leader told me that he's not interested in what people will say about him in ten years. He's interested in what his leaders of leaders of leaders are doing in 300 years. As crazy as that may sound, it forced him to think generationally. It changed his entire approach. He now asks new questions like, "How will what I'm doing now impact people generations from now?" In his case, it also caused him to stop pursuing wealth and launch a coaching and leadership organization.

What you do matters. What you do could matter for generations to come. The question is, are you willing to prepare, lead, and take territory to leave a legacy as a true kingdom driven leader?

WHAT WOULD YOU LIKE ON YOUR TOMBSTONE?

The concept of planning a legacy is not a new one. We saw early in this book that kings were intentional about trying to keep their lineage on the throne. To plan your legacy, you need to think about the ending.

Admittedly, there can be tension between your mission, which might be to share the gospel with one person, and a legacy meant to last centuries. However, it could be that the one person you're meant to influence is going to be the next Mother Theresa or Billy Graham. The idea of leaving a legacy is that it forces you to think beyond the present with strategic thoughts about the future. Another way to put it is that it forces you to think about who you want to become.

One helpful exercise is to imagine what people might say about you at your funeral. Take some time to imagine what they might say now. Now think about what you'd *want* them to say. Is there a difference between the two? Your legacy planning can be as easy as figuring out what you need to change in your life to ensure that people say what you want them to about you at your funeral.

This book is all about you becoming a more intentional kingdom driven leader that makes a lasting impact. We covered foundational principles as well as principles in which we can grow in order to increase our influence to grow God's kingdom. We looked at kings with enduring legacies to inform us on what to do to leave the kind of legacy that lasts long beyond our lives. If you follow in Jesus' footsteps and apply these lessons, there's no doubt that you'll leave a legacy as a great kingdom driven leader.

Conclusion

When I started the journey of writing this book, it started as God showing me the patterns of kings from the Old Testament and how certain characteristics matched the life of Christ. Combined with my passion for business and business as a mission field, I found myself meeting others that were either doing it or in the process of becoming more missional.

What I set out to create in this book is a guide to help you reference back to see what the Bible says about being a great kingdom driven leader.

The Old Testament taught it, the New Testament confirmed it, and if you needed any further convincing, secular research has proven it out.

Choose to be intentional today about growing as a kingdom driven leader. Whether you are starting out or have been on this journey for some time, examine your kingdom or your life, if you will. In what area(s) are you weak? In what area(s) are you strong?

Every day you should self-evaluate your journey to become a better kingdom driven leader. Ask yourself,

» Am I completely submitted? For me, I feel like I'm never at a full 100 percent and must constantly re-evaluate my priorities.
» Am I talking with Christ daily, reading His word? Am I doing this as a way to check a box, or am I engaging with His word and in conversation with Him?
» Am I doing everything with integrity and excellence? How about the

littlest of things that don't matter to anyone – the stuff that only God and I see?
- Am I serving others? As I review my days' activities, was I more selfish today or selfless?
- What got me excited today? Was it something related to God's kingdom? While most of these questions are useful in examining one's heart, this one might help you identify areas of your life that you might want to pursue more deeply or cut out. For example, if politics are getting you "excited," then you might consider volunteering for a cause, or it could mean that you might need to stop watching the news.
- How's my pride? If you're asking these questions of yourself, I'd say you're teachable and humble, but as leaders, we must check ourselves here.
- Am I tithing? I know this isn't a salvation issue. However, I believe that tithing keeps my heart more humble when it comes to money.
- Am I growing my giving above the tithe? What is my plan to grow in this area?
- Am I growing in wisdom? Do I have wise counsel I can count on? If not, how is my plan going to surround myself with wise, godly counsel?
- Am I growing my connections with others for the kingdom?
- Am I putting myself in situations that would make it easy for the enemy to attack me?
- What am I doing to actively pursue my kingdom legacy?

You'll notice that there are two sets of questions. One set deals specifically with your heart, and the other deal specifically with your growth. To be more like Christ, you'll have to check your heart and continue to push forward in your spiritual growth. When things aren't going well for you, this becomes an easy check. Check your heart first, then check whether you are growing or not.

CONCLUSION

> "For we are God's masterpiece. He has created us anew in Christ Jesus, so we can do the good things he planned for us long ago."
> — **Ephesians 2:10 NLT**

A kingdom driven leader isn't a title; it's a state of mind. As Paul says, you are a masterpiece, created on purpose and for a purpose. Kingdom driven leaders need to see the big picture, but we also always need to remember who our Father is and how our mission could simply be to share His love with one other person.

Now is the time to work toward becoming more like Christ in every area of your life. Every merger, every hiring and firing, and every new opportunity won't be as fruitful without Christ's wisdom permeating everything you do. Let's all collectively work toward making our lives more missional to expand the kingdom and truly become kingdom driven leaders!

Let's Pray.

> Heavenly Father,
>
> I ask that you open my eyes, ears, and mind to clearly understand my calling. Reveal to me areas that I need to grow in to become more like you, the King of kings. Help me see the life-giving connections that you've placed in my life. Help me connect with others to expand your kingdom. Today, I submit my time, treasure, and talent on your altar. Make me usable and use me for your Kingdom purpose. Give me the supernatural grace and confidence in my unique mission and keep my eyes from comparing my mission to others. Protect my heart from pride and lust as we move forward. Clothe me in your kingly righteous armor in Jesus' name.
>
> Amen.

Acknowledgements

I want to thank my wife, who supported me throughout this whole process. She was one of my first editors and lovingly helped me make my first edit.

I want to thank my mom, who also helped me refine the ideas and constantly reminded me that she believed in me.

I want to thank Charlie, who coached and mentored me when all I had was a few thousand words and no outline. Thanks to Dr. Rob, who was willing to believe in me enough to connect me to Charlie. Thanks to Monika, who helped me edit the initial drafts and encouraged me along the way.

I want to thank Jace, Bobby, Toksy, Joseph, Taiye, and the rest of the king's group for providing such outstanding prayer and support along the way.

I want to thank Carolyn Reed, my editor.

Special thanks to John. Your feedback was invaluable.

Notes

[1] Catalyst, https://www.catalystleader.com/, accessed 8/2020
[2] SBA, SBA.GOV, https://www.sba.gov/sites/default/files/advocacy/Frequently-Asked-Questions-Small-Business-2018.pdf, Page 2 (accessed 7/16/2020)
[3] The Coca-Cola Company, "Our Purpose", https://www.coca-colacompany.com/company/purpose-and-vision (accessed 7/16/2020) The Coca-Cola Company, "
[4] 2019 Business & Sustainability Report", https://investors.coca-colacompany.com/ (accessed 7/16/2020)
[5] Huffington Post, https://www.huffpost.com/entry/how-to-solve-the-world-wa_b_1104367, (accessed 7/16/2020)
[6] Chick-fil-A, Who We Are, Corporate Purpose, https://www.chick-fil-a.com/about/who-we-are (accessed 7/16/2020)
[7] Chick-fil-A, Giving Back, https://www.chick-fil-a.com/about/giving-back (accessed 7/16/2020)
[8] Chick-fil-A, Remarkable Futures Program, https://www.chick-fil-a.com/remarkable-futures-scholarships (accessed 7/16/2020)
[9] Wikipedia, Hemosiderosis, https://en.wikipedia.org/wiki/Hemosiderosis (accessed 7/16/2020)
[10] *Kaplan, Justin, ed. (2002). "Reinhold Niebuhr (1892–1971)". Bartlett's Familiar Quotations (17th ed.). p. 735. (attributing the prayer to Niebuhr in 1943)*
[11] Kouzes, James M., and Barry Z. Posner. The Leadership Challenge:

How to Make Extraordinary Things Happen in Organizations. Sixth edition. Hoboken, New Jersey: John Wiley & Sons, Inc, 2017

[12] Thayer and Smith. "Greek Lexicon entry for Merimna". "The KJV New Testament Greek Lexicon", Word 3308

[13] Harvard Business Review, The Power of Small Wins, Teresa Amabile and Steven J. Kramer, https://hbr.org/2011/05/the-power-of-small-wins (accessed 7/16/2020)

[14] Life.Church, "Wild Life with John Eldredge - Part 4" September 21, 2017, video, 6:45, https://www.youtube.com/watch?v=buEjeQnz27o

[15] van Minden, Jack J.R. (2005). Alles over psychologische tests (in Dutch). Business Contact. p. 207. ISBN 978-90-254-0415-4.

[16] *Patrick M. Lencioni (2010). "The Five Dysfunctions of a Team: A Leadership Fable", p.41*

[17] Hybels, Bill, Holy Discontent: Fueling the Fire That Ignites Personal Vision, Book Description, Zondervan; ITPE edition (May 27, 2007)

[18] "Humility." Merriam-Webster.com Dictionary, Merriam-Webster, https://www.merriam-webster.com/dictionary/humility. Accessed 5 Aug. 2020.

[19] Spider-Man. 2002. [film] Directed by S. Raimi. USA: Columbia Pictures Corporation & Marvel Enterprises.

[20] https://marriagetoday.com/

[21] Lewis, C S. Mere Christianity.p 101, New York: Macmillan, 1960. Print.

[22] Warren, Rick. The Purpose-Driven Life: What on Earth Am I Here For? p.134, Grand Rapids, Mich: Zondervan, 2002. Print.

[23] NY Times, https://www.nytimes.com/2013/06/20/business/in-head-hunting-big-data-may-not-be-such-a-big-deal.html, (accessed 8/2020)

[24] Harvard Business Review, https://hbr.org/2014/05/the-best-leaders-are-humble-leaders, (accessed 8/2020)

[25] Thayer and Smith. "Greek Lexicon entry for Hagios". "The KJV New Testament Greek Lexicon" Word 40

[26] Lipsey Water, https://lipseywater.com/articles/spring-water-vs-purified-

water/ (8/2020)

²⁷ Maxwell, John, The 21 Irrefutable Laws of Leadership, p 127, Harper Collins

²⁸ MSN Money, https://www.msn.com/en-in/money/photos/the-20-richest-people-of-all-time/ss-BBsg8nX#image=17, (accessed 8/2020)

²⁹ Lencioni, Patrick. The Ideal Team Player: How to Recognize and Cultivate The Three Essential Virtues. Germany, Wiley, 2016.

³⁰ "Excellence", Vocabulary.com https://www.vocabulary.com/dictionary/excellence, (accessed 8/2020)

³¹ Sinek, Simon. Start with Why. Penguin Books, 2011.

³² How great leaders inspire action". TEDxPuget Sound Talk, www.ted.com. September 2009. (accessed 8/2020)

³³ Stanley, Andy, Making Vision Stick (Leadership Library), Zondervan (July 30, 2007)

³⁴ Koch Industries, https://www.kochind.com/about/business-philosophy, (accessed 8/2020)

³⁵ Young-Eisendrath, Polly, and Terence Dawson. The Cambridge Companion to Jung., 2008., p73

³⁶ *You might have noticed a small contradiction there. When you come across these seeming contradictions you must examine the Word more closely. Could both things be true? In this case, the answer is yes. He could have removed all the high places in every town and left some that were not in towns. He could have intended to remove them all and failed. There are several explanations that make it possible for this to be true*

³⁷ "Religion." Merriam-Webster.com Dictionary, Merriam-Webster, https://www.merriam-webster.com/dictionary/religion. Accessed 31 Aug. 2020.

³⁸ "Culture." Merriam-Webster.com Dictionary, Merriam-Webster, https://www.merriam-webster.com/dictionary/culture. Accessed 31 Aug. 2020.

³⁹ Duhigg, Charles, author. The Power of Habit: Why We Do What We

Do in Life and Business. New York: Random House Trade Paperbacks, 2014.

[40] Biggs, Michael (2013), "Prophecy, Self-Fulfilling/Self-Defeating", Encyclopedia of Philosophy and the Social Sciences, SAGE Publications, Inc.

[41] Kelledy L., Lyons B. (2019) Circular Causality in Family Systems Theory. In: Lebow J.L., Chambers A.L., Breunlin D.C. (eds) Encyclopedia of Couple and Family Therapy. Springer, Cham. https://doi.org/10.1007/978-3-319-49425-8_248

[42] For a more in-depth look at getting free from strongholds, read, Robert Morris's, "Set Free" and watch his series under the same title online at http://gatewaypeople.com.

[43] Zacharias, Ravi K. The Grand Weaver: How God Shapes Us Through the Events of Our Lives. Grand Rapids, Mich: Zondervan, 2007. Print. Pg 187

[44] Ellicott, C J. An Old Testament Commentary for English Readers. New York: E.P. Dutton, 1890. Print.

[45] https://www.ancient.eu/Tyre/ (accessed 8/2020)

[46] https://en.wikipedia.org/wiki/Tyre,_Lebanon (accessed 8/2020)

[47] Duhigg, Charles. The Power of Habit: Why We Do What We Do In Life And Business. New York: Random House, 2012. Print.

[48] Comparing two methods for estimating network size, Christopher McCarty; Peter D Killworth; H Russell Bernard; Eugene C Johnsen; Human Organization; Spring 2001; 60, 1; pg. 28

[49] "You can expect what you inspect" (management adage), Barry Popik, https://www.barrypopik.com/index.php/new_york_city/entry/you_can_expect_what_you_inspect_management_adage (accessed 8/2020)

[50] Miller, Donald, and OverDrive Inc. Building a Storybrand: Clarify Your Message so Customers Will Listen. [New York]: HarperCollins Leadership, an imprint of HarperCollins, 2017

[51] Morris, Robert, The Blessed Life, Bethany House Publishers; Revised,

NOTES

Updated ed. Edition (September 20, 2016)

[52] Victory Church, https://victoryatl.com/messages-item/10justandgenerous/, Dennis Rouse, Min 23, Accessed 8/2020

[53] Ramsey, Dave. Entreleadership: 20 Years of Practical Business Wisdom from the Trenches. New York: Howard Books, 2011. Print.

[54] Breakthrough To Success Event, Jack Canfield, https://www.jackcanfield.com/breakthrough-to-success/ , accessed 8/2020

[55] Gateway Church, Robert Morris, https://gatewaypeople.com/series/more-than-words?sermon=dominion, accessed 8/2020

[56] Folkman, Jack Zenger Joseph. "What Great Listeners Actually Do." Harvard Business Review, 20 July 2017, hbr.org/2016/07/what-great-listeners-actually-do.

[57] Folkman, Jack Zenger Joseph. "What Great Listeners Actually Do." Harvard Business Review, 20 July 2017, hbr.org/2016/07/what-great-listeners-actually-do.

[58] Wikipedia, See Notes from *Ancient Near Eastern Texts*, p. 288 https://en.wikipedia.org/wiki/Hezekiah

[59] Pritchard, J.B., editor; *Ancient Near Eastern Texts Relating to the Old Testament*, 287-8. Copyright ©1950, 1955, 1969 by Princeton University Press. Reprinted by permission of Princeton University Press.

[60] Smith, Michael W., Surrounded (Fight My Battles), 2017, Rocketown Records/The Fuel Music

[61] Maxwell, John C. The 21 Irrefutable Laws of Leadership: Follow Them and People Will Follow You. Nashville, Tenn.: Thomas Nelson Publishers, 1998. Print.

[62] "lust v.1." OED Online. Oxford University Press, September 2020. Web. 10 October 2020.

[63] Lewis, C. S. Mere Christianity: a Revised and Amplified Edition, with a New Introduction, of the Three Books Broadcast Talks, Christian Behavior, and Beyond Personality. William Collins, a Division of HarperCollins Publishers, 2017.

[64] Lewis, C. S. Mere Christianity: a Revised and Amplified Edition, with a New Introduction, of the Three Books Broadcast Talks, Christian Behavior, and Beyond Personality. William Collins, a Division of HarperCollins Publishers, 2017

[65] Brown-Driver-Briggs Hebrew and English Lexicon, Unabridged, Electronic Database.
Copyright © 2002, 2003, 2006 by Biblesoft, Inc.

[66] Ludwig, Dean & Longenecker, Clinton (1990). The Bathsheba Syndrome. _Proceedings of the International Association for Business and Society_ 1:622-640.

[67] Ludwig, Dean & Longenecker, Clinton (1990). The Bathsheba Syndrome. _Proceedings of the International Association for Business and Society_ 1:622-640.

[68] Columbia Pictures presents a Marvel Enterprises/Laura Ziskin production; producers, Laura Ziskin, Ian Bryce; screenplay writer, David Koepp ; director, Sam Raimi. Spider-Man. Culver City, Calif.: Columbia TriStar Home Entertainment, 2002.

[69] Gladiator. Universal City, CA: DreamWorks Home Entertainment: Universal Studios, 2000.

www.ingramcontent.com/pod-product-compliance
Lightning Source LLC
Chambersburg PA
CBHW020901080526
44589CB00011B/384